Two Story
HOME PLANS
Premiere Edition

Cover Photography by Glen Graves
Cover & 4/C Interior Layout by Paula Mennone

LIBRARY OF CONGRESS NO.: 94-073700
ISBN: 0-938708-58-9

Submit all Canadian plan orders to:
The Garlinghouse Company
20 Cedar Street North
Kitchener, Ontario N2H 2WB

Canadian Orders Only: 1-800-561-4169
Fax #: 1-519-743-1282
Customer Service #: 1-519-743-4169

PRICE CODE C

Photography by Fred Mudge
The photographed home has been modified to suit individual tastes...

OUTSTANDING DESIGN

This beautiful stucco and stone design opens to a formal foyer that leads through double doors into a well-designed library which is also conveniently accessible from the master bedroom. The master bedroom offers a vaulted ceiling and a huge bath area. Other features of this home are an oversized living room with a fireplace, an open kitchen and a connecting dining room. A utility room and half-bath are located next to a two-car garage. One other select option in this design is the separate cedar closet to use for off-season clothes storage.

First floor — 1,671 sq. ft.
Second floor — 505 sq. ft.
Basement — 1,661 sq. ft.
Garage — 604 sq. ft.
Foundation — Basement
Bedrooms — Three
Baths — 2(Full), 1(Half)

Total living area — 2,176 sq. ft.

An
EXCLUSIVE DESIGN
By Karl Kreeger

DESIGN NO. 10555

P9-BIO-218

COUNTRY COMFORTS MAKE FOR A WELCOMING DESIGN

From the sprawling front porch to the two-way fireplace that warms the hearth room and living room, this house says "Welcome" to all who enter. Even your houseplants will love the cozy, sunny atmosphere of this country classic. A central hallway links the formal, bayed dining room with the spacious kitchen at the rear of the house. Relax over an informal meal in the adjoining hearth room, or out on the deck when the weather's warm. It's accessible from both the hearth room and soaring, wide open living room. Relish in the privacy of your first-floor master suite, which features a bath with every amenity, and a huge, walk-in closet. Step upstairs for a great view of active areas, where you'll find three more bedrooms, each adjoining a full bath.

The soaring hearth room, steps away from the adjoining deck, is a great spot for formal or informal gatherings and portrays a cozy warmth with its stone fireplace.

Outdoor entertaining is a breeze with your wood deck located off the hearth room. Rear views are as exciting as front views in this perfect design....

PRICE CODE D

Photography by Glen Graves

An
EXCLUSIVE DESIGN
By Karl Kreeger

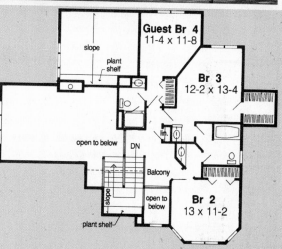

Second Floor

Guest Br 4
11-4 x 11-8

Br 3
12-2 x 13-4

Br 2
13 x 11-2

slope · plant shelf · open to below · DN · Balcony · open to below · plant shelf · lin.

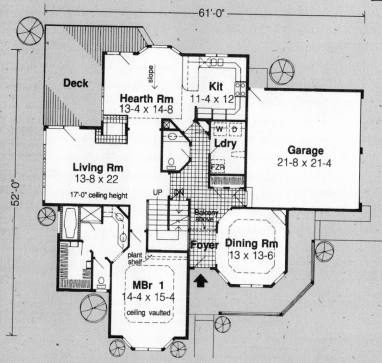

61'-0"

52'-0"

Deck

Hearth Rm
13-4 x 14-8

Kit
11-4 x 12

Ldry

Garage
21-8 x 21-4

Living Rm
13-8 x 22

17'-0" ceiling height

W D · FZR · UP · DN · Balcony above

plant shelf

Foyer

Dining Rm
13 x 13-6

MBr 1
14-4 x 15-4

ceiling vaulted

First Floor

PLAN INFO:

FIRST FLOOR	1,737 SQ. FT.
SECOND FLOOR	826 SQ. FT.
BASEMENT	1,728 SQ. FT.
FOUNDATION	BASEMENT
BEDROOMS	FOUR
BATHS	3(FULL), 1(HALF)
SQ. FT. TOTAL	2,563 SQ. FT.

DESIGN NO. 20144

SIMPLY ELEGANT DESIGN WITH LOADS OF STORAGE SPACE

This simple design's exterior features a large picture window and rock front. On the first floor past the foyer is a spacious living room with its own wood-burning fireplace. The dining room lies in front of the living room and next to the kitchen. From the kitchen to the right is the breakfast room with access to a large outdoor wooden deck. A half-bath and laundry facilities are other rooms on the first floor. On the second floor are three bedrooms. Two of these bedrooms share a full bath with its own skylight, while the master bedroom has its own private bath and walk-in closet. One final feature of this plan is the large amount of storage space available in the two-car garage.

Look down upon the spacious Living Room, with its cozy fireplace and steps away from the adjoining Dining Room, from the balcony located off the second floor hallway.

Serving is a breeze with the location of the Breakfast Room next to the Kitchen. Or step out to the Deck when the weather's warm.

Photography by John Ehrenclou

SECOND FLOOR

An
EXCLUSIVE DESIGN
By Karl Kreeger

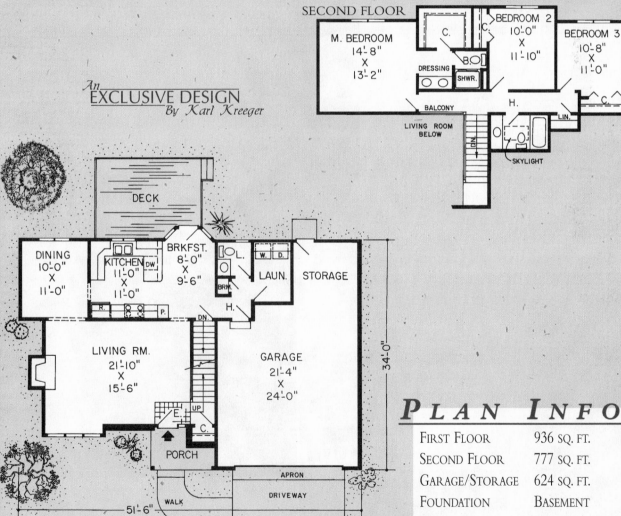

M. BEDROOM
14'-8"
X
13'-2"

C.

C.

BEDROOM 2
10'-0"
X
11'-10"

BEDROOM 3
10'-8"
X
11'-0"

DRESSING

B.

SHWR.

H.

LIN.

BALCONY

LIVING ROOM BELOW

DN

SKYLIGHT

C.

DECK

DINING
10'-0"
X
11'-0"

KITCHEN
11'-0"
X
11'-0"

DW

BRKFST.
8'-0"
X
9'-6"

L.

W. D.

LAUN.

STORAGE

BRM.

R.

P.

H.

DN

LIVING RM.
21'-10"
X
15'-6"

GARAGE
21'-4"
X
24'-0"

E.

UP

C.

PORCH

WALK

APRON

DRIVEWAY

51'-6"

34'-0"

FIRST FLOOR

PLAN INFO:

FIRST FLOOR	936 SQ. FT.
SECOND FLOOR	777 SQ. FT.
GARAGE/STORAGE	624 SQ. FT.
FOUNDATION	BASEMENT
BEDROOMS	THREE
BATHS	2(FULL), 1(HALF)
SQ. FT. TOTAL	**1,713 SQ. FT.**

COMFORT AND CONVENIENCE IN AN ELEGANT SETTING

Transom windows, skylights, and an open plan combine to make this sturdy brick classic a sun-filled retreat you'll love coming home to. The soaring ceilings of the foyer are mirrored in the fireplaced family room, a perfect place for informal gatherings. Its proximity to the island kitchen with built-in bar and adjoining breakfast room makes your mealtime efforts easier. When you want to entertain in style, choose the formal living and dining rooms just inside the front door. Down a short hall off the foyer, you'll find a luxurious master suite featuring a vaulted bath with garden spa. Enjoy the family room view from the upstairs balcony that leads to two more bedrooms and a full bath with double vanities.

This tiled Foyer is quite spacious, leads to the Dining Room on the right or the Living Room on the left, and makes for a grand entrance into a great home.

This Kitchen and the Breakfast Room flow together into one open area for added convenience. The center island is great for really quick meals or snacks while studying.

Photography by Beth Singer

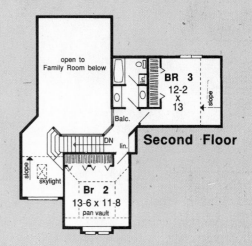

open to
Family Room below

BR 3
12-2
x
13

slope

Balc.

DN   lin.

slope

skylight

Second Floor

Br 2
13-6 x 11-8
pan vault

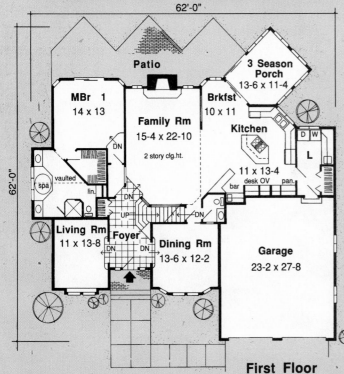

62'-0"

62'-0"

Patio

3 Season Porch
13-6 x 11-4

MBr 1
14 x 13

Brkfst
10 x 11

Family Rm
15-4 x 22-10

2 story clg. ht.

Kitchen

DN

11 x 13-4

D W

L

vaulted

desk OV pan.

bar

spa

lin.

DN

UP

DN

Living Rm
11 x 13-8

Foyer

DN   DN

DN

Dining Rm
13-6 x 12-2

Garage
23-2 x 27-8

First Floor

PLAN INFO:

FIRST FLOOR	1,859 SQ. FT.
SECOND FLOOR	579 SQ. FT.
BASEMENT	1,859 SQ. FT.
GARAGE	622 SQ. FT.
FOUNDATION	BASEMENT
BEDROOMS	THREE
BATHS	2(FULL), 1(HALF)
SQ. FT. TOTAL	2,438 SQ. FT.

CONTEMPORARY DESIGN FEATURES SUNKEN LIVING ROOM

Wood adds its warmth to the contemporary features of this solar design. Generous use of southern glass doors and windows, an air-lock entry, skylights and a living room fireplace reduce energy needs. R-26 insulation is used for floors and sloping ceilings. Decking rims the front of the home and provides access through sliding glass doors to a bedroom/den area and living room. The dining room lies up several steps from the living room and is separated from it by a half-wall. The dining room flows into the kitchen through an eating bar. A second floor landing balcony overlooks the living room. Two bedrooms, one with its own private deck, and a full bath complete the second level.

Step down to your sun-filled Living Room, warmed by a towering fireplace and accessible to a large wrap-around deck.

This home is very interesting from any view — intricate angles, many windows and skylights, and an enormous rear deck combine for overall good looks.

Photography by Beth Singer
The photographed home has been modified to suit individual tastes...

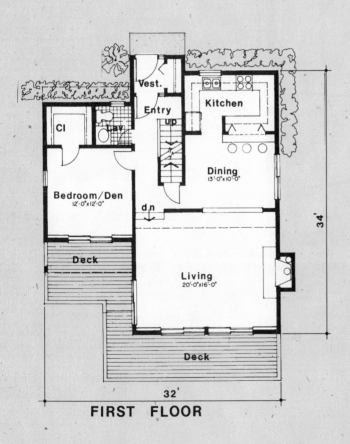

FIRST FLOOR

- Vest.
- Entry
- up
- Kitchen
- Cl
- Lav.
- Bedroom/Den 12'-0"x12'-0"
- dn
- Dining 13'-0"x10'-0"
- Deck
- Living 20'-0"x16'-0"
- Deck
- 32'
- 34'

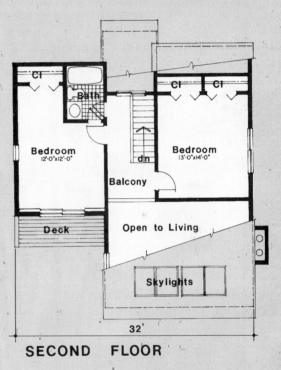

SECOND FLOOR

- Cl
- Bath
- Bedroom 12'-0"x12'-0"
- Cl
- Cl
- Bedroom 13'-0"x14'-0"
- Balcony
- dn
- Deck
- Open to Living
- Skylights
- 32'

PLAN INFO:

FIRST FLOOR	911 SQ. FT.
SECOND FLOOR	576 SQ. FT.
BASEMENT	911 SQ. FT.
FOUNDATION	BASEMENT
BEDROOMS	THREE
BATHS	1(FULL), 1(HALF)
SQ. FT. TOTAL	1,487 SQ. FT.

DESIGN NO. 26112

DRAMATIC AWARD WINNING ENERGY SAVER

Step inside this three-bedroom solar beauty and you'll know why it won awards for its ingenious design. Twin greenhouses off the living and family rooms provide dramatic views and a constant climate throughout the house for energy efficiency. Giant cutouts and floor grates in the upstairs bedrooms insure a continuous flow of solar warmth. And, when the sun goes down, heat-holding brick floors and a massive fireplace will help keep the energy bills down. You'll appreciate the efficient galley kitchen that serves the dining room, family room, and outdoor deck with ease. Two full baths adjoin the bedrooms upstairs and down for added convenience in the morning rush.

This sun filled Family Room enjoys magnificent views of the adjoining Greenhouse and contains a cozy fireplace — sit back and relax....

Enjoy cooking with ease — abundant counter and cabinet space allow two cooks to get the job done with efficiency — allowing more time for relaxing dining.

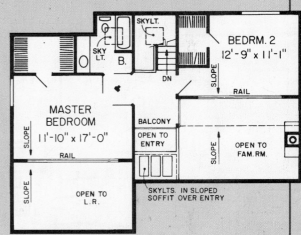

BEDRM. 2
12'-9" x 11'-1"

SKYLT.

SKY
LT.

B.

DN

SLOPE

RAIL

MASTER
BEDROOM
11'-10" x 17'-0"

SLOPE

BALCONY

OPEN TO
ENTRY

SLOPE

OPEN TO
FAM. RM.

RAIL

SLOPE

OPEN TO
L.R.

SKYLTS. IN SLOPED
SOFFIT OVER ENTRY

SECOND FLOOR

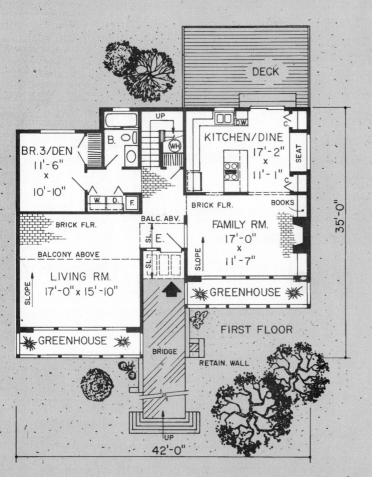

DECK

UP

B.

BR.3/DEN
11'-6"
x
10'-10"

KITCHEN/DINE
17'-2"
x
11'-1"

WH

DW.

C.

SEAT

W. D. F.

BRICK FLR.

BOOKS

BRICK FLR.

BALC. ABV.

SL.

E.

SL.

35'-0"

BALCONY ABOVE

SL.

FAMILY RM.
17'-0"
x
11'-7"

SLOPE

SLOPE

LIVING RM.
17'-0" x 15'-10"

GREENHOUSE

GREENHOUSE

FIRST FLOOR

BRIDGE

RETAIN. WALL

UP

42'-0"

PLAN INFO:

FIRST FLOOR	1,218 SQ. FT.
SECOND FLOOR	654 SQ. FT.
FOUNDATION	CRAWL SPACE
BEDROOMS	THREE
BATHS	2(FULL)
SQ. FT. TOTAL	**1,872 SQ. FT.**

PRICE CODE D

An
EXCLUSIVE DESIGN
By Karl Kreeger

PLAN INFO:

FIRST FLOOR	1,789 SQ. FT.
SECOND FLOOR	568 SQ. FT.
BASEMENT	1,789 SQ. FT.
GARAGE	529 SQ. FT.
FOUNDATION	BASEMENT
BEDROOMS	THREE
BATHS	2(FULL), 1(HALF)
SQ. FT. TOTAL	**2,357 SQ. FT.**

First floor plan:

DECK

KIT./BRKFST.
14'-4"x22'-4"

LIVING ROOM
17'-0"x23'-4"
(11'-0" CLG.)

M. BEDROOM
14'-10"x15'-4"

BAR

CLG. FAN

TV

CLG. FAN

ISLAND

DESK BOOKS

C.

B.

SKYLIGHT

8' CLG.

9' CLO—11' CLG.

H.

L. LIN.

SLOPE

DW

O.

P.

UP

DN

SLOPE

FOYER

C.

W. D.

LAUNDRY

C.

SHWR.

55'-0"

SLOPE

SLOPE

DINING
12'-2"x12'-4"

?

FIRST FLOOR

GARAGE
22'-4"x22'-8"

61'-0"

BEDROOM 3
11'-4"x12'-6"

C.

L.

B.

BEDROOM 2
11'-4"x11'-10"
10' CLG.

H.

DN

8' CLG.

SLOPE

SLOPE

CEDAR CLOSET

ATTIC STOR.

C.

SECOND FLOOR

Two-WAY FIREPLACE WARMS COMMON AREAS FOR COZY LIVING

Stucco, fieldstone, and rough-hewn timbers grace the elegant exterior of this three bedroom family home. But with abundant windows, high ceilings, and an open plan, this cheerful abode is a far cry from the chilly tudor castle of long ago. Flanked by a vaulted formal dining room and a stairway to the upstairs bedrooms, full bath, and built-in cedar closet, the central foyer leads to a spacious living room, kept comfortable in any season by a ceiling fan. Nearby, the first-floor master suite is loaded with amenities: a walk-in closet, skylit double vanities, and a sunken tub. Notice the cooktop island in the kitchen, the built-in bar adjacent to the living room, and the rear deck accessible through French doors in the breakfast room.

PRICE CODE **B**

Photography by Lauri Soloman

opt. **DECK**

opt. slab/ crawl space

LIVING RM.
14'-0"
X
17'-0"

KIT.
10'-8"
X
11'-8"

BRKFST.
10'-0"
X
9'-4"

LDRY.

W D

DINING
11'-4"
X
11'-8"

FOYER

GARAGE
21'-4"
X
21'-8"

COVERED
PORCH

FIRST
FLOOR

44'-0"

48'-0"

PLAN INFO:

FIRST FLOOR	909 SQ. FT.
SECOND FLOOR	854 SQ. FT.
BASEMENT	899 SQ. FT.
GARAGE	491 SQ. FT.
FOUNDATION	BASEMENT, SLAB CRAWL SPACE
BEDROOMS	THREE
BATHS	2(FULL), 1(HALF)
SQ. FT. TOTAL	**1,763 SQ. FT.**

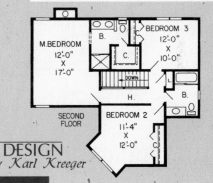

M.BEDROOM
12'-0"
X
17'-0"

BEDROOM 3
12'-0"
X
10'-0"

BEDROOM 2
11'-4"
X
12'-0"

SECOND
FLOOR

An
EXCLUSIVE DESIGN
By Karl Kreeger

COVERED PORCH OFFERED IN FARM-STYLE TRADITIONAL

This pleasant Traditional design has a farmhouse flavor exterior that incorporates a covered porch and features a circle wood louver on its garage, giving this design a feeling of sturdiness. Inside, on the first level, to the right of the foyer, is a formal dining room complete with a bay window and an elevated ceiling. To the left of the foyer is the cozy living room with a wood-burning fireplace. The kitchen, connected to the breakfast room, provides room for laundry facilities. A half-bath is also featured on the first floor. The master bedroom, on the second floor, has its own private bath and walk-in closet. The other two bedrooms share a full bath and one has an interesting shape. A two-car garage is also added into this design.

PRICE CODE D

The photographed home has been modified to suit individual tastes…

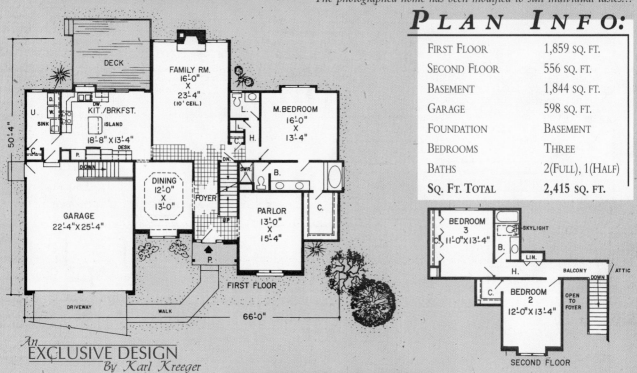

PLAN INFO:

FIRST FLOOR	1,859 SQ. FT.
SECOND FLOOR	556 SQ. FT.
BASEMENT	1,844 SQ. FT.
GARAGE	598 SQ. FT.
FOUNDATION	BASEMENT
BEDROOMS	THREE
BATHS	2(FULL), 1(HALF)
SQ. FT. TOTAL	**2,415 SQ. FT.**

An EXCLUSIVE DESIGN *By Karl Kreeger*

ELEGANT BRICK FACADE TOPS A GREAT FLOOR PLAN

There's a taste of Tudor in this three-bedroom family home. You'll see it in the brick facade, in the tiled foyer, and also in the fireplaced family room with ten-foot ceilings. But, it's easy to see how convenient this plan is, too. The island kitchen and breakfast nook are adjacent to a gracious formal dining room and outdoor deck, perfect for a summer supper outdoors. The first-floor master suite means you won't have to trek down the stairs for your morning coffee. It is also secluded from the other bedrooms for added privacy. The kids will love their upstairs bath. A skylight assures a sunny atmosphere at wakeup time. This plan has good looks and practicality rolled into one.

PRICE CODE **B**

PLAN INFO:

FIRST FLOOR	990 SQ. FT.
SECOND FLOOR	721 SQ. FT.
BASEMENT	934 SQ. FT.
GARAGE	429 SQ. FT.
FOUNDATION	BASEMENT
BEDROOMS	THREE
BATHS	2(FULL), 1(HALF)
SQ. FT. TOTAL	**1,711 SQ. FT.**

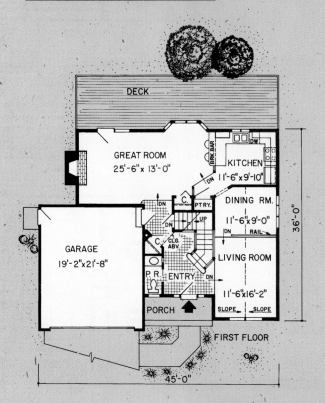

FIRST FLOOR

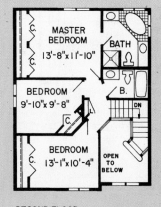

SECOND FLOOR

TWO STORY ENTRY EXUDES AN AIR OF CHARM AND BEAUTY

From the dramatic, two-story entry to the full-length deck off the massive Great room, this is a modern plan in a classic package. Cathedral ceilings soar over the formal dining and sunken living rooms, which are separated by an open railing. The corner kitchen efficiently serves formal and family eating areas. Can't you imagine a table overlooking the deck in the sunken Great room's sunny bay? Up the angular staircase, two bedrooms, each with a huge closet, share a full bath. You'll have your own private bath, including double vanities and a sun-washed raised tub, in the master suite located at the rear of the house.

PRICE CODE B

An
EXCLUSIVE DESIGN
By Karl Kreeger

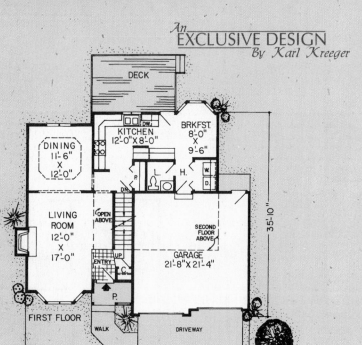

DECK

KITCHEN
12'-0" X 8'-0"

BRKFST.
8'-0"
X
9'-6"

DINING
11'-6"
X
12'-0"

LIVING
ROOM
12'-0"
X
17'-0"

OPEN
ABOVE

SECOND
FLOOR
ABOVE

GARAGE
21'-8" X 21'-4"

35'-10"

ENTRY
UP

FIRST FLOOR

WALK

DRIVEWAY

42'-0"

PLAN INFO:

FIRST FLOOR	877 SQ. FT.
SECOND FLOOR	910 SQ. FT.
BASEMENT	877 SQ. FT.
GARAGE	458 SQ. FT.
FOUNDATION	BASEMENT
BEDROOMS	THREE
BATHS	2(FULL), 1(HALF)
SQ. FT. TOTAL	**1,787 SQ. FT.**

BEDROOM 2
11'-8"
X
10'-0"

MAST. BEDROOM
14'-4"
X
13'-6"

C.

C.

BEDROOM 3
12'-0"
X
13'-6"

OPEN
TO
ENTRY
BELOW

SHWR

SKYLT

PLANT
SHELF

SECOND FLOOR

SHELTERED PORCH MAKES FOR AN INVITING ENTRANCE

Enjoy the beauty and tradition of a two-story home. From the spacious, tiled entry, with a handy coat closet, to the seclusion of second floor bedrooms, you'll appreciate the classic features that distinguish a two-story home. You'll also delight in the modern touches that make this plan unique: the handsome window treatment in the living room; the oversized master bedroom with walk-in closet and deluxe, skylit bath; the efficient kitchen and charming breakfast nook; and the sweeping outdoor deck. Two additional bedrooms, each with their own walk-in closet, share a full bath. A plant shelf, located near the staircase landing, is just another special feature that makes this a really great home for anyone.

PRICE CODE C

An
EXCLUSIVE DESIGN
By Upright Design

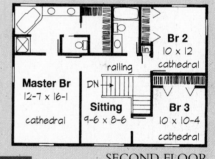

crawl access

Dining

furn. w/h

PLAN INFO:

FIRST FLOOR	1,034 SQ. FT.
SECOND FLOOR	944 SQ. FT.
BASEMENT	944 SQ. FT.
GARAGE/STORAGE	684 SQ. FT.
FOUNDATION	BASEMENT, SLAB CRAWL SPACE
BEDROOMS	FOUR
BATHS	2(FULL), 1(HALF)
SQ. FT. TOTAL	1,978 SQ. FT.

First Floor:

- Living 21-2 x 12-4 decor clg.
- Kitchen 14-11 x 12-4
- Storage/Shop 16-2 x 12-7
- Den/Guest 10 x 10
- Dining 10 x 12-3 decor clg.
- Garage 23-2 x 19-3

39'-6"

FIRST FLOOR   67'-6"

Second Floor:

- Master Br 12-7 x 16-1 cathedral
- railing
- Br 2 10 x 12 cathedral
- DN
- Sitting 9-6 x 8-6
- Br 3 10 x 10-4 cathedral

SECOND FLOOR

A VERY POPULAR DESIGN FOR ENJOYABLE LIVING IN THE 90'S

This delightful home's wrap-around covered porch recalls the warmth and charm of days past — lounging in the porch swing and savoring life. Inside, a spacious foyer welcomes guests and provides easy access to the formal dining room, secluded den/guest room (which might serve as your home office), and the large living room. Ceilings downstairs are all 9' high, with decorative vaults in the living and dining rooms. The kitchen, with its island/breakfast bar, is large enough for two people to work in comfortably. The adjacent laundry room also serves as a mudroom for boots and clothes, and leads directly to the garage, which features an ample storage/shop area at the rear. Upstairs, three bedrooms, each with cathedral ceilings, share a cheery, sunlit sitting area that also features a cathedral ceiling. For privacy, the master bedroom is separated from the other bedrooms, and boasts a palatial bathroom, complete with a whirlpool tub. If room to relax is what you're after, this home is loaded with irresistible features.

PRICE CODE B

PLAN INFO:

MAIN FLOOR	728 SQ. FT.
UPPER FLOOR	573 SQ. FT.
LOWER FLOOR	379 SQ. FT.
GARAGE	240 SQ. FT.
FOUNDATION	BASEMENT
BEDROOMS	THREE
BATHS	2 (FULL)
SQ. FT. TOTAL	**1,680 SQ. FT.**

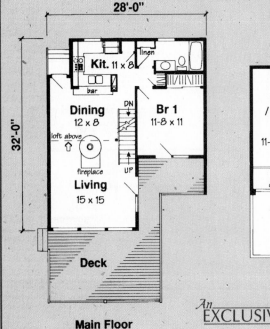

28'-0"

32'-0"

Kit. 11 x 8

linen

Dining 12 x 8

Br 1 11-8 x 11

loft above

DN

UP

fireplace

Living 15 x 15

bar

Deck

Main Floor

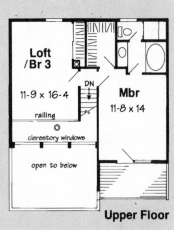

Loft /Br 3

11-9 x 16-4

DN

Mbr 11-8 x 14

railing

clerestory windows

open to below

Upper Floor

An **EXCLUSIVE DESIGN** *By Marshall Associates*

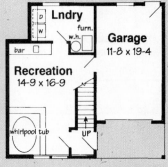

Lndry

furn.

D W

w.h.

Garage 11-8 x 19-4

bar

Recreation 14-9 x 16-9

whirlpool tub

UP

Lower Floor

VACATION HAVEN WITH MANY VIEWS – RELAX AND ENJOY!

This home is a vacation haven with views from every room whether it is situated on a lake or a mountaintop. The main floor features a living room and dining room split by a fireplace. The kitchen flows into the dining room and is gracefully separated by a bar. There is a bedroom and a full bath on the main floor. The second floor has a bedroom or library loft, with clerestory windows, which opens above the living room. The master bedroom and bath are also on the top floor. The lower floor has a large recreation room with a whirlpool tub, a bar, a laundry room and a garage. This home has large decks, for outdoor entertaining, and windows on one entire side of the plan.

PRICE CODE C

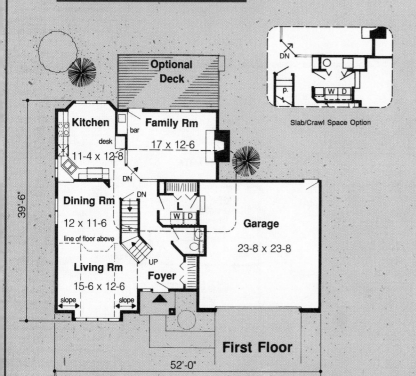

Optional Deck

Kitchen

desk   bar

11-4 x 12-8

Family Rm

17 x 12-6

DN

Dining Rm

12 x 11-6

line of floor above

DN

Living Rm

15-6 x 12-6

slope   slope

UP

Foyer

L

W D

Garage

23-8 x 23-8

First Floor

39'-6"

52'-0"

DN

P

W D

Slab/Crawl Space Option

PLAN INFO:

FIRST FLOOR	1,108 SQ. FT.
SECOND FLOOR	786 SQ. FT.
BASEMENT	972 SQ. FT.
GARAGE	567 SQ. FT.
FOUNDATION	BASEMENT, SLAB CRAWL SPACE
BEDROOMS	THREE
BATHS	2(FULL), 1(HALF)
SQ. FT. TOTAL	**1,894 SQ. FT.**

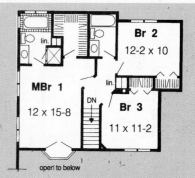

lin.

lin.

Br 2

12-2 x 10

MBr 1

12 x 15-8

DN

Br 3

11 x 11-2

open to below

Second Floor

TWO STORY WINDOW WALL IS A FEAST FOR THE EYES

It's hard to miss the focal point of this magnificent Contemporary home; the window wall that graces the dramatic two-story living room is a feast for the eyes, inside and out. And the open plan of this three-bedroom beauty adds even more excitement to the plans spacious ambience. Eat in the dining room that adjoins the living room, or have a snack by the fire in the sunken family room overlooking the rear deck. The nearby kitchen, with an angled counter design, is convenient to both. Three bedrooms share the second floor with two full baths. Be sure to notice the unique balcony area and large walk-in closet off the master suite.

PRICE CODE C

PLAN INFO:

FIRST FLOOR	1,060 SQ. FT.
SECOND FLOOR	990 SQ. FT.
BASEMENT	1,060 SQ. FT.
GARAGE	462 SQ. FT.
FOUNDATION	BASEMENT
BEDROOMS	THREE
BATHS	2(FULL), 1(HALF)
SQ. FT. TOTAL	2,050 SQ. FT.

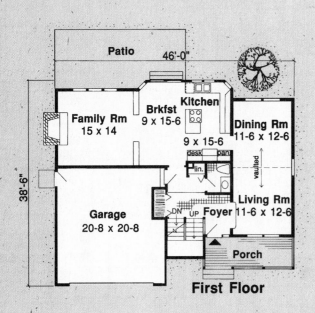

First Floor

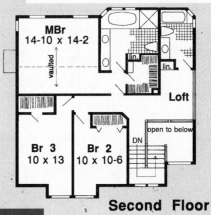

Second Floor

VAULTED CEILINGS LET THIS COMPACT GEM FEEL QUITE SPACIOUS

Thanks to vaulted ceilings and an absence of unnecessary walls, this compact gem feels larger than it really is. Step into the foyer and look up to a ceiling two stories high, an open staircase, and a spacious living and dining room arrangement with vaulted ceilings. At the core of the house, an efficient island kitchen opens to a sunny breakfast room with sliders to the rear patio. Whether you're serving a formal dinner, or a snack in the fireplaced family room, you're never more than a few steps away. Walk up the U-shaped stairs to a loft overlooking the scene below, which serves as a link to the three bedrooms and hall bath. The master suite features its own private bath with garden tub and double vanities.

PRICE CODE C

PLAN INFO:

FIRST FLOOR	1,079 SQ. FT.
SECOND FLOOR	750 SQ. FT.
GARAGE	548 SQ. FT.
FOUNDATION	BASEMENT, SLAB CRAWL SPACE
BEDROOMS	THREE
BATHS	2(FULL), 1(HALF)
SQ. FT. TOTAL	1,829 SQ. FT.

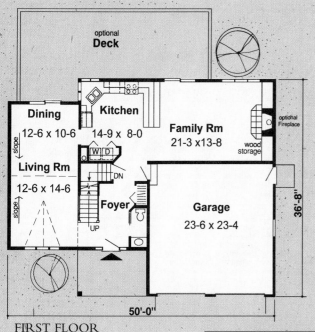

optional **Deck**

Dining 12-6 x 10-6

Kitchen 14-9 x 8-0

Family Rm 21-3 x13-8

optional Fireplace

wood storage

W D

Living Rm 12-6 x 14-6

DN

Foyer

UP

Garage 23-6 x 23-4

36'-8"

50'-0"

FIRST FLOOR

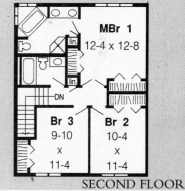

D W

Slab/Crawlspace Option

MBr 1 12-4 x 12-8

DN

Br 3 9-10 x 11-4

Br 2 10-4 x 11-4

SECOND FLOOR

CHARMING TWO-STORY WITH MODERN APPOINTMENTS

Enter into the spacious foyer, walk past the powder room and sloped-ceilinged living/dining room arrangement and head right into the fireplaced family room. Look to your right and view the modern kitchen with plenty of counter space and a breakfast bar for added convenience. Upstairs, you'll find two large bedrooms and a spacious master suite complete with a tub, step-in shower and double vanities in the master bath. For more than ample storage space, use the spacious, two-car garage. This Traditional home has an open floor plan for easy living and all the amenities you look for when buying a new home. Look it over — could this be your new dream home?

PRICE CODE E

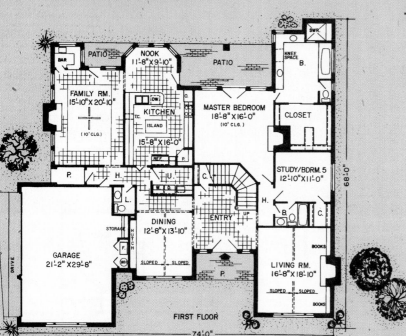

FIRST FLOOR

74'-0"

68'-0"

PLAN INFO:

FIRST FLOOR	2,849 SQ. FT.
SECOND FLOOR	1,086 SQ. FT.
GARAGE	721 SQ. FT.
FOUNDATION	SLAB
BEDROOMS	FIVE
BATHS	4(FULL), 1(HALF)
SQ. FT. TOTAL	**3,935 SQ. FT.**

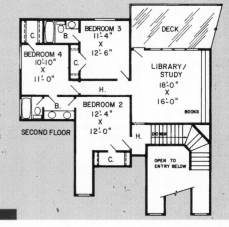

SECOND FLOOR

SPACIOUS FIVE BEDROOM DESIGN HAS STUNNING ENTRY

Vaulted-ceilings, a gently curving staircase, and high, arched windows make the entry to this spacious, five-bedroom home an airy celebration of light and space. A short hall leads from the formal dining room to the cozy family room, island kitchen, and sunny breakfast nook with adjoining brick patio. Warmed by its own fireplace, the master bedroom shares a private

wing on the first floor with a bedroom that could double as a study. The second floor deck off the library is a great place to enjoy a sunny afternoon. And, don't worry about storage. Two pantries, a room-sized wetbar, and walk-in closets in every bedroom mean you'll never have to worry about clutter.

PRICE CODE C

PLAN INFO:

FIRST FLOOR	1,280 SQ. FT.
SECOND FLOOR	735 SQ. FT.
GREENHOUSE	80 SQ. FT.
PLAYHOUSE	80 SQ. FT.
FOUNDATION	CRAWL SPACE
BEDROOMS	THREE
BATHS	2(FULL), 1(HALF)
SQ. FT. TOTAL	**2,015 SQ. FT.**

MAIN FLOOR PLAN

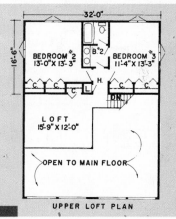

UPPER LOFT PLAN

OPEN PLAN IS ACCENTED BY LOFT, WINDOWS AND DECKS

The first floor living space of this inviting home combines the family room and dining room for comfortable family living. The large kitchen shares a preparation/eating bar with the dining room for added convenience. The ample utility room is designed with a pantry, plus plenty of room for a freezer, washer and dryer. Also on the first floor is the master suite with its two closets and five-piece bath which opens into a greenhouse making it quite a unique room. The second floor is highlighted by a loft which overlooks the first floor living space and makes for a cozy sitting area. The two upstairs bedrooms each have double closets and share a four-piece, compartmentalized bath.

DESIGN NO. 10500

PRICE CODE E

MASTER
BEDROOM
17'-0"
X
15'-4"

GREAT ROOM
17'-0"
X
23'-4"

BREAKFAST
11'-4"
X
9'-6"

KITCHEN
19'-10" X 15'-8"

DINING
ROOM
12'-10"
X
13'-4"

GARAGE
23'-4"
X
23'-4"

FOYER

PORCH

PATIO

60'-4"

72'-0"

FIRST FLOOR

An
EXCLUSIVE DESIGN
By Karl Kreeger

PLAN INFO:

FIRST FLOOR	2,188 SQ. FT.
SECOND FLOOR	1,083 SQ. FT.
BASEMENT	2,188 SQ. FT.
GARAGE	576 SQ. FT.
FOUNDATION	BASEMENT
BEDROOMS	FOUR
BATHS	3(FULL), 1(HALF)
SQ. FT. TOTAL	3,271 SQ. FT.

BEDROOM 4
10'-8"
X
13'-0"

UPPER GREAT
ROOM

LOFT
9'-8"
X
7'-8"

BEDROOM 2
10'-8"
X
15'-6"

BEDROOM 3
13'-0"
X
13'-4"

UPPER FOYER

SECOND FLOOR

CLASSIC TUDOR PLAN BLENDS WITH DISTINCTIVE EXTERIOR

*L*ots of living is packed into this well-organized design. The expansive Great room is accented by a massive fireplace and a beamed, cathedral ceiling. The kitchen and breakfast area include a charming and efficient angled cooking center, while the formal dining room is convenient yet protected from noise for intimate gatherings. Indulge yourself in the master suite with its luxurious 5-piece bath, including a raised tile tub. An elegant curved staircase leads you to the upper level. Three bedrooms and a loft, which looks upon the foyer, are located on the second floor. Each bedroom has a walk-in closet and direct access to a full bath. This just might be the perfect design!

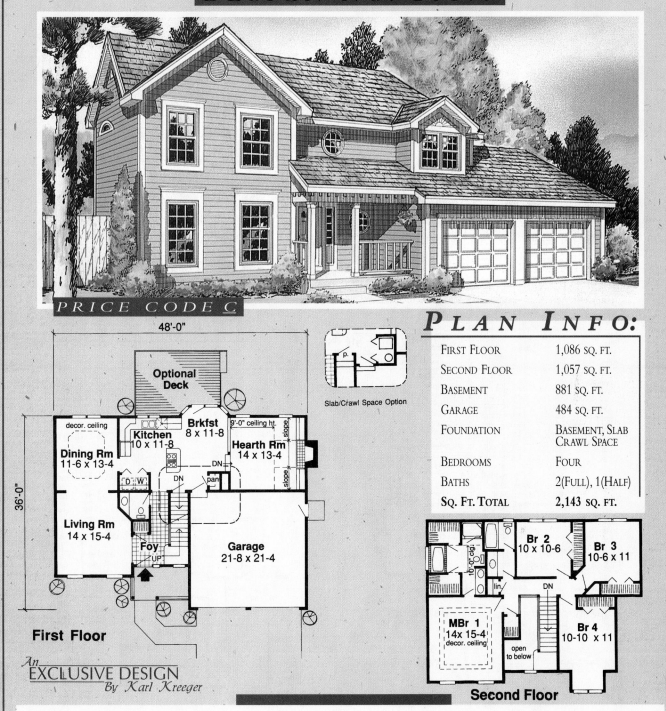

PRICE CODE C

48'-0"

Optional Deck

Slab/Crawl Space Option

36'-0"

decor. ceiling

Dining Rm 11-6 x 13-4

Kitchen 10 x 11-8

Brkfst 8 x 11-8

9'-0" ceiling ht.

slope

Hearth Rm 14 x 13-4

slope

D W

DN

DN

pan

Living Rm 14 x 15-4

Foy

UP

Garage 21-8 x 21-4

First Floor

An EXCLUSIVE DESIGN *By Karl Kreeger*

PLAN INFO:

FIRST FLOOR	1,086 SQ. FT.
SECOND FLOOR	1,057 SQ. FT.
BASEMENT	881 SQ. FT.
GARAGE	484 SQ. FT.
FOUNDATION	BASEMENT, SLAB CRAWL SPACE
BEDROOMS	FOUR
BATHS	2(FULL), 1(HALF)
SQ. FT. TOTAL	**2,143 SQ. FT.**

10'-0" clg.

lin.

Br 2 10 x 10-6

Br 3 10-6 x 11

DN

MBr 1 14x 15-4 decor. ceiling

open to below

Br 4 10-10 x 11

Second Floor

ENTERTAIN WITH EASE – BUILD THIS CAREFREE DESIGN

Enjoy the impressive staircase as you enter the foyer of this home. The formal living room and dining room provide for classic entertaining space. For a more contemporary gathering, take advantage of the roomy gourmet kitchen with its range-top island, and the open flow into the windowed breakfast area. Just over the railing the sunken hearth room awaits you.

Take a step down and appreciate its well-designed sloping ceilings and space. Upstairs, find three large bedrooms, a full bath, plus a master bedroom suite. This room features an elegant decorative ceiling, and an original bath and dressing room arrangement. Take full advantage of the whirlpool tub, for quiet relaxation, and double vanities.

PRICE CODE B

An
EXCLUSIVE DESIGN
By Karl Kreeger

PLAN INFO:

FIRST FLOOR	901 SQ. FT.
SECOND FLOOR	864 SQ. FT.
BASEMENT	901 SQ. FT.
GARAGE	594 SQ. FT.
FOUNDATION	BASEMENT
BEDROOMS	THREE
BATHS	2(FULL), 1(HALF)
SQ. FT. TOTAL	1,765 SQ. FT.

First Floor

Deck
Dining 11-4 x 15-4
Kit 10 x 11-4
desk
ceiling height 13'-4"
Living Rm 20-8 x 13-4
Garage 21-4 x 21-8
Foy
38'-0"
47'-0"

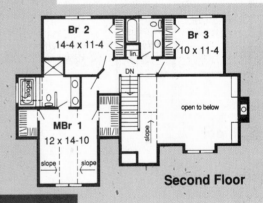

Second Floor

Br 2 14-4 x 11-4
Br 3 10 x 11-4
MBr 1 12 x 14-10
open to below

DRAMA ON A GRAND SCALE UPON ENTERING THIS HOME

The Traditional clapboard exterior of this tidy home is quite deceiving. Step inside and you'll find drama on a grand scale. The central foyer, crowned by a balcony, slopes upward to meet the high ceilings of the fireplaced living room. At the rear of the house, you'll find a skylit dining room with a three-sided view of the adjoining deck. Just across the counter, the gourmet kitchen features a built-in desk and loads of cabinets. Three bedrooms share the second floor with two full baths. Rear bedrooms share the hall bath, but the master suite boasts a luxury bath complete with double vanities, garden tub and two ample sized closets. Please notice the generous closet and storage space throughout this exceptional, compact home.

PRICE CODE D

An
EXCLUSIVE DESIGN
By Karl Kreeger

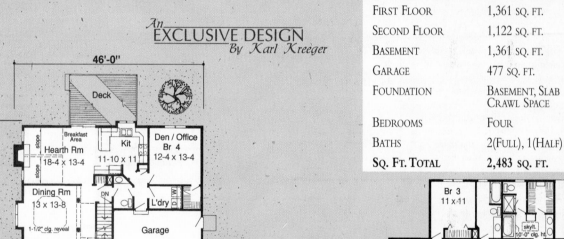

46'-0"

45'-0"

Deck

Breakfast Area

Hearth Rm
18-4 x 13-4

Kit
11-10 x 11

Den / Office
Br 4
12-4 x 13-4

Dining Rm
13 x 13-8
1-1/2" clg. reveal

DN

L'dry

D W

Living Rm
13 x 15-4

UP

Foyer

Garage
21-4 x 21-4

slope

First Floor

Br 3
11 x 11

skylt.

10'-0" clg. ht.

lin.

Balcony DN

sl.

Br 2
13-6 x 11

MBr 1
21 x 15-6

slope

foyer
below

sl.

sl.

sl.

sl.

Sitting Area
15 x 7-8

Second Floor

PLAN INFO:

FIRST FLOOR	1,361 SQ. FT.
SECOND FLOOR	1,122 SQ. FT.
BASEMENT	1,361 SQ. FT.
GARAGE	477 SQ. FT.
FOUNDATION	BASEMENT, SLAB CRAWL SPACE
BEDROOMS	FOUR
BATHS	2(FULL), 1(HALF)
SQ. FT. TOTAL	**2,483 SQ. FT.**

EVERY ROOM HAS ITS OWN SPECIAL CHARM AND CHARACTER

Generous, well-placed windows and angular ceilings give every room of this Traditional charmer a cheerful open atmosphere. The living and dining rooms flow together off the foyer, adorned by the classic elegance of a palladium window, columns and decorative ceilings. Family areas at the rear of the house include a toasty hearth room adjoining the efficient kitchen. And, for warm-weather dining, just step out to the deck off the breakfast room. One bedroom, tucked behind the garage, is just across from the powder room. You'll find the other bedrooms upstairs. With its skylit, double-vanity bath, cozy sitting area, and room-sized closet, the master suite over the garage is the crowning glory of this exquisite home.

DELUXE VACATION CHALET

DESIGN NO. 9964

This romantic chalet design would be equally appealing along an ocean beach or mountain stream. Restful log fires will add atmosphere in the sizable recreation room bordering the patio of this chalet. Upstairs, another fireplace warms the living and dining rooms which are accessible to the large wooden sun deck. Four bedrooms and two baths are outlined. The home is completely insulated for year round convenience and contains washer and dryer space.

First floor — 896 sq. ft.
Second floor — 457 sq. ft.
Basement — 864 sq. ft.
Foundation — Basement
Bedrooms — Four
Baths — Two

Total living area — 1,353 sq. ft.

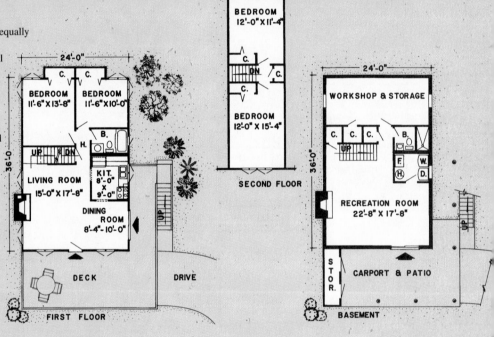

MASTER SUITE CROWNS PLAN

DESIGN NO. 10394

The master bedroom suite occupies the entire second level of this passive solar design. The living room rises two stories in the front, as does the foyer, and can be opened to the master suite to aid in air circulation. Skylights in the sloping ceilings of the kitchen and master bath give abundant light to these areas. Angled walls, both inside and out, lend a unique appeal. An air-lock entry, 2x6 exterior studs, 6-inch concrete floor, and generous use of insulation help make this an energy efficient design.

First floor — 1,306 sq. ft.
Second floor — 472 sq. ft.
Garage — 576 sq. ft.
Foundation — Bsmt., Slab, Crawl Space
Bedrooms — Three
Baths — Two

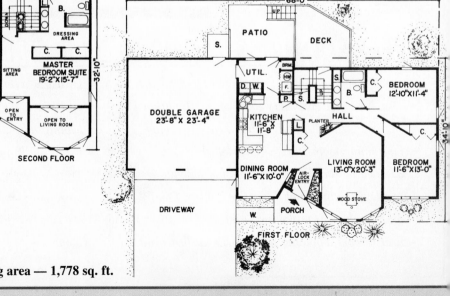

Total living area — 1,778 sq. ft.

VICTORIAN DETAILS ENHANCE FACADE

DESIGN NO. 10593

A charming porch shelters the entrance of this four bedroom home with a delightful country kitchen. In colder climates, the closed vestibule cuts heat loss. Off the central foyer, the cozy living room shares a fireplace with the family room, which contains a bar and access to the patio and screened porch for entertaining. The bay-windowed breakfast room is handy for quick meals. Or, use the formal dining room with an octagonal recessed ceiling. All the bedrooms, located on the second floor, have walk-in closets.

First floor — 1,450 sq. ft.
Second floor — 1,341 sq. ft.
Basement — 1,450 sq. ft.
Garage — 629 sq. ft.
Covered porch — 144 sq. ft.
Wood storage — 48 sq. ft.
Foundation — Basement
Bedrooms — Four
Baths — 2(Full), 1(Half)

Total living area — 2,791 sq. ft.

An
EXCLUSIVE DESIGN
By Karl Kreeger

PRICE CODE A

RUSTIC EXTERIOR; COMPLETE HOME

DESIGN NO. 34600

Although rustic in appearance, the interior of this cabin is quiet, modern and comfortable. Small in overall size, it still contains three bedrooms and two baths in addition to a large, two-story living room with exposed beams. As a hunting/fishing lodge or mountain retreat, this compares well.

First floor — 1,013 sq. ft.
Second floor — 315 sq.ft.
Basement — 1,013 sq. ft.
Foundation — Basement, Slab, Crawl Space
Bedrooms — Three
Baths — Two

Total living area —1,328 sq. ft.

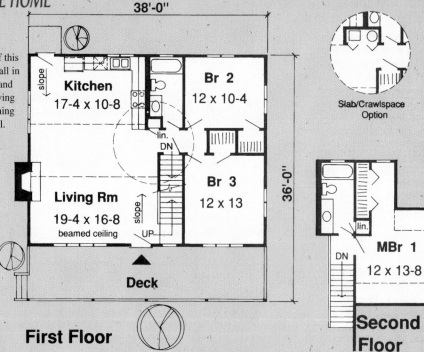

38'-0"

Kitchen
17-4 x 10-8

Br 2
12 x 10-4

slope

lin.
DN

Br 3
12 x 13

Living Rm
19-4 x 16-8
beamed ceiling

UP
slope

36'-0"

▲
Deck

First Floor

Slab/Crawlspace Option

lin.

MBr 1
12 x 13-8

DN

Second Floor

FARMHOUSE FLAVOR

An **EXCLUSIVE DESIGN**
By Karl Kreeger

DESIGN NO. 10785

The charm of an old-fashioned farmhouse combines with sizzling contemporary excitement in this three-bedroom home. Classic touches abound, from the clapboard exterior with its inviting, wrap-around porch to the wood stove that warms the entire house. Inside, the two-story foyer, crowned by a plant ledge high overhead, affords a view of the soaring, skylit living room and rear deck beyond sliding glass doors. To the right, there's a formal dining room with bay window, just steps away from the kitchen. The well-appointed master suite completes the first floor. Upstairs, you'll find a full bath, two more bedrooms, each with a walk-in closet, and a cozy gable sitting nook.

skylight
open to below

Balcony

Br 2
10-4 x 14

DN

Br 3
11 x 14

plant ledge

slope

Optional Deck

Living Rm
13 x 19-6

Ldry
W D
pan

wood stove

MBr 1
13-6 x 14

Kitchen
11 x 12

DN

Dining Rm
12-10 x 13-6

Foyer
▲

39'-0"

47'-0"

First floor — 1,269 sq. ft.
Second floor — 638 sq. ft.
Basement — 1,269 sq. ft.
Foundation — Basement, Slab, Crawl Space
Bedrooms — Three
Baths — 2(Full), 1(Half)

Total living area — 1,907 sq. ft.

WONDERFUL VIEWS EVERYWHERE

DESIGN NO. 20068

Consider this home if your backyard is something special in each season. Both living and dining areas offer broad views across the deck to the beautiful scenery beyond. Even the balcony on the second floor captures it all. The open floor plan in the interior of the home brings the view to the kitchen and front hall as well. The master bedroom, with a fabulous walk-in closet and lavish bath, maintains its privacy to the side while indulging in the view of the backyard. The second floor bedrooms are notable for their oversized closets.

First floor — 1,266 sq. ft.
Second floor — 489 sq. ft.
Basement — 1,266 sq. ft.
Garage — 484 sq. ft.
Foundation — Basement
Bedrooms — Three
Baths — 2(Full), 1(Half)

Total living area — 1,755 sq. ft.

An
EXCLUSIVE DESIGN
By Karl Kreeger

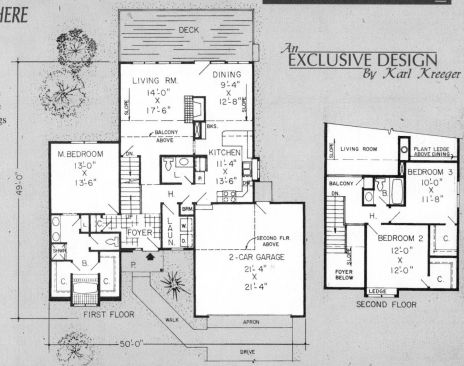

PRICE CODE A

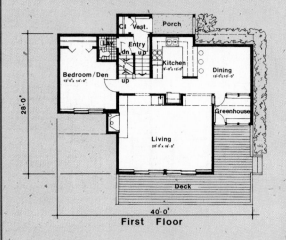

First Floor

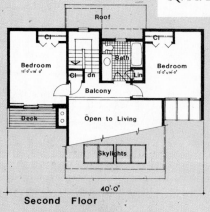

Second Floor

PLAN INFO:

FIRST FLOOR	902 SQ. FT.
SECOND FLOOR	567 SQ. FT.
FOUNDATION	BASEMENT
BEDROOMS	THREE
BATHS	1(FULL), 1(HALF)
SQ. FT. TOTAL	**1,469 SQ. FT.**

PASSIVE SOLAR AND CONTEMPORARY FEATURES UNITE

Numerous south-facing glass doors and windows, skylights and a greenhouse clue the exterior viewer to this passive solar Contemporary design. For minimum heat loss, 2x6 studs for R-19 insulation are used in exterior walls, and R-33 insulation is used in all sloping ceilings. The living room employs a concrete slab floor for solar gain. Basement space is located under the kitchen, dining room, lower bedroom and den. A northern entrance through a vestibule and French doors channels you upward to the first floor living area. A unique feature on this level is the skylit living room ceiling which slants two stories. Second story rooms are lit by clerestory windows. Two balconies are on this level: an exterior one off the bedroom and an interior one overlooking the living room.

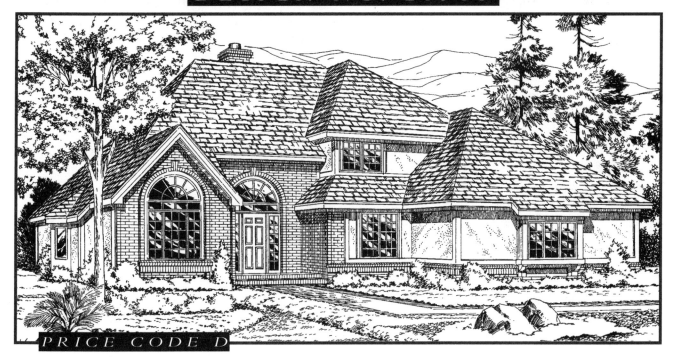

PRICE CODE D

SPACIOUS STUCCO DESIGN

No. 20368

■ This plan features:

— Three bedrooms

— Two and one half baths

■ A vaulted foyer flanked by a soaring Living Room with huge palladium windows

■ A Family Room with a massive two-way fireplace

■ A Master Suite with garden spa, private deck access, and a walk-in closet

FIRST FLOOR — 1,752 SQ. FT.
SECOND FLOOR — 620 SQ. FT.
BASEMENT — 1,726 SQ. FT.
GARAGE — 714 SQ. FT.

TOTAL LIVING AREA:
2,372 SQ. FT.

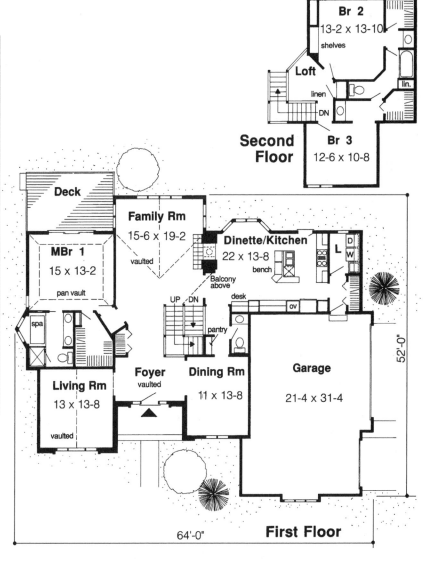

Second Floor

Br 2
13-2 x 13-10
shelves
Loft
linen
lin.
DN
Br 3
12-6 x 10-8

Deck

Family Rm
15-6 x 19-2
vaulted

MBr 1
15 x 13-2
pan vault

spa

Dinette/Kitchen
22 x 13-8
bench
Balcony above
desk
ov
pantry
UP   DN

Living Rm
13 x 13-8
vaulted

Foyer
vaulted

Dining Rm
11 x 13-8

Garage
21-4 x 31-4

52'-0"

64'-0"

First Floor

PRICE CODE F

SURROUND YOURSELF WITH LUXURY

No. 10615

■ This plan features:

— Five bedrooms

— Five full baths

■ Luxurious surroundings in all bedrooms

■ A tiled foyer and a grand staircase with a landing that leads to both wings

■ A vast Living Room for formal entertaining and a Kitchen designed to serve the eating areas and Family Room

■ A patio, pool, second floor deck and courtyard

FIRST FLOOR — 4,075 SQ. FT.
SECOND FLOOR — 1,179 SQ. FT.
GARAGE — 633 SQ. FT.

TOTAL LIVING AREA:
5,254 SQ. FT.

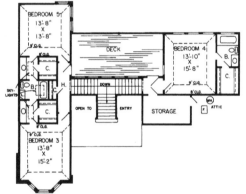

PRICE CODE E

TODAY'S AMENITIES, YESTERDAY'S OLD-FASHIONED CHARM

No. 10805

■ This plan features:

— Three bedrooms

— Two and one half baths

■ Wide corner boards, clapboard siding, and a full-length covered porch lending a friendly air to this classic home

■ A central entry opening to a cozy Den on the right, a sunken Living Room with adjoining Dining Room on the left

■ An informal Dining Nook accented by bay windows

■ A Master Suite spanning the rear of the home including a huge, walk-in closet, a private bath with double vanities, and a whirlpool tub

FIRST FLOOR — 1,622 SQ. FT.
SECOND FLOOR — 1,156 SQ. FT.

TOTAL LIVING AREA:
2,778 SQ. FT.

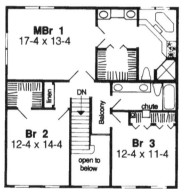

Second Floor

MBr 1
17-4 x 13-4

Br 2
12-4 x 14-4

Br 3
12-4 x 11-4

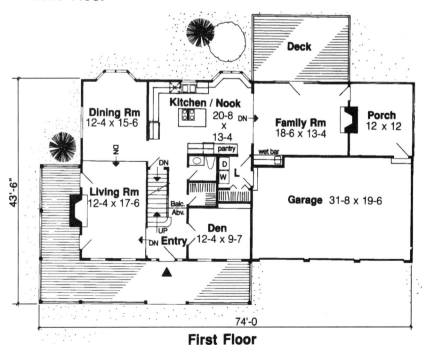

First Floor

Deck

Dining Rm
12-4 x 15-6

Kitchen / Nook
20-8 x 13-4

Family Rm
18-6 x 13-4

Porch
12 x 12

pantry

wet bar

Living Rm
12-4 x 17-6

Garage 31-8 x 19-6

Den
12-4 x 9-7

Entry

43'-6"

74'-0"

PRICE CODE C

No. 20050

This plan features:

— Three bedrooms

— Two full and one half baths

■ A beautiful front door surrounded by windows leads into a tiled, vaulted Foyer and expansive Living Room

■ A sloped ceiling, a wall of windows and a large fireplace enhance the Living Room

■ A formal Dining Room with a decorative ceiling conveniently adjacent to the Kitchen

■ A Kitchen equipped with a corner sink, a cooktop island/snack bar and a built-in pantry

■ A Master Suite featuring a double closet and a Bath with a raised garden tub and double vanity

■ Two additional bedrooms on the second floor

FIRST FLOOR — 1,303 SQ. FT.
SECOND FLOOR — 596 SQ. FT.
BASEMENT — 1,303 SQ. FT.
GARAGE — 460 SQ. FT.

TOTAL LIVING AREA :
1,899 SQ. FT.

PERFECT FOR ENTERTAINING

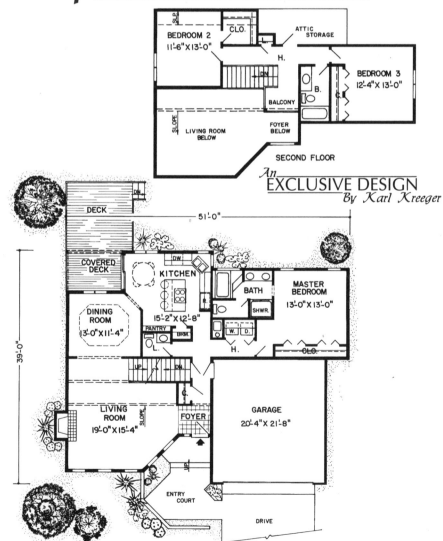

An
EXCLUSIVE DESIGN
By Karl Kreeger

PRICE CODE D

THE PERFECT HOME

No. 20199

■ This plan features:

— Four bedrooms

— Three and one half baths

■ A stunning fireplace in the Breakfast/Hearth Room with a built-in TV cabinet and plant shelf

■ A spacious Living Room with ten-foot ceiling height

■ A decorative ceiling enhancing the elegant Dining Room

■ An efficient Kitchen with all the amenities

■ A sloped ceiling in the Master Suite and a private full bath with walk-in closet

■ Three additional bedrooms, one with a private bath and two with walk-in closets

FIRST FLOOR — 1,760 SQ. FT.
SECOND FLOOR — 785 SQ. FT.
BASEMENT — 1,760 SQ. FT.
GARAGE — 797 SQ. FT.

TOTAL LIVING AREA:
2,545 SQ. FT.

An
EXCLUSIVE DESIGN
By Karl Kreeger

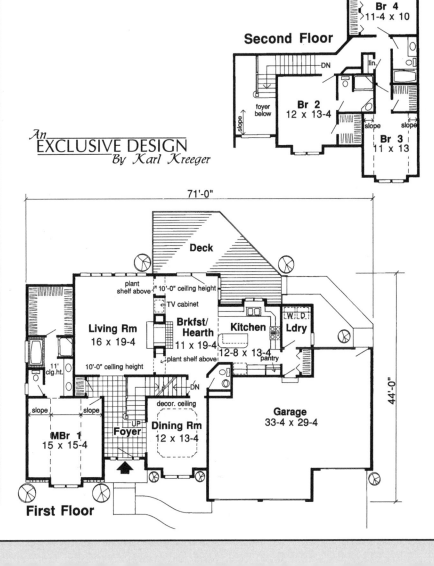

PRICE CODE E

FAMILY LIVING ON TWO LEVELS

No. 20090

■ This plan features:

— Four bedrooms

— Two and one half baths

■ A stacked window gracing the facade of this spacious, four-bedroom classic

■ A formal Parlor and Dining Room, both with decorative ceilings, off the foyer

■ Family areas at the rear of the house arranged for convenient access to the Kitchen

■ A sky-lit Breakfast room with a surrounding outdoor deck

■ A cozy fireplace in the Family Room

■ A first floor Master Suite with double vanities, a walk-in closet, and an elegant recessed ceiling

FIRST FLOOR — 1,933 SQ. FT.
SECOND FLOOR — 918 SQ. FT.
BASEMENT — 1,933 SQ. FT.
GARAGE— 484 SQ. FT.

TOTAL LIVING AREA:
2,851 SQ. FT.

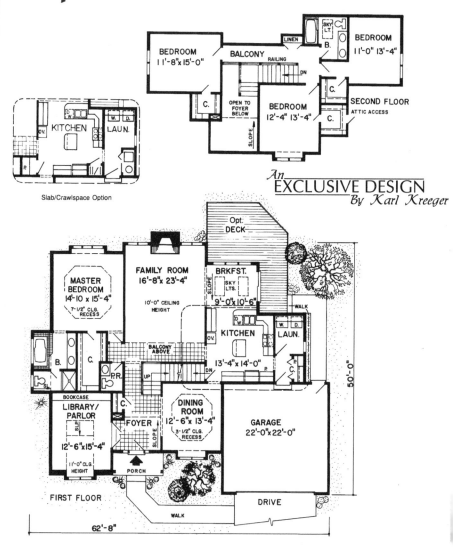

Slab/Crawlspace Option

An
EXCLUSIVE DESIGN
By Karl Kreeger

PRICE CODE D

BAY WINDOWS AND SKYLIGHTS BRIGHTEN THIS HOME

No. 10673

■ This plan features:

— Four bedrooms

— Two and one half baths

■ A Kitchen equipped with a pantry and Breakfast Nook leading onto a brick patio

■ An oversized Living Room with skylights and a fireplace

■ A Master Suite containing a whirlpool tub

FIRST FLOOR — 1,265 SQ. FT.
SECOND FLOOR — 1,210 SQ. FT.
BASEMENT — 1,247 SQ. FT.
GARAGE — 506 SQ. FT.

TOTAL LIVING AREA:
2,475 SQ. FT.

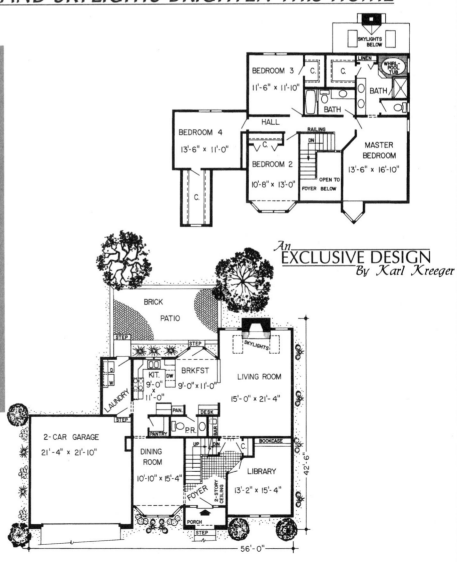

An EXCLUSIVE DESIGN *By Karl Kreeger*

PRICE CODE F

TUDOR FOR TODAY AND TOMORROW

No. 10761

■ This plan features:

— Four bedrooms

— Three and one half baths

■ Double doors opening to a huge entry foyer flanked by a formal Dining Room and a sunken Living Room

■ The cozy elegance of a book-lined Library

■ A Kitchen with a range top island and a sunny Breakfast room

■ A Master Suite with a fireplace, sitting area, and his-and-her closets

FIRST FLOOR — 1,926 SQ. FT.
SECOND FLOOR — 1,606 SQ. FT.
BASEMENT — 1,926 SQ. FT.
GARAGE — 840 SQ. FT.

TOTAL LIVING AREA:
3,532 SQ. FT.

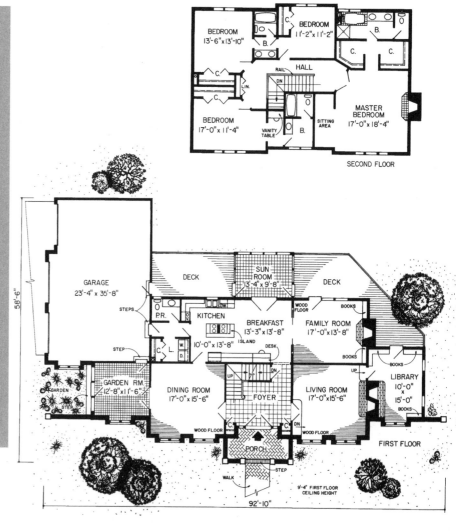

PRICE CODE C

HIGH IMPACT FAMILY HOME

No. 20111

■ This plan features:

— Four bedrooms

— Two and one half baths

■ A balcony linking the upstairs bedrooms and a skylit bath dividing a two-story foyer

■ A massive fireplace in the open Living Room

■ A well-situated Kitchen handy to both the formal Dining Room and sunny Breakfast area

■ A convenient, private first-floor Master Suite with a garden tub, step-in shower, and walk-in closet

FIRST FLOOR — 1,680 SQ. FT.
SECOND FLOOR — 514 SQ. FT.
BASEMENT — 1,045 SQ. FT.
GARAGE — 635 SQ. FT.

TOTAL LIVING AREA:
2,194 SQ. FT.

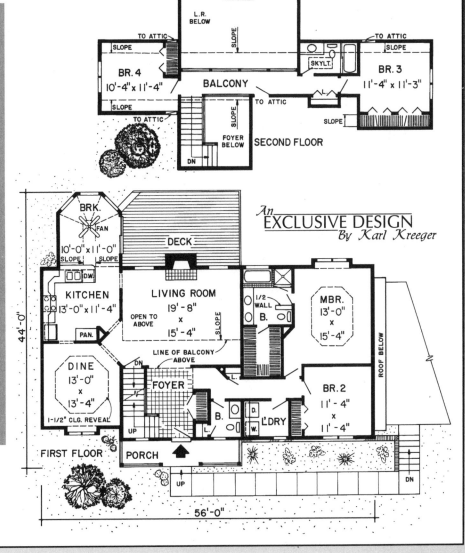

An
EXCLUSIVE DESIGN
By Karl Kreeger

PRICE CODE A

WELL ORGANIZED FLOOR PLAN

No. 20303

■ This plan features:

— Three bedrooms

— Two full baths

■ An air-lock vestibule entry that keeps the chill outside

■ A cozy sitting nook in the Living Room

■ A well-equipped Kitchen with a Breakfast nook

■ A sky-lit hall bath shared by two of the bedrooms

■ A Master Suite with his-n-her closets and a sky-lit private full bath

FIRST FLOOR — 885 SQ. FT.
SECOND FLOOR — 368 SQ. FT.
BASEMENT — 715 SQ. FT.

TOTAL LIVING AREA:
1,253 SQ. FT.

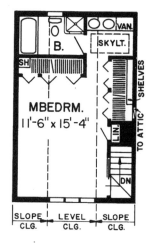

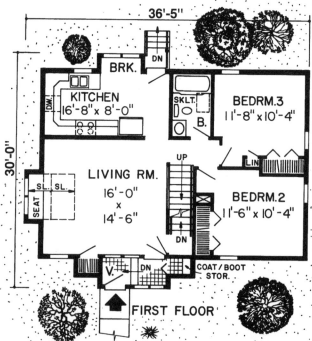

PRICE CODE C

STYLISH AND PRACTICAL PLAN

No. 20069

■ This plan features:

— Three bedrooms

— Two and one half baths

■ A Kitchen with a Breakfast Area large enough for most informal meals

■ A spacious Living Room with a fireplace

■ A formal Dining Room with a decorative ceiling for comfortable entertaining

■ A first floor Master Bedroom providing a private retreat and lavish Master Bath

FIRST FLOOR — 1,340 SQ. FT.
SECOND FLOOR — 651 SQ. FT.
BASEMENT — 1,322 SQ. FT.

TOTAL LIVING AREA:
1,991 SQ. FT.

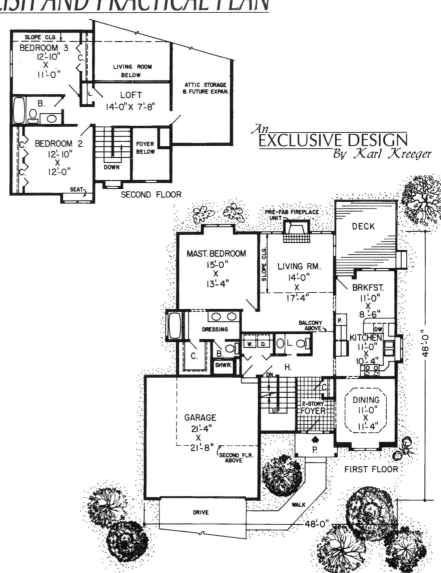

An
EXCLUSIVE DESIGN
By Karl Kreeger

PRICE CODE D

ROOM FOR FAMILY ACTIVITIES

No. 10649

■ This plan features:

— Three bedrooms

— Two and one half baths

■ A Family Room warmed by a fireplace, contains lots of windows, French doors, a wetbar and access to the covered porch

■ A Kitchen centered between a bay window breakfast nook and a formal Dining Room

■ Window seats adorning the front bedrooms

FIRST FLOOR — 1,285 SQ. FT.
SECOND FLOOR — 930 SQ. FT.
GARAGE — 492 SQ. FT.

**TOTAL LIVING AREA:
2,215 SQ. FT.**

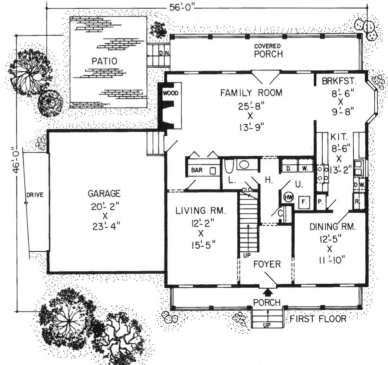

PRICE CODE D

TRADITION WITH MANY MODERN AMENITIES

No. 24246

- ■ This plan features:
- — Three bedrooms
- — Three full baths
- ■ A sloped, two-story ceiling in the Foyer giving a definite impression of distinguished elegance
- ■ A double door entrance into the formal Living Room adding anticipation while the corner fireplace adds warmth and atmosphere to the room
- ■ A built-in china alcove in the formal Dining Room
- ■ A U-shaped Kitchen directly accessed form the Dining Room
- ■ A built-in pantry, breakfast bar, double sink and ample counter and storage space in the Kitchen adding to its efficiency
- ■ A second corner fireplace accenting the Family Room
- ■ A whirlpool corner tub, two vanities, a separate shower and a walk-in closet in the Master Suite
- ■ A full bath, easily accessible from the two additional bedrooms

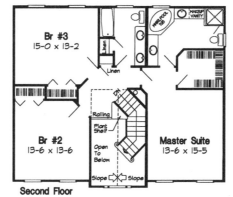

Second Floor

FIRST FLOOR — 1,354 SQ. FT.
SECOND FLOOR — 1,071 SQ. FT.
BASEMENT — 1,358 SQ. FT.
GARAGE — 578 SQ. FT.

TOTAL LIVING AREA:
2,425 SQ. FT.

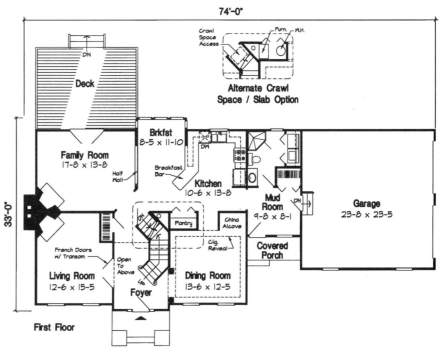

First Floor

PRICE CODE D

EMBRACING WRAP-AROUND PORCH

No. 24255

■ This plan features:

— Three bedrooms

— Two full and one half bath

■ A skylit, vaulted ceiling in the Family Room with a fireplace

■ A modern, well-equipped Kitchen with cooktop island, double sink and ample storage and counter space

■ A vaulted ceiling in the Living Room which flows easily into the Dining Room

■ A Master Bedroom with a vaulted ceiling and skylit, private Master Bath

■ Additional bedrooms share a full hall bath

FIRST FLOOR — 1,370 SQ. FT.
SECOND FLOOR — 1,000 SQ. FT.
BONUS ROOM — 194 SQ. FT.
GARAGE — 667 SQ. FT.

TOTAL LIVING AREA:
2,370 SQ. FT.

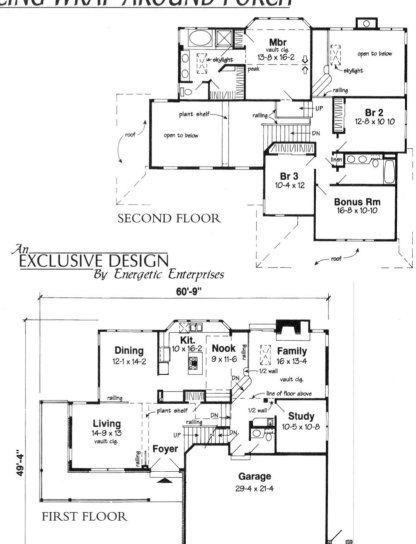

SECOND FLOOR

An
EXCLUSIVE DESIGN
By Energetic Enterprises

FIRST FLOOR

PRICE CODE E

WINDOW STUDDED BRICK FACADE

No. 20353

■ This plan features:

— Three bedrooms

— Three full and one half bath

■ A sky-lit Foyer with a balcony above

■ A formal Dining Room made spacious by a vaulted ceiling

■ A large island Kitchen with peninsula counter that serves a glass-walled Breakfast area equipped with an adjoining pantry

■ A built-in bar in the huge Family Room with a cozy fireplace that is just steps away from the elegant Parlor

■ A magnificent Master Suite with pan vault ceiling, fireplace, circular spa, two-way access to a private deck and large walk-in closet

■ Two additional bedrooms each with a full bath

FIRST FLOOR — 1,807 SQ. FT.
SECOND FLOOR — 1,359 SQ. FT.
BASEMENT — 1,807 SQ. FT.
GARAGE — 840 SQ. FT.

TOTAL LIVING AREA:
3,166 SQ. FT.

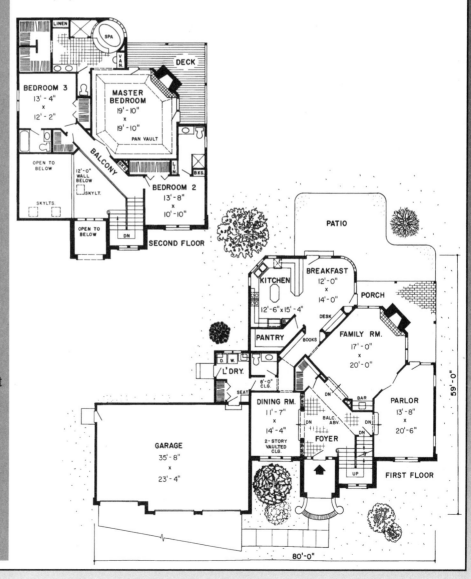

PRICE CODE B

SAVOR THE SUMMER

No. 24242

■ This plan features:

— Four bedrooms

— Two and a half baths

■ A efficient home with a friendly front Porch and a practical back porch

■ A cozy fireplace and a boxed window with a built-in seat in the Living Room

■ A formal Dining Room opening to front entrance and Kitchen

■ A well-equipped Kitchen with an old-fashion booth and ample cabinet and counter space adjoining Laundry area and back porch

■ A convenient, first floor Master Suite with two closet and a private Bath

■ Three additional bedrooms, on second floor, sharing a full hall bath

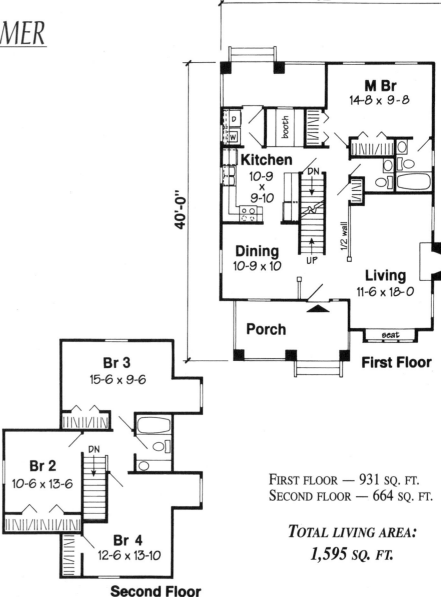

FIRST FLOOR — 931 SQ. FT.
SECOND FLOOR — 664 SQ. FT.

TOTAL LIVING AREA:
1,595 SQ. FT.

PRICE CODE E

UPDATED SALTBOX DESIGN

No. 20404

■ This plan features:

— Five bedrooms

— Three full baths

■ Flower boxes and a friendly front porch introducing an updated saltbox

■ A formal Dining Room and Parlor adjoining the open Foyer offers a classic arrangement with a contemporary approach

■ A wonderful gathering place, where the Kitchen, Breakfast area, and Family Room join together, enhanced by a cozy fireplace and a wall of windows overlooking the Deck

■ A Guest Suite including a full Bath with handicap access

■ A private Deck and luxurious Bath highlighting the Master Suite

■ A Balcony that links two, optional three, bedrooms and a full bath together on the second floor

FIRST FLOOR — 2,285 SQ. FT.
SECOND FLOOR — 660 SQ. FT.
GARAGE — 565 SQ. FT.

TOTAL LIVING AREA:
2,945 SQ. FT.

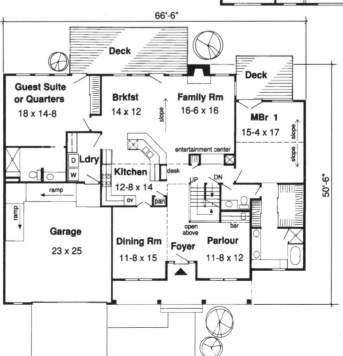

PRICE CODE F

HEARTH ROOM HIGHLIGHTS PLAN

No. 10527

■ This plan features:

— Four bedrooms

— Three full and one half baths

■ A cozy Hearth Room off the efficient Kitchen

■ A large, sunken Family Room highlighted by a built-in bar and a fireplace flanked by bookcases

■ A Master Bedroom including two walk-in closets and a five-piece bath

FIRST FLOOR — 1,697 SQ. FT.
SECOND FLOOR — 1,624 SQ. FT.
BASEMENT — 1,697 SQ. FT.
GARAGE — 586 SQ. FT.

TOTAL LIVING AREA:
3,321 SQ. FT.

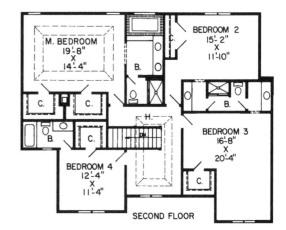

SECOND FLOOR

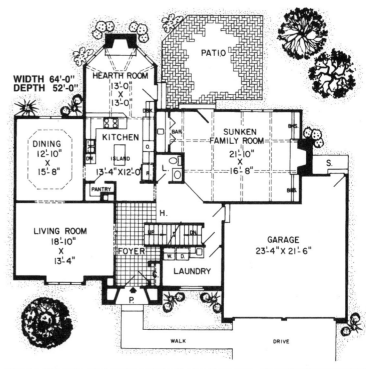

WIDTH 64'-0"
DEPTH 52'-0"

An
EXCLUSIVE DESIGN
By Karl Kreeger

BUILT-IN BEAUTY

No. 20155

■ This plan features:

— Four bedrooms

— Four and one half bath

■ An L-shaped Living and Dining Room arrangement with a fireplace flanked by bookcases and a decorative ceiling in the Dining area

■ A gourmet Kitchen with range-top island/snack bar, built-in pantry and double sinks

■ A massive fireplace, with wood storage, that separates the Hearth/Breakfast Room from the sky-lit Sun Room

■ A Master Suite with a decorative ceiling, walk-in closet, elegant bath and private access to the screened porch

■ Three additional bedrooms that share use of a full hall bath

FIRST FLOOR — 2,800 SQ. FT.
SECOND FLOOR — 1,113 SQ. FT.
BASEMENT — 2,800 SQ. FT.
SCREEN PORCH — 216 SQ. FT.
GARAGE — 598 SQ. FT.

TOTAL LIVING AREA:
3,913 SQ. FT.

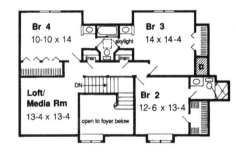

Second Floor

An
EXCLUSIVE DESIGN
By Karl Kreeger

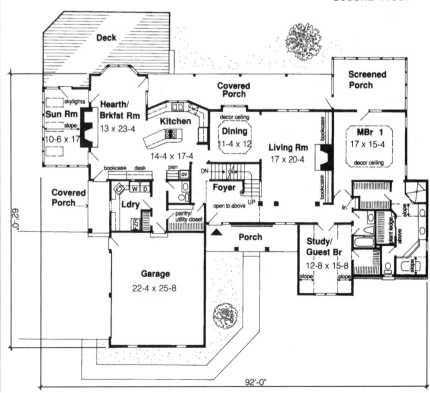

PRICE CODE B

ANGULAR FIREPLACE ADDS INTEREST

No. 20125

■ This plan features:

— Three bedrooms

— Two and a half baths

■ A cozy fireplaced Living Room and an elegant formal Dining Room

■ A Master Suite with walk-in closet and private Master Bath

■ Two additional bedrooms sharing a full hall bath

FIRST FLOOR — 1,340 SQ. FT.
SECOND FLOOR — 455 SQ. FT.
BASEMENT — 347 SQ. FT.
GARAGE — 979 SQ. FT.

TOTAL LIVING AREA:
1,795 SQ. FT.

An
EXCLUSIVE DESIGN
By Karl Kreeger

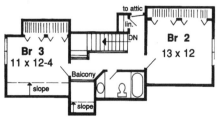

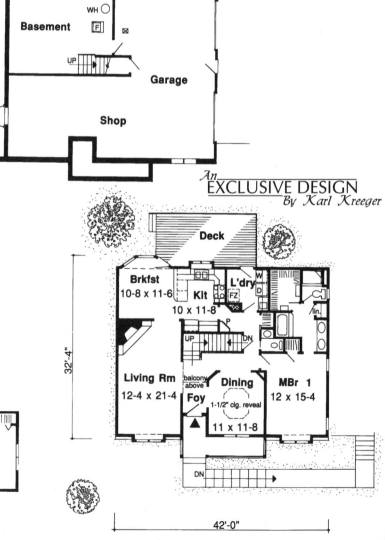

PRICE CODE C

DINE ON THE DECK

No. 10679

■ This plan features:

— Three bedrooms

— Two and one half baths

■ A rear-facing Master Suite with his-n-her walk-in closets and a luxurious bath overlooking the deck

■ A sunken Living Room with expansive stacked windows and sloping ceilings

■ A range-top island Kitchen open to the Dining area

■ A Sewing Room, Laundry Room and large Garage

FIRST FLOOR — 1,445 SQ. FT.
SECOND FLOOR — 739 SQ. FT.
BASEMENT — 1,229 SQ. FT.
GARAGE — 724 SQ. FT.

TOTAL LIVING AREA:
2,184 SQ. FT.

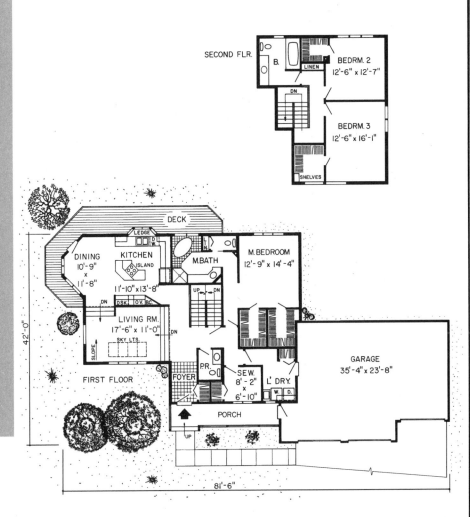

PRICE CODE E

BALCONY PROVIDES A SPLENDID VIEW

No. 20097

■ This plan features:

— Three bedrooms

— Two and one half baths

■ A Living Room with a two-story ceiling pierced by a skylight

■ Living and Dining Rooms flow together into one spacious unit

■ A handy Kitchen with a breakfast bar peninsula

■ A large Master Bedroom with an abundance of closet space and a private bath with a separate shower and tub

FIRST FLOOR — 1,752 SQ. FT.
SECOND FLOOR — 897 SQ. FT.
BASEMENT — 1,752 SQ. FT.
GARAGE — 531 SQ. FT.

TOTAL LIVING AREA:
2,649 SQ. FT.

An
EXCLUSIVE DESIGN
By Karl Kreeger

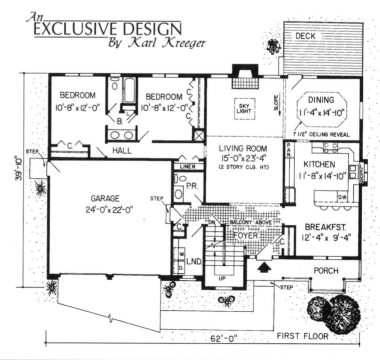

PRICE CODE D

GABLED GRACE

No. 20176

■ This plan features:

— Four bedrooms

— Three full and one half bath

■ An angular Kitchen with built-in pantry, double sinks, peninsula counter that opens to the sunny Breakfast bay and the Hearth Room

■ A cozy fireplace that warms the Hearth Room, Breakfast bay and Kitchen

■ A sloped ceiling with skylights in the Living Room

■ A Master Suite with private Master Bath and a walk-in closet

■ Three additional bedrooms, two with walk-in closets, one with a private bath

FIRST FLOOR — 1,625 SQ. FT.
SECOND FLOOR — 916 SQ. FT.
BASEMENT — 1,618 SQ. FT.
GARAGE — 521 SQ. FT.

TOTAL LIVING AREA:
2,541 SQ. FT.

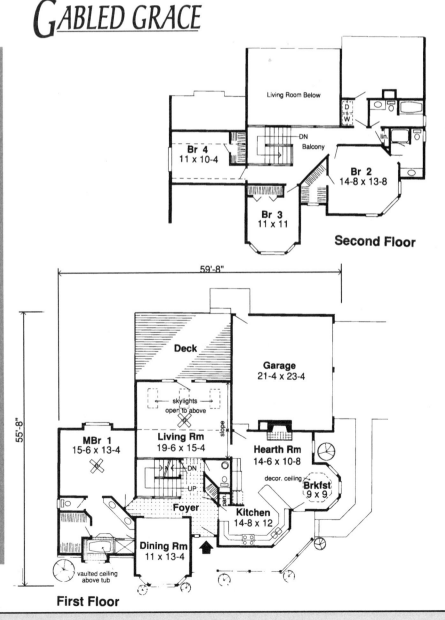

Second Floor

First Floor

PRICE CODE F

BALCONY OFFERS SWEEPING VIEWS

No. 10778

■ This plan features:

— Three bedrooms

— Three and one half baths

■ A Living Room and formal Dining Room located off the foyer

■ A convenient island Kitchen steps away from both the Dining Room and the Three Season Porch

■ A cozy Master Suite including a fireplace and large bath area

FIRST FLOOR — 1,978 SQ. FT
SECOND FLOOR — 1,768 SQ. FT.
BASEMENT — 1,978 SQ. FT.

TOTAL LIVING AREA:
3,746 SQ. FT.

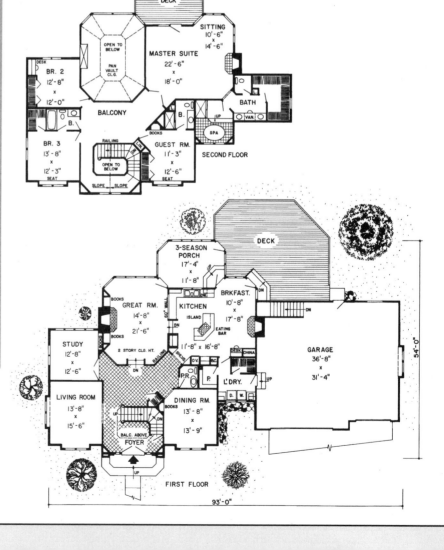

PRICE CODE B

OUTDOOR-LOVERS DREAM

No. 20055

■ This plan features:

— Three bedrooms

— Two and one half baths

■ Sloped ceilings

■ An efficient Kitchen with cooktop peninsula and easy access to Breakfast or Dining Room

■ A Master Suite featuring soaring ceilings and a private dressing area flanked by a full bath and walk-in closet

■ A large Living room that adjoins a deck

FIRST FLOOR — 928 SQ. FT.
SECOND FLOOR — 773 SQ. FT.
BASEMENT — 910 SQ. FT.
GARAGE — 484 SQ. FT.

TOTAL LIVING AREA:
1,701 SQ. FT.

An
EXCLUSIVE DESIGN
By Karl Kreeger

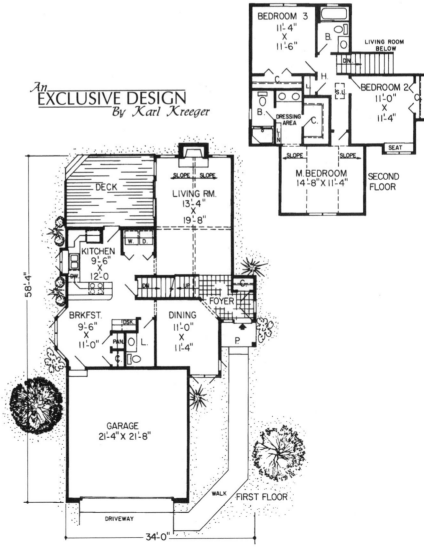

PRICE CODE B

*A*RCHES GRACE CLASSIC FACADE

No. 10677

■ This plan features:

— Three bedrooms

— Two and one half baths

■ Built-in planters and half walls to define rooms

■ A balcony that connects three upstairs bedrooms

■ Double sinks and built-in vanities in the Master Bath

■ Ample closet space

First floor — 932 sq. ft.
Second floor — 764 sq. ft.
Garage — 430 sq. ft.
Basement — 920 sq. ft.

Total living area:
1,696 sq. ft.

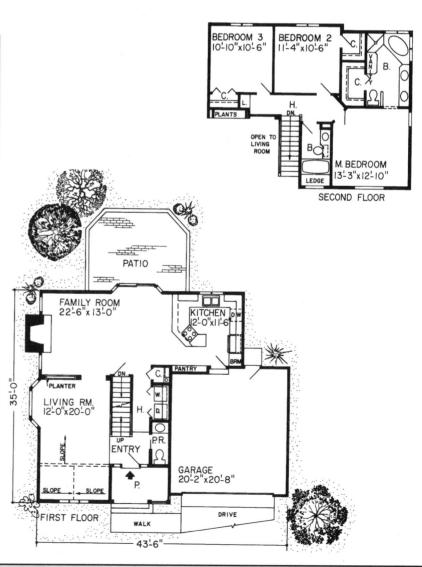

PRICE CODE E

EXCELLENT CHOICE FOR SLOPING LOT

No. 9714

■ This plan features:

— Three bedrooms

— Three full baths

■ A Family Room on the lower level facing the front, and opening onto the lower level

■ A sun deck on the upper level adjoining the Living and Dining Rooms

■ A tiled country Kitchen with a cooking island and a built-in laundry room

FIRST FLOOR — 1,748 SQ. FT.
SECOND FLOOR — 932 SQ. FT.
GARAGE — 768 SQ. FT.

TOTAL LIVING AREA:
2,680 SQ. FT.

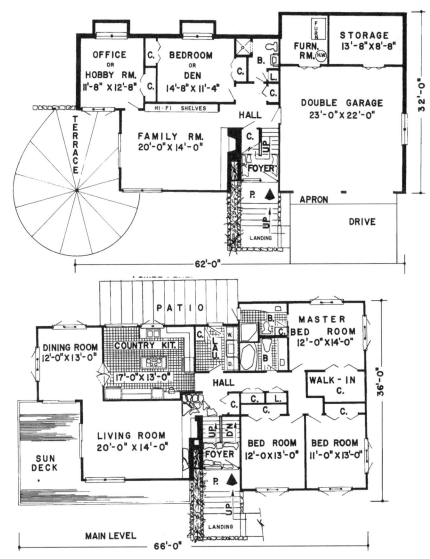

PRICE CODE F

*V*ERANDA MIRRORS TWO-STORY BAY

No. 10780

- This plan features:

— Four bedrooms

— Two and one half baths

- A huge foyer flanked by the formal Parlor and Dining Room

- An island Kitchen with an adjoining pantry

- A Breakfast bay and sunken Gathering Room located at the rear of the home

- Double doors opening to the Master Suite and the book-lined Master Retreat

- An elegant Master Bath including a raised tub and adjoining cedar closet

FIRST FLOOR — 2,108 SQ. FT.
SECOND FLOOR — 2,109 SQ. FT.
BASEMENT — 1,946 SQ. FT.
GARAGE — 764 SQ. FT.

TOTAL LIVING AREA:
4,217 SQ. FT.

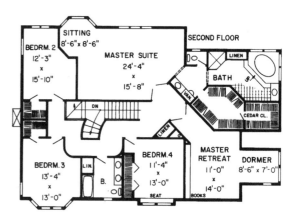

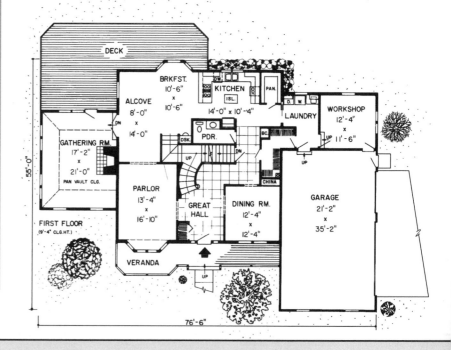

PRICE CODE B

CONTEMPORARY WITH A COUNTRY FLAIR

No. 20203

■ This plan features:

— Three bedrooms

— Two and a half baths

■ A fireplaced Living Room flowing easily into the Dining Room with decorative ceiling

■ A Master Suite with a walk-in closet and private Master Bath

■ Two additional bedrooms sharing a sky-lit full bath

FIRST FLOOR — 1,229 SQ. FT.
SECOND FLOOR — 515 SQ. FT.
GARAGE — 452 SQ. FT.

TOTAL LIVING AREA:
1,744 SQ. FT.

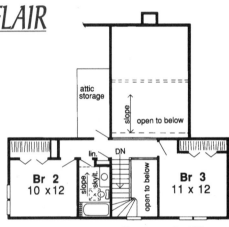

Second Floor

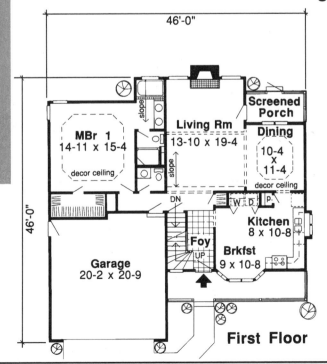

First Floor

An
EXCLUSIVE DESIGN
By Karl Kreeger

PRICE CODE B

FIRST-TIME OWNER'S DELIGHT

No. 20063

- This plan features:
- — Three bedrooms
- — Two and one half baths
- A distinctive exterior of wood veneer siding with a large, multi-paned picture window
- A foyer leading directly into the Living Room which has a wood burning fireplace and opens to the Dining Room
- A laundry room conveniently placed between the Kitchen and the Garage
- A Master Bedroom on the first floor with a full bath and a walk-in closet
- A loft area open to the Living Room below

FIRST FLOOR — 1,161 SQ. FT.
SECOND FLOOR — 631 SQ. FT.

TOTAL LIVING AREA: 1,792 SQ. FT.

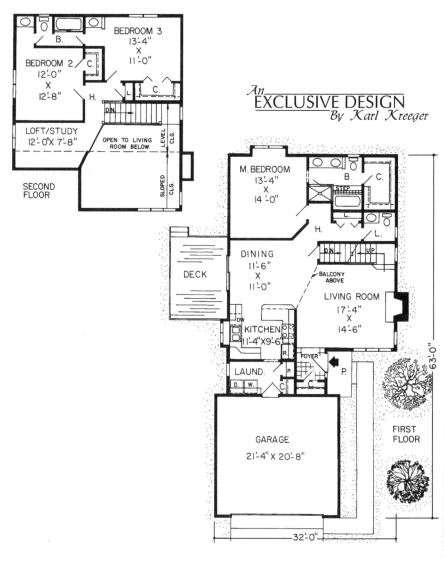

PRICE CODE C

COUNTRY CHARM

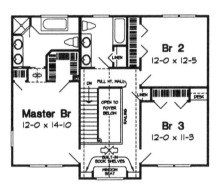

Second Floor

FIRST FLOOR — 1,095 SQ. FT.
SECOND FLOOR — 952 SQ. FT.
GARAGE — 480 SQ. FT.
BASEMENT — 1,095 SQ. FT.

TOTAL LIVING AREA:
2,047 SQ. FT.

No. 24245

■ This plan features:
— Three bedrooms
— Two full and one half baths

■ Formal areas flanking the entry hall

■ A Living Room that includes a wonderful fireplace

■ Direct access from the formal Dining Room to the Kitchen

■ A U-shaped Kitchen including a breakfast bar, built-in pantry and planning desk and a double sink

■ A Mudroom entry that will help keep the dirt from play or muddy shoes away from the rest of the home

■ A sunny Breakfast Nook providing a cheerful place to start your day

■ An expansive Family Room with direct access to the rear wood deck

■ A Master Suite highlighted by a walk-in closet and a private Master Bath

■ Two additional bedrooms, one with a built-in desk, share a full hall bath with a double vanity

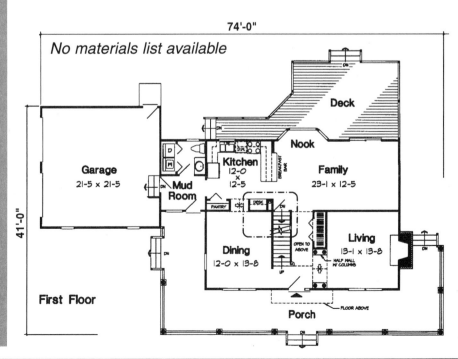

No materials list available

First Floor

PRICE CODE E

FARMHOUSE FLAVOR, FAMILY STYLE DESIGN

No. 99205

- ■ This plan features:
- — Four bedrooms
- — Two full and two half baths
- ■ A sunny Breakfast bay with easy access to the efficient Kitchen
- ■ A large and spacious Family Room with a fireplace and a pass-through to the Kitchen
- ■ Sliders that link the Family and Dining Rooms with the rear terrace
- ■ A private Master Suite with his-and-her walk-in closets, a dressing room with built-in vanity and a convenient step-in shower

FIRST FLOOR — 1,590 SQ. FT.
SECOND FLOOR — 1,344 SQ. FT.

TOTAL LIVING AREA: 2,934 SQ. FT.

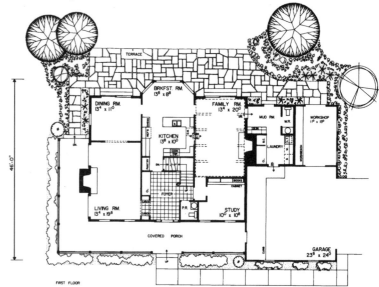

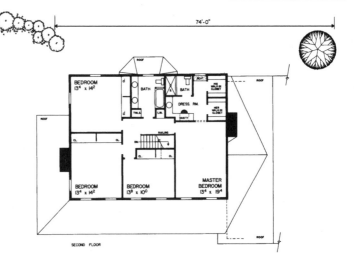

PRICE CODE A

CONTEMPORARY TRADITIONS

No. 99339

■ This plan features:

— Three bedrooms

— Two full baths

■ A vaulted ceiling in the Living Room with a half-round transom window and a fireplace

■ A Dining area flowing into either the Kitchen or the Living Room with sliders to the deck

■ A main floor Master Suite with corner windows, walk-in closet, and private access to a full Bath

■ Two additional bedrooms on the second floor, one with a walk-in closet, having use of a full Bath

FIRST FLOOR — 857 SQ. FT.
SECOND FLOOR — 446 SQ. FT.

TOTAL LIVING AREA:
1,303 SQ. FT.

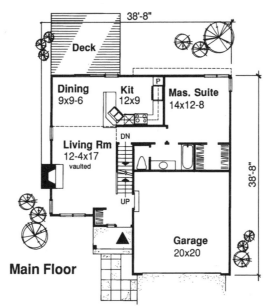

38'-8"

Deck

Dining 9x9-6

Kit 12x9

Mas. Suite 14x12-8

Living Rm 12-4x17 vaulted

DN

UP

Garage 20x20

38'-8"

Main Floor

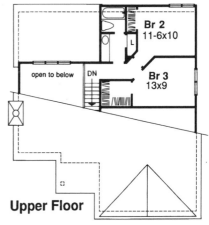

Br 2 11-6x10

open to below

DN

Br 3 13x9

Upper Floor

PRICE CODE C

TWO-SINK BATHS EASE RUSH

No. 90622

- This plan features:
- — Four bedrooms
- — Two full and one half baths
- A wood beam ceiling in the spacious Family Room
- An efficient, island Kitchen with a sunny bay window dinette
- A formal Living Room with a heat-circulating fireplace
- A large Master Suite with a walk-in closet and a private Master Bath
- Three additional bedrooms sharing a full hall bath

FIRST FLOOR — 983 SQ. FT.
SECOND FLOOR — 1,013 SQ. FT.
MUDROOM — 99 SQ. FT.
GARAGE — 481 SQ. FT.

**TOTAL LIVING AREA:
2,095 SQ. FT.**

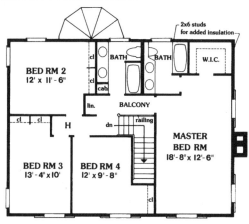

SECOND FLOOR PLAN

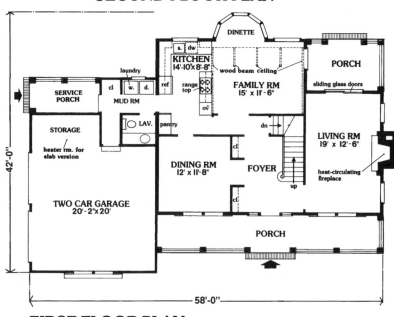

FIRST FLOOR PLAN

PRICE CODE D

No. 90450

■ This plan features:

— Four bedrooms

— Two or three full and one half baths

■ A large two-story Great Room with a fireplace and access to a wood deck

■ A secluded Master Suite with two walk-in closets and a private, lavish, Master Bath

■ A large island Kitchen serving the formal Dining Room and the sunny Breakfast Nook with ease

■ Three additional bedrooms, two with walk-in closets, sharing a full hall bath

■ An optional Bonus Room with a private entrance from below

■ An optional basement or crawl space foundation — please specify when ordering

FIRST FLOOR — 1,637 SQ. FT.
SECOND FLOOR — 761 SQ. FT.
OPT. BATH & CLOSET — 106 SQ. FT.
OPT. BONUS — 347 SQ. FT.

TOTAL LIVING AREA:
2,398 SQ. FT.

ELEGANT BRICK TWO-STORY

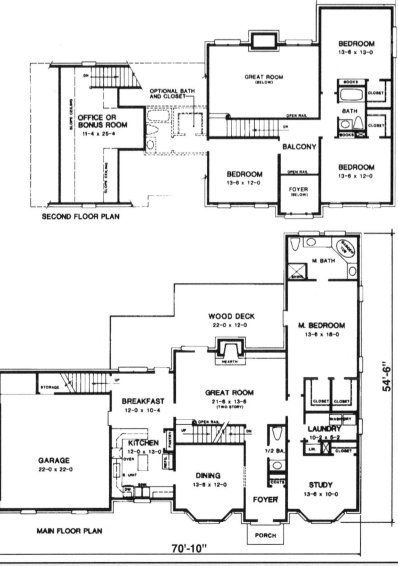

PRICE CODE E

A DISTINCTIVE HOME

An **EXCLUSIVE DESIGN**
By Britt J. Willis

No. 24559

■ This plan features:

— Three bedrooms

— Three full baths

■ An attention getting elevation for great curb appeal

■ A large Kitchen highlighted by a snack bar/island and extensive counter and cabinet space

■ A decorative ceiling adding elegance to the formal Dining Room

■ A Great Room with a focal point fireplace adding warmth and atmosphere to the room

■ A pan vaulted ceiling in the Master Suite that includes a whirlpool tub, step-in shower and double vanity

■ Two additional bedrooms that share a full hall bath

FIRST FLOOR — 1,552 SQ. FT.
SECOND FLOOR — 1,064 SQ. FT.
GARAGE — 708 SQ. FT.

TOTAL LIVING AREA:
2,616 SQ. FT.

Alternate Crawl Space/Slab Option

Second Floor

No materials list available

First Floor

PRICE CODE E

COUNTRY ESTATE

No. 99605

■ This plan features:

— Four bedrooms

— Two full and one half baths

■ A decorative circular stair and curved corners in the Foyer

■ A sunken Living Room with a heat-circulating fireplace and a tray ceiling

■ A Family Room with a heat-circulating fireplace

■ A fully equipped Kitchen with a built-in pantry and ample counter space

■ A formal Dining Room and a Dinette eating area

■ A Master Suite with a private Study, walk-in closet and lavish Master Bath

■ Three additional bedrooms that share a full hall bath

FIRST FLOOR — 1,352 SQ. FT.
SECOND FLOOR — 1,416 SQ. FT.
BASEMENT — 894 SQ. FT.

TOTAL LIVING AREA:
2,768 SQ. FT.

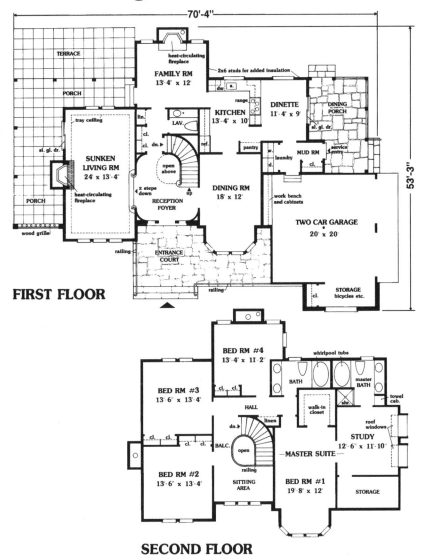

FIRST FLOOR

SECOND FLOOR

PRICE CODE C

COUNTRY LIVING IN ANY NEIGHBORHOOD

No. 90436

■ This plan features:

— Three bedrooms

— Two full and two half baths

■ An expansive Family Room with fireplace

■ A Dining Room and Breakfast Nook lit by flowing natural light from bay windows

■ A first floor Master Suite with a double vanitied bath that wraps around his-n-her closets

■ An optional basement, slab or crawl space foundation — please specify when ordering

FIRST FLOOR — 1,477 SQ. FT.
SECOND FLOOR — 704 SQ. FT.
BASEMENT — 1,374 SQ. FT.

**TOTAL LIVING AREA:
2,181 SQ. FT.**

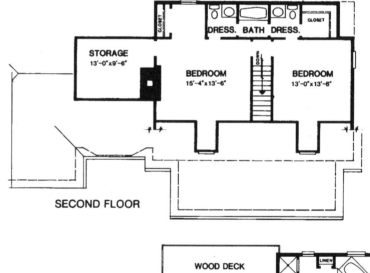

SECOND FLOOR

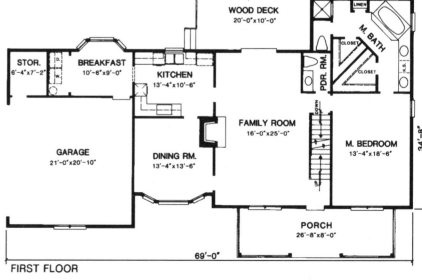

FIRST FLOOR

PRICE CODE D

TRADITONAL RANCH HAS MANY MODERN FEATURES

No. 90444

■ This plan features:

— Three bedrooms

— Three full baths

■ A vaulted-ceiling Great Room with skylights and a fireplace

■ A double L-shaped Kitchen with an eating bar opening to a bayed Breakfast Room

■ A Master Suite with a walk-in closet, corner garden tub, separate vanities and a linen closet

■ Two additional bedrooms each with a walk-in closet and built-in desk, sharing a full hall bath

■ A loft that overlooks the Great Room which includes a vaulted ceiling and open rail balcony

■ A basement or crawl space foundation — please specify when ordering

FIRST FLOOR — 1,996 SQ. FT.
LOFT — 305 SQ. FT.

TOTAL LIVING AREA:
2,301 SQ. FT.

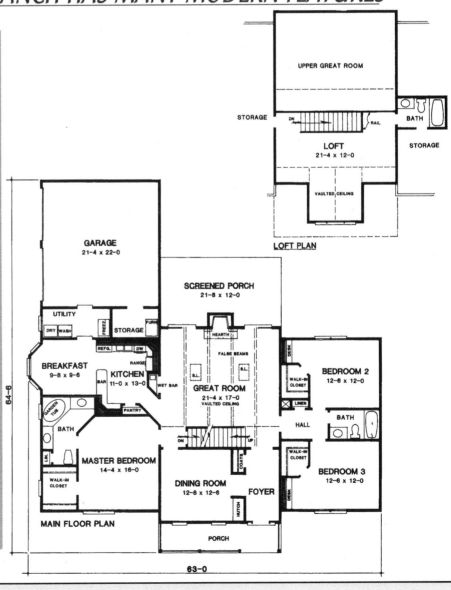

PRICE CODE B

MODIFIED CAPE WITH PASSIVE SOLAR FEATURES

No. 10386

■ This plan features:

— Three bedrooms

— Two baths

■ A solar greenhouse on the south side of the home employing energy storage rods and water to capture the sun's warmth

■ Triple glazed windows for energy efficiency

■ A Living Room accentuated by a heat-circulating fireplace

■ Sliding doors leading from the sitting area of the Master Bedroom to a private patio

■ A Garage with a large storage area

FIRST FLOOR — 1,164 SQ. FT.
SECOND FLOOR — 574 SQ. FT.
BASEMENT — 1,164 SQ. FT.
GARAGE & STORAGE AREA — 574 SQ. FT.
GREENHOUSE — 238 SQ. FT.

**TOTAL LIVING AREA:
1,738 SQ. FT.**

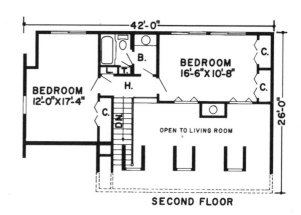

SECOND FLOOR

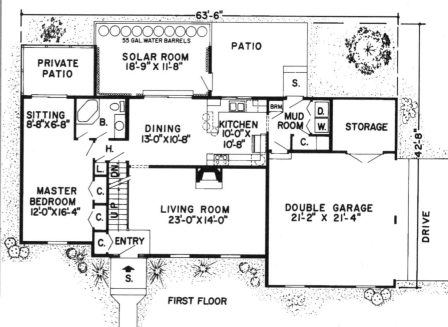

FIRST FLOOR

PRICE CODE A

TRADITION COMBINED WITH CONTEMPORARY

No. 99327

■ This plan features:

— Three bedrooms

— Two full baths

■ A vaulted ceiling in the Entry

■ A formal Living Room with a fireplace and a half-round transom

■ A Dining Room with sliders to the deck and easy access to the Kitchen

■ A main floor Master Suite with corner windows, walk-in closet and private Bath access

■ Two additional bedrooms that share a full hall Bath

FIRST FLOOR — 858 SQ. FT.
SECOND FLOOR — 431 SQ. FT.
BASEMENT — 858 SQ. FT.

TOTAL LIVING AREA:
1,289 SQ. FT.

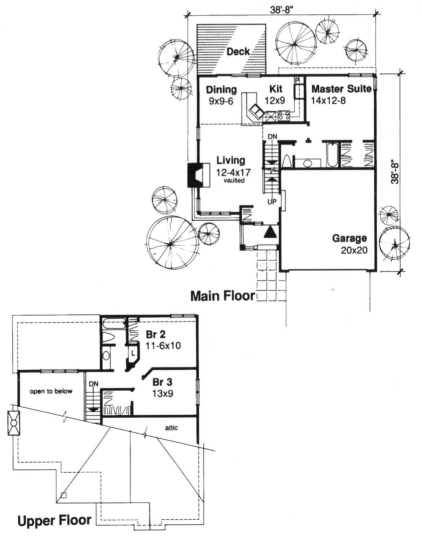

Main Floor

Upper Floor

PRICE CODE C

TRADITIONAL ELEMENTS COMBINE IN FRIENDLY COLONIAL

No. 90606

■ This plan features:

— Four bedrooms

— Two and one half baths

■ A beautiful circular stair ascending from the central foyer and flanked by the formal Living Room and Dining Room

■ Exposed beams, wood paneling, and a brick fireplace wall in the Family Room

■ A separate dinette opening to an efficient Kitchen

FIRST FLOOR — 1,099 SQ. FT.
SECOND FLOOR — 932 SQ. FT.

TOTAL LIVING AREA:
2,031 SQ. FT.

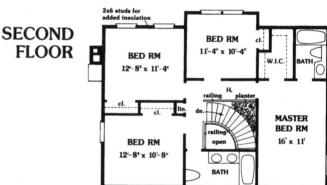

SECOND FLOOR

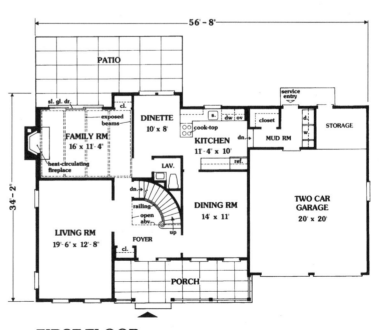

FIRST FLOOR

PRICE CODE B

SECOND FLOOR BALCONY OVERLOOKS GREAT ROOM

No. 24610

■ This plan features:

— Three bedrooms

— Two full and one half baths

■ A Great Room with a focal point fireplace and a two story ceiling

■ An efficient Kitchen with an island, double sinks, built-in pantry and ample storage and counter space

■ A first floor Laundry Room

■ A Dining Room with access to both the Kitchen and the outside

■ A Master Suite with a private master Bath and a walk-in closet

■ Two additional bedrooms with ample closet space that share a full hall bath

FIRST FLOOR — 891 SQ. FT.
SECOND FLOOR — 894 SQ. FT.
GARAGE — 534 SQ. FT.
BASEMENT — 891 SQ. FT.

TOTAL LIVING AREA:
1,785 SQ. FT.

An
EXCLUSIVE DESIGN
By Greg Stafford

No materials list available

PRICE CODE E

ELEGANT AND INVITING

No. 10689

■ This plan features:

— Five bedrooms

— Three and one half baths

■ Wrap-around verandas and a three-season porch

■ An elegant Parlor with a parquet floor and a formal Dining Room separated by a half-wall

■ An adjoining Kitchen with a Breakfast bar and nook

■ A Gathering Room with a fireplace, soaring ceilings and access to the porch

FIRST FLOOR — 1,580 SQ. FT.
SECOND FLOOR — 1,164 SQ. FT.
BASEMENT — 1,329 SQ. FT.
GARAGE — 576 SQ. FT.

TOTAL LIVING AREA:
2,744 SQ. FT.

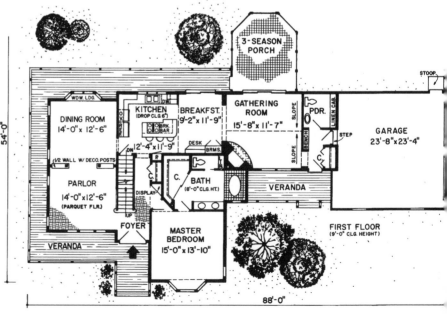

PRICE CODE A

CONTEMPORARY CLASSIC WITH A CUSTOM LOOK

No. 99314

■ This plan features:

— Two bedrooms

— Two and a half baths

■ A well-appointed Kitchen with an angular Nook

■ A two-story Great Room accentuated by a massive fireplace and glass sliders to the rear Deck

■ A bump-out window seat and private Bath with double vanities in the Master Suite

FIRST FLOOR — 1,044 SQ. FT.
SECOND FLOOR — 454 SQ. FT.

**TOTAL LIVING AREA:
1,498 SQ. FT.**

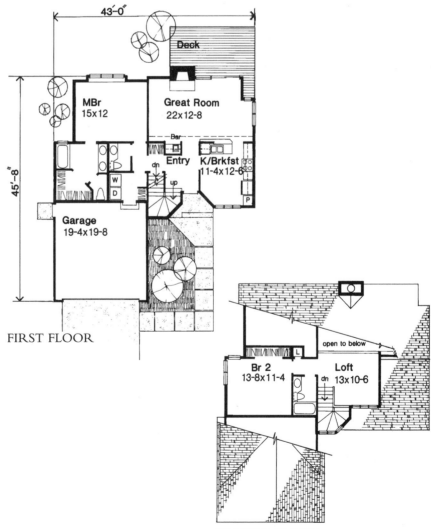

FIRST FLOOR

SECOND FLOOR

PRICE CODE A

YEAR ROUND RETREAT

No. 90613

■ This plan features:

— Three bedrooms

— Two full baths

■ A Living Room with a dramatic sloping ceiling and a wood burning stove

■ A Kitchen and Living Room opening onto the rear deck

■ A Master Suite with a full bath, linen closet and ample closet space

FIRST FLOOR — 960 SQ. FT.
SECOND FLOOR — 465 SQ. FT.

TOTAL LIVING AREA: 1,425 SQ. FT.

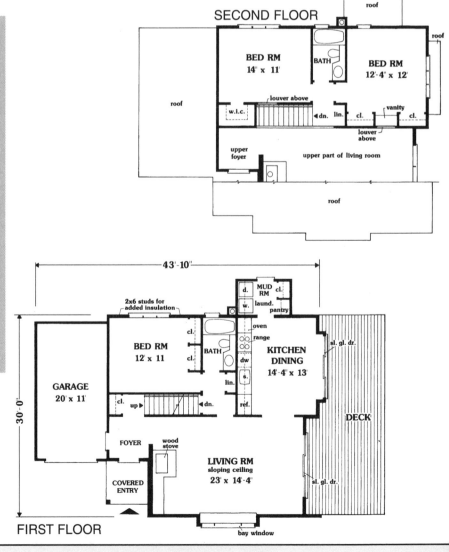

PRICE CODE B

RUSTIC WARMTH

No. 90440

- This plan features:
- — Three bedrooms
- — Two full baths
- A fireplaced Living Room with built-in bookshelves
- A fully-equipped Kitchen with an island
- A sunny Dining Room with glass sliders to a wood deck
- A first floor Master Suite with walk-in closet and lavish Master Bath
- An optional basement or crawl space foundation — please specify when ordering

FIRST FLOOR — 1,100 SQ. FT.
SECOND FLOOR — 664 SQ. FT.
BASEMENT — 1,100 SQ. FT.

TOTAL LIVING AREA:
1,764 SQ. FT.

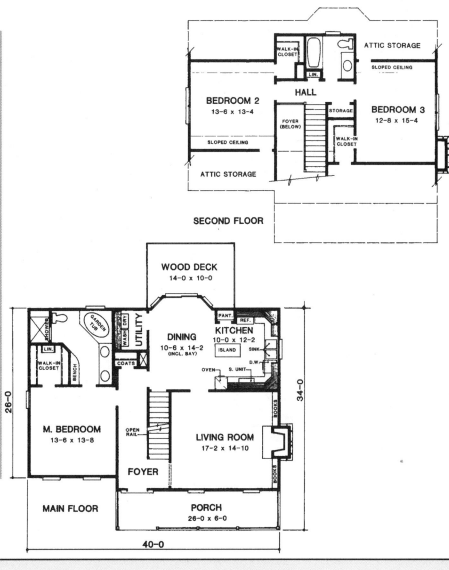

PRICE CODE D

CALL THIS HOME

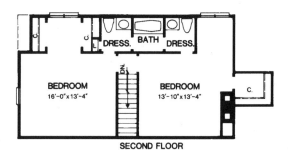

No. 90424

■ This plan features:

— Three bedrooms

— Two full and one half baths

■ A covered porch in the front and a screened porch in the back to take advantage of seasonal weather

■ A Great Room with a stone fireplace that occupies the center of the home

■ An island Kitchen that flows directly into the Dining Room and the Breakfast Bay

■ A secluded Master Bedroom with a five-piece bath and his-n-her walk-in closets

■ Two upstairs bedrooms, each with plenty of closet space and private access to a shared bath

■ A slab foundation only

FIRST FLOOR — 1,535 SQ. FT.
SECOND FLOOR — 765 SQ. FT.
BASEMENT — 1,091 SQ. FT.

TOTAL LIVING AREA:
2,300 SQ. FT.

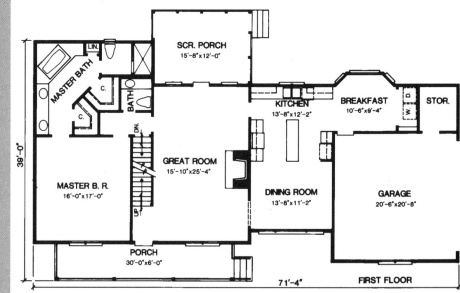

PRICE CODE D

CLASSIC COLONIAL STYLE

No. 90449

■ This plan features:

— Three bedrooms

— Two full and one half baths

■ A large Family Room with a fireplace and built-in book shelves having French doors leading to an outdoor deck

■ A spacious, efficient Kitchen open to the Breakfast Room which has a sunny bay

■ A Master Suite with a large private bath including a garden tub and separate shower

■ A second floor laundry convenient to the bedrooms

■ An optional bonus room so the house can expand with your family

■ An optional basement or crawl space foundation — please specify when ordering

FIRST FLOOR — 1,138 SQ. FT.
SECOND FLOOR — 1,124 SQ. FT.
OPTIONAL BONUS — 284 SQ. FT.
BASEMENT — 1,124 SQ. FT.
GARAGE — 484 SQ. FT.

TOTAL LIVING AREA:
2,262 SQ. FT.

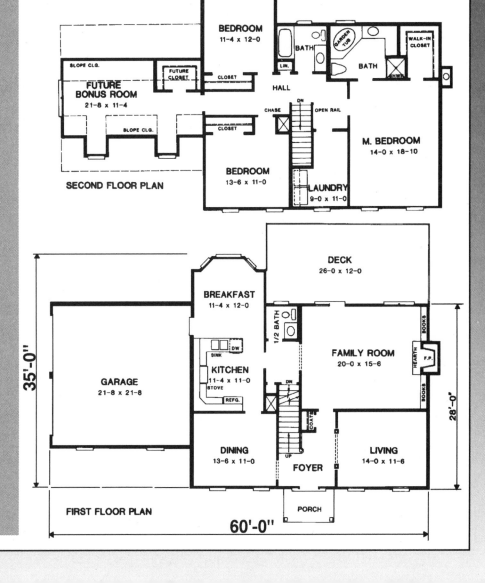

PRICE CODE E

LIVING IN STYLE

No. 24555

■ This plan features:

— Four bedrooms

— Two full and one half baths

■ Bayed windows in the formal Living Room, Dining Room and the Family Room

■ A sunken Family Room with a focal point fireplace

■ Decorative ceilings crowning the formal Living Room, Dining Room and the Master Bedroom

■ An open layout between the island Kitchen and the Breakfast area giving a feeling of space

■ A Master Suite with a master Bath and two walk-in closets

■ Three additional bedrooms with ample closet space that share use of a full hall bath

FIRST FLOOR — 1,544 SQ. FT.
SECOND FLOOR — 1,214 SQ. FT.
GARAGE — 800 SQ. FT.

TOTAL LIVING AREA:
2,758 SQ. FT.

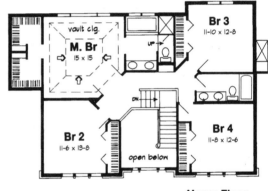

Upper Floor

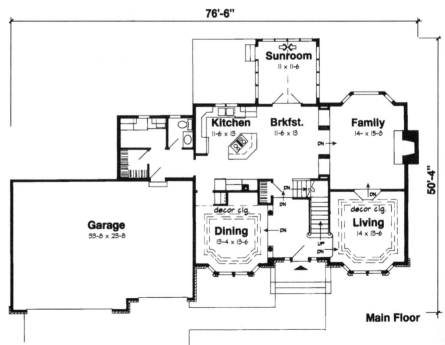

Main Floor

PRICE CODE A

AFFORDABLE CHARM

No. 99362

- ■ This plan features:
- — Three bedrooms
- — Two and one half baths
- ■ An eat-in Kitchen leading out onto the patio
- ■ A Living Room which can be expanded behind the Garage
- ■ A Master Suite with vaulted ceilings and a walk-in closet
- ■ A two-car Garage

FIRST FLOOR — 669 SQ. FT.
SECOND FLOOR — 727 SQ. FT.

TOTAL LIVING AREA:
1,396 SQ. FT.

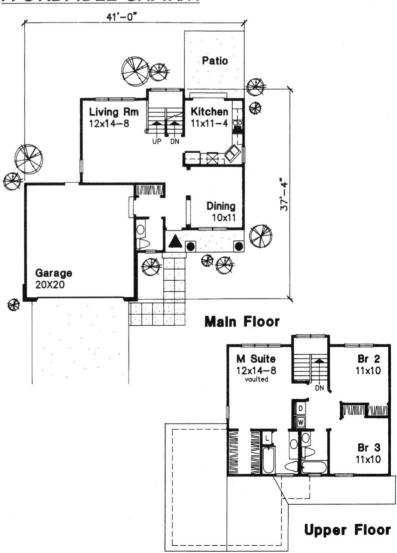

Main Floor

Upper Floor

PRICE CODE C

FIRST FLOOR MASTER SUITE IS SPECIAL

No. 90624

■ This plan features:

— Three bedrooms

— Two and one half baths

■ A two story foyer lit from above by a skylight

■ Access to the terrace or Garage through the Family Room

■ A heat-circulating fireplace

■ A Master Suite with vaulted ceilings and spectacular windows

FIRST FLOOR — 1,360 SQ. FT.
SECOND FLOOR — 613 SQ. FT.
BASEMENT — 1,340 SQ. FT.
GARAGE — 462 SQ. FT.

TOTAL LIVING AREA:
1,973 SQ. FT.

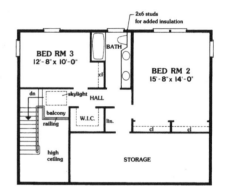

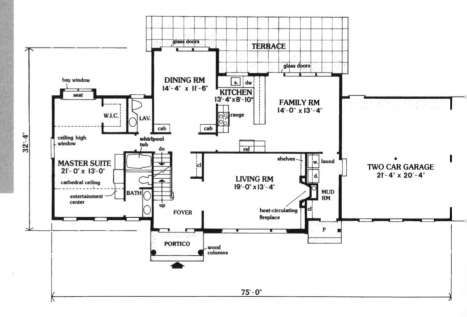

PRICE CODE D

ROMANCE PERSONIFIED

No. 90439

■ This plan features:

— Three bedrooms

— Two full and one half baths

■ A spacious Family Room including a fireplace flanked by bookshelves

■ A sunny Breakfast Bay and adjoining country Kitchen with a peninsula counter

■ An expansive Master Suite spanning the width of the house including built-in shelves, walk-in closet, and a private bath with every amenity

■ A full bath that serves the two other bedrooms tucked into the gables at the front of the house

■ An optional basement or crawl space foundation — please specify when ordering

FIRST FLOOR — 1,366 SQ. FT.
SECOND FLOOR — 1,196 SQ. FT.
BASEMENT — 1,250 SQ. FT.
GARAGE — 484 SQ. FT.

TOTAL LIVING AREA:
2,562 SQ. FT.

SECOND FLOOR

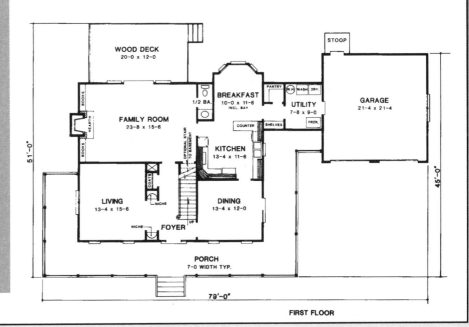

FIRST FLOOR

PRICE CODE D

COUNTRY STYLE FOR TODAY

No. 99620

■ This plan features:

— Four bedrooms

— Two full and one half baths

■ Two bay windows in the formal Living Room with a heat-circulating fireplace to enhance the mood and warmth

■ A spacious formal Dining Room with a bay window and easy access to the Kitchen

■ An octagon-shaped Dinette defined by columns, dropped beams and a bay window

■ An efficient island Kitchen with ample storage and counter space

■ A Master Suite equipped with a large whirlpool tub plus a double vanity

■ Three additional bedrooms that share a full hall bath

FIRST FLOOR — 1,132 SQ. FT.
SECOND FLOOR — 1,020 SQ. FT.
BASEMENT — 1,026 SQ. FT.
GARAGE & STORAGE — 469 SQ. FT.
LAUNDRY/MUDROOM — 60 SQ. FT.

**TOTAL LIVING AREA:
2,212 SQ. FT.**

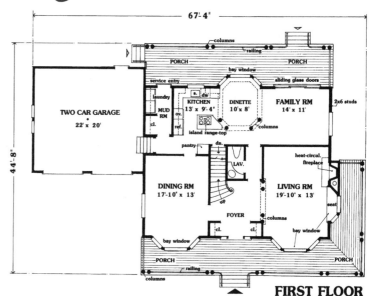

FIRST FLOOR

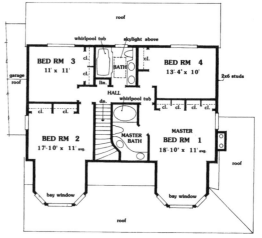

SECOND FLOOR

PRICE CODE A

COMFORT EXPRESSED IN A CONTEMPORARY DESIGN

No. 10567

- This plan features:
— Three bedrooms
— Two full baths
- A Kitchen with an open, non-partitioned Dining Area
- A Living Room with a skylight adding more natural light to the room
- A secluded Master Bedroom with a sitting room, walk-in closets, and a full bath

FIRST FLOOR — 1,046 SQ. FT.
SECOND FLOOR — 375 SQ. FT.
BASEMENT — 1,046 SQ. FT.
GARAGE — 472 SQ. FT.

TOTAL LIVING AREA:
1,421 SQ. FT.

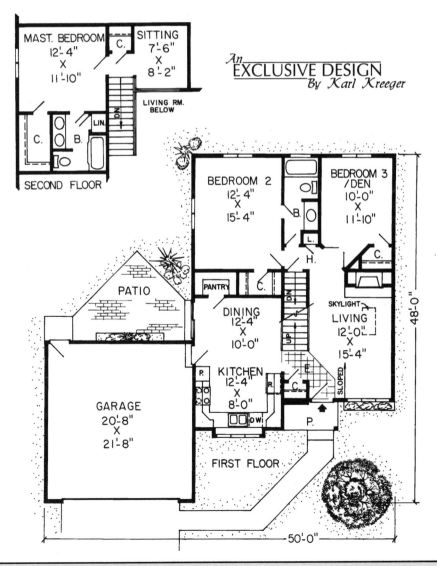

An
EXCLUSIVE DESIGN
By Karl Kreeger

PRICE CODE D

Warm and Inviting

No. 24264

■ This plan features:

— Four bedrooms

— Two full and one half bath

■ A see-through fireplace between the Living Room and the Family Room

■ A gourmet Kitchen with an island, built-in pantry, and double sink

■ A Master Bedroom with a vaulted ceiling

■ A Master Bath with large double vanity, linen closet, corner tub, separate shower, compartmented toilet, and huge walk-in closet

■ Three additional bedrooms, one with walk-in closet share full hall Bath

FIRST FLOOR — 1,241 SQ. FT.
SECOND FLOOR — 1,170 SQ. FT.

**TOTAL LIVING AREA:
2,411 SQ. FT.**

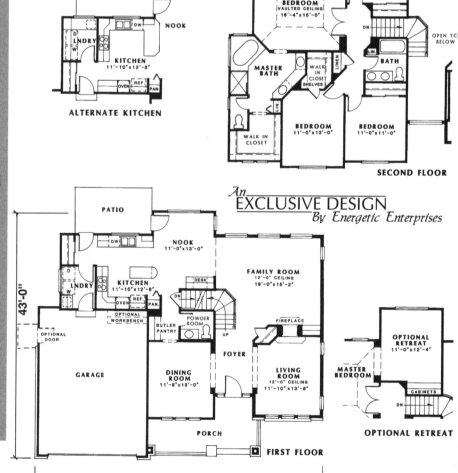

An
EXCLUSIVE DESIGN
By Energetic Enterprises

No materials list available

PRICE CODE F

BIG COUNTRY HOME HAS TRADITIONAL CHARM

No. 99239

■ This plan features:

— Three bedrooms

— Two full and two half baths

■ An elegant Living Room with a stone fireplace including an unusual Music Alcove, complete with custom built-ins for audio equipment

■ An adjoining Library having floor-to-ceiling, built-in bookcases and a second cozy fireplace

■ A formal Dining Room with a wall of windows and access to the back Porch

■ A wonderful Country Kitchen with its own fireplace, sitting/dining area, cooktop, snack bar and double sink

■ An incredible Master Suite with a large, luxurious Dressing/Bath equipped with a whirlpool tub, two vanities, an oversized shower, a walk-in closet and a wall closet

FIRST FLOOR — 2,026 SQ. FT.
SECOND FLOOR — 1,386 SQ. FT.
GARAGE — 576 SQ. FT.

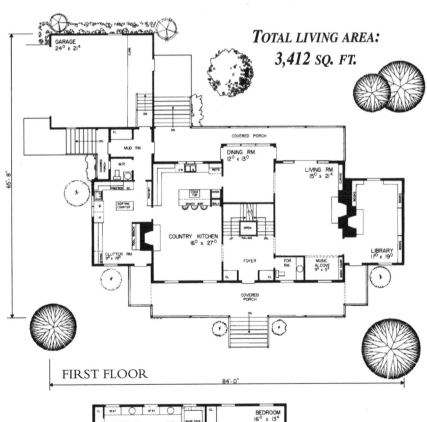

TOTAL LIVING AREA: 3,412 SQ. FT.

FIRST FLOOR

SECOND FLOOR

PRICE CODE D

TRADITIONAL FARMHOUSE

No. 99626

■ This plan features:

— Four bedrooms

— Two full and one half baths

■ A decorative circular stairway enhancing the Foyer

■ A heat-circulating fireplace in both the Family Room and the formal Living Room

■ An efficient, well-appointed Kitchen with a built-in pantry, double sinks and ample cabinet and counter space

■ A Master Suite equipped with a walk-in closet, and a large Master Bath

■ Three additional bedrooms that share a full hall bath

FIRST FLOOR — 1,183 SQ. FT.
SECOND FLOOR — 1,103 SQ. FT.
BASEMENT — 1,116 SQ. FT.
GARAGE & STORAGE — 467 SQ. FT.
PORCHES — 283 SQ. FT.

**TOTAL LIVING AREA:
2,286 SQ. FT.**

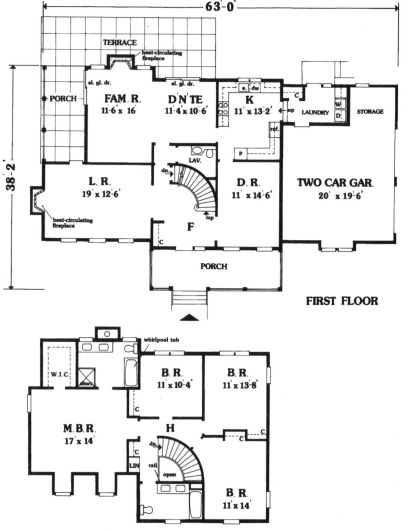

FIRST FLOOR

SECOND FLOOR

PRICE CODE B

FIREPLACE EQUIPPED FAMILY ROOM

An
EXCLUSIVE DESIGN
By Marshall Associates

No. 24326

■ This plan features:

— Four bedrooms

— Two full baths and one half bath

■ A lovely front porch shading the entrance

■ A spacious Living Room that opens into the Dining Area which flows into the efficient Kitchen

■ A Family Room equipped with a cozy fireplace and sliding glass doors to a patio

■ A Master Suite with a large walk-in closet and a private bath with a step-in shower

■ Three additional bedrooms that share a full hall bath

FIRST FLOOR — 692 SQ. FT.
SECOND FLOOR — 813 SQ. FT.
BASEMENT — 699 SQ. FT.
GARAGE — 484 SQ. FT.

TOTAL LIVING AREA:
1,505 SQ. FT.

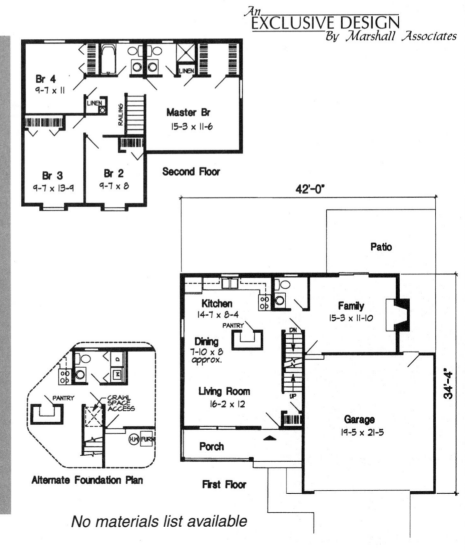

Br 4
9-7 x 11

Master Br
15-3 x 11-6

Br 3
9-7 x 13-9

Br 2
9-7 x 8

Second Floor

42'-0"

Patio

Kitchen
14-7 x 8-4

PANTRY

Family
15-3 x 11-10

Dining
7-10 x 8
approx.

DN

Living Room
16-2 x 12

UP

34'-4"

Garage
19-5 x 21-5

Porch

First Floor

PANTRY

CRAWL SPACE ACCESS

HW FURN

Alternate Foundation Plan

No materials list available

PRICE CODE E

No. 90443

- This plan features:
- — Three bedrooms
- — Two full and one half baths
- A Master Suite with two closets and a private bath with separate shower, corner tub and dual vanities
- A large Dining Room with a bay window, adjacent to the Kitchen
- A formal Living Room for entertaining and a cozy Family Room with fireplace for informal relaxation
- Two upstairs bedrooms with walk-in closets sharing a full hall bath
- A Bonus Room to allow the house to grow with your needs
- An optional basement or crawl space foundation — please specify when ordering

FIRST FLOOR — 1,927 SQ. FT.
SECOND FLOOR — 832 SQ. FT.
BONUS ROOM — 624 SQ. FT.
BASEMENT — 1,674 SQ. FT.

TOTAL LIVING AREA:
2,759 SQ. FT.

TRADITIONAL THAT HAS IT ALL

SECOND FLOOR

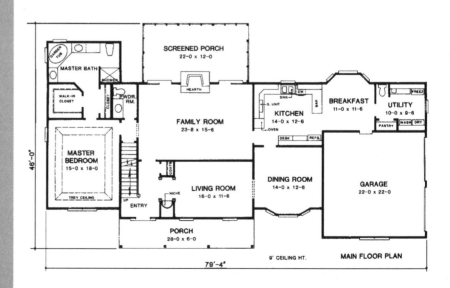

MAIN FLOOR PLAN

PRICE CODE E

TRADITIONAL ENERGY SAVER

No. 20071

- This plan features:

— Four bedrooms

— Three and one half baths

- A heat storing floor in the sun room adjoining the Living Room and Breakfast Room

- A Living Room with French doors and a massive fireplace

- A balcony overlooking the soaring two-story foyer and Living Room

- An island Kitchen centrally-located between the formal and informal Dining Rooms

FIRST FLOOR — 2,186 SQ. FT.
SECOND FLOOR — 983 SQ. FT.
BASEMENT — 2,186 SQ. FT.
GARAGE — 704 SQ. FT.

TOTAL LIVING AREA:
3,169 SQ. FT.

An
EXCLUSIVE DESIGN
By Karl Kreeger

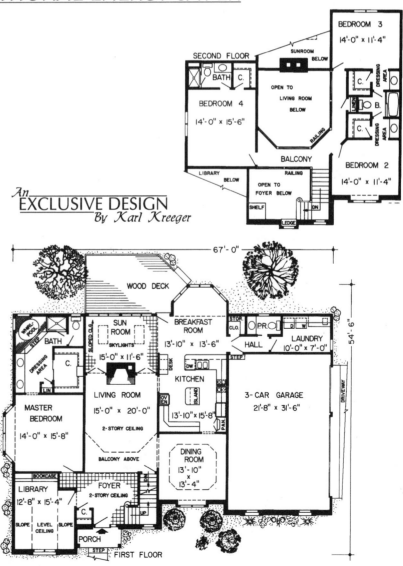

PRICE CODE C

OPEN PLAN BRIGHTENS CONTEMPORARY

No. 90506

■ This plan features:

— Three bedrooms

— Two full and one half baths

■ A covered entrance into practical, tile floors from an open Entry to the Nook/Kitchen area, 1st floor Bath and laundry area

■ A graceful landing staircase and balcony overlook a Great Room with a vaulted ceiling that opens into a comfortable Dining area

■ An efficient Kitchen opening both to a distinctive, octagon-shaped Nook and the Dining area

■ A Master Suite with another distinctive and a plush Bath featuring two closets, two vanities, and a window tub

■ On the second floor, two additional bedrooms sharing a full hall bath, and a Play Room that doubles as a storage area

FIRST FLOOR — 996 SQ. FT.
SECOND FLOOR — 942 SQ. FT.

**TOTAL LIVING AREA :
1,938 SQ. FT.**

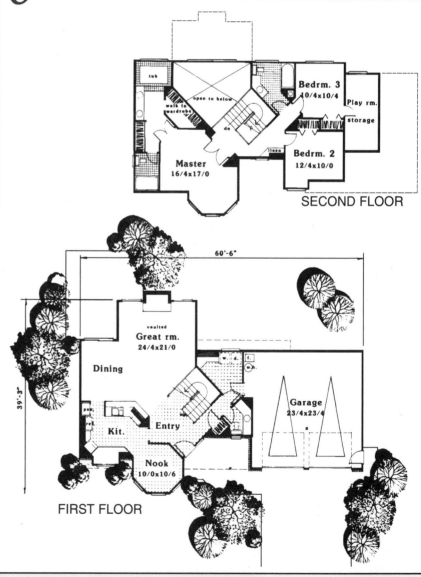

SECOND FLOOR

FIRST FLOOR

PRICE CODE C

BUILT IN ENTERTAINMENT CENTER FOR FAMILY FUN

No. 90615

■ This plan features:

— Four bedrooms

— Two and one half baths

■ A heat-circulating fireplace in the Living Room framed by decorative pilasters that support dropped beams

■ A convenient mudroom providing access to the two-car Garage

■ A spacious Master Suite with a separate dressing area

■ An optional slab foundation

FIRST FLOOR — 1,094 SQ. FT.
SECOND FLOOR — 936 SQ. FT.
GARAGE — 441 SQ. FT.

TOTAL LIVING AREA:
2,030 SQ. FT.

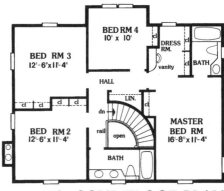

SECOND FLOOR PLAN

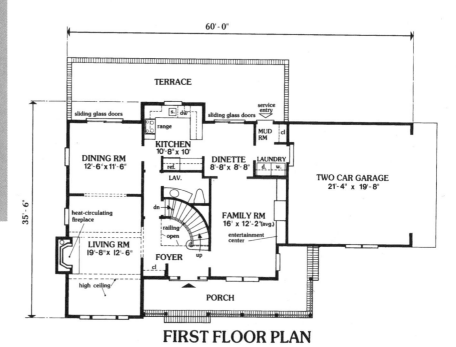

FIRST FLOOR PLAN

PRICE CODE D

VAULTED CEILINGS IN THE LIVING ROOM AND MASTER SUITE

No. 24269

■ This plan features:

— Three or four bedrooms

— Two full and one half baths

■ A vaulted ceiling in the Living Room adding to its spaciousness

■ A formal Dining Room with easy access to both the Living Room and the Kitchen

■ An efficient Kitchen with double sinks, and ample storage and counter space

■ An informal Eating Nook with a built-in pantry

■ A Master Suite with a vaulted ceiling and luxurious Master Bath and two walk-in closets

■ Two additional bedrooms share a full bath

FIRST FLOOR — 1,115 SQ. FT.
SECOND FLOOR — 1,129 SQ. FT.
BASEMENT — 1,096 SQ. FT.
GARAGE — 415 SQ. FT.

**TOTAL LIVING AREA:
2,244 SQ. FT.**

No materials list available

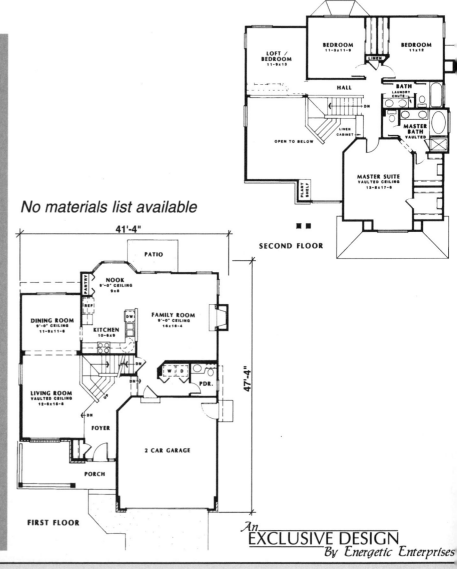

An
EXCLUSIVE DESIGN
By Energetic Enterprises

PRICE CODE E

*L*ARGE WRAP-AROUND PORCH ADDS A TOUCH OF COUNTRY

No. 24403

- This plan features:

— Three or four bedrooms

— Three full baths

- A large welcoming, wrap-around porch adding an old-fashioned country feel

- An elegant Dining Room topped by a decorative ceiling treatment

- An expansive Family Room equipped with a massive fireplace with built-in bookshelves

- An informal Breakfast Room conveniently enhanced by a built-in planning desk

- Peninsula counter, a built-in pantry, and ample counter and cabinet space in the Kitchen

- Two additional bedrooms sharing a full, compartmented hall bath

FIRST FLOOR — 1,378 SQ. FT.
SECOND FLOOR — 1,269 SQ. FT.
BASEMENT — 1,378 SQ. FT.
GARAGE — 717 SQ. FT.
PORCH — 801 SQ. FT.

TOTAL LIVING AREA:
2,647 SQ. FT.

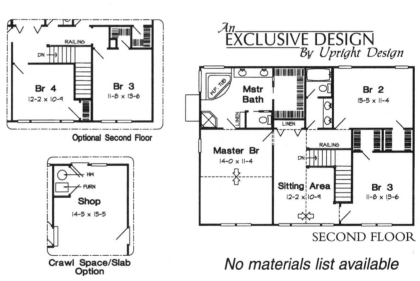

An EXCLUSIVE DESIGN
By Upright Design

No materials list available

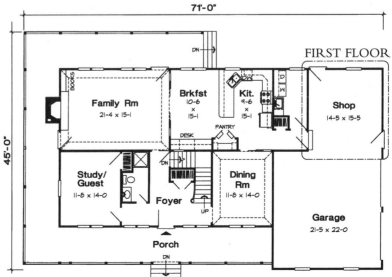

An
EXCLUSIVE DESIGN
By Patrick Morabito, A.I.A. Architect

PRICE CODE E

No. 93335

■ This plan features:

— Four bedrooms

— Two full and one half baths

■ A sheltered Entry with welcoming sidelights, and an open Foyer with a landing staircase

■ A formal Dining Room crowned by a stepped ceiling, accenting its unique shape

■ A cozy, quiet Den with built-in book shelves, offering an at-home office

■ An expansive Great Room, with a tray ceiling accenting a two-way fireplace and windows on three sides, with an atrium door to deck

■ A private Master Suite equipped with a lavish Bath, including a corner window, whirlpool tub, a double vanity and two walk-in closets

■ Three additional bedrooms, on the second floor, with ample closet space, sharing a large hall bath

FIRST FLOOR — 2,164 SQ. FT.
SECOND FLOOR — 773 SQ. FT.

TOTAL LIVING AREA:
2,937 SQ. FT.

DECORATIVE CEILINGS ENHANCE INTERIO

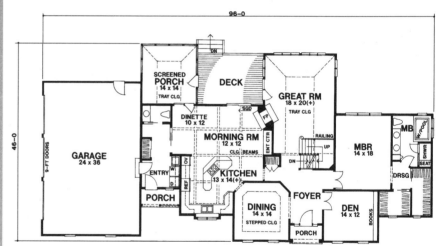

No materials list available

FIRST FLOOR

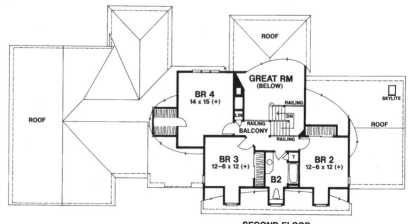

SECOND FLOOR

PRICE CODE F

ACCENT ON SPIRAL STAIRCASE

No. 10537

■ This plan features:

— Four bedrooms

— Four and one half baths

■ A roomy kitchen complete with a pantry and lots of cabinet space

■ A unique Morning Room complemented by a large fireplace and an entrance to the patio for year round enjoyment

■ Four bedrooms, each with walk-in closets and private baths

FIRST FLOOR — 3,282 SQ. FT.
SECOND FLOOR — 956 SQ. FT.
BASEMENT — 3,235 SQ. FT.
GARAGE — 936 SQ. FT.

TOTAL LIVING AREA:
4,238 SQ. FT.

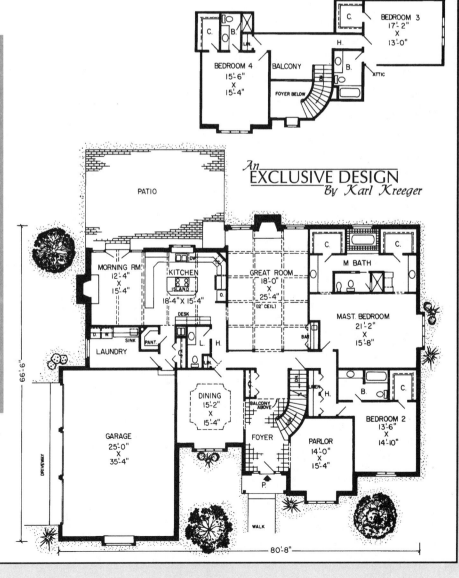

An
EXCLUSIVE DESIGN
By Karl Kreeger

PRICE CODE C

TRADITIONAL INTERIOR

No. 24554

■ This plan features:

— Four bedrooms

— Three full and one half baths

■ A unique railing defining formal Living Room space with double doors leading to the Family Room

■ A Family Room with a cozy fireplace and triple window view of backyard opens to Kitchen area

■ An ideally located Kitchen with a center work island adjoins the Breakfast bay, formal Dining Room, laundry area, and Garage

■ A comfortable Master Suite with a vaulted ceiling includes a walk-in closet, a private Bath with an oval window tub, double vanity and separate shower

■ Three additional bedrooms with closets, sharing a full hall bath

FIRST FLOOR — 1,063 SQ. FT.
SECOND FLOOR — 979 SQ. FT.

TOTAL LIVING AREA:
2,042 SQ. FT.

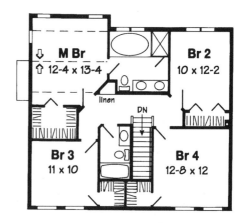

An **EXCLUSIVE DESIGN**
By Britt J. Willis

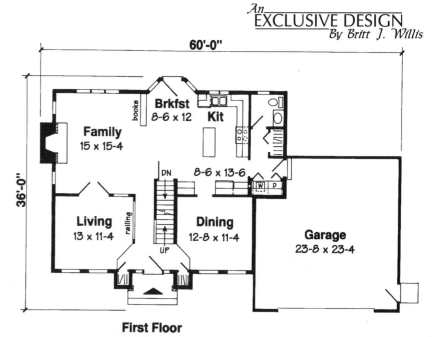

First Floor

PRICE CODE D

COUNTRY STYLE FOR TODAY

No. 91700

- ■ This plan features:
- — Three bedrooms
- — Two full and one half baths
- ■ A wide wrap-around porch for a farmhouse style
- ■ A spacious Living Room with double doors and a large front window
- ■ A garden window over the double sink in the huge, country Kitchen with two islands, one a butcher block, and the other an eating bar
- ■ A corner fireplace in the Family Room enjoyed throughout the Nook and Kitchen, thanks to an open layout
- ■ A Master Suite with a spa tub, and a huge walk-in closet as well as a shower and double vanities

FIRST FLOOR — 1,785 SQ. FT.
SECOND FLOOR — 621 SQ. FT.

TOTAL LIVING AREA:
2,406 SQ. FT.

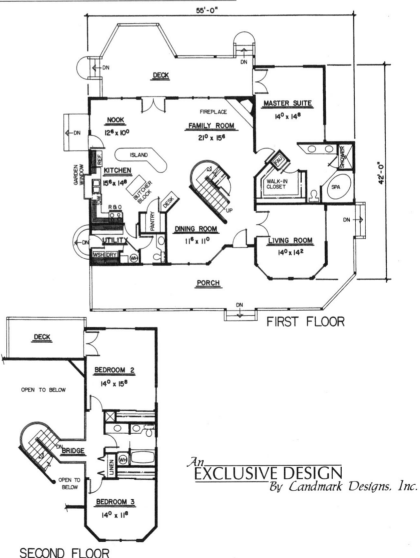

An
EXCLUSIVE DESIGN
By Landmark Designs, Inc.

PRICE CODE E

A FIREPLACE IN THE MASTER SUITE

An
EXCLUSIVE DESIGN
By Energetic Enterprises

No. 24266

- This plan features:
- — Three or four bedrooms
- — Three full baths
- Vaulted ceilings in both the Family Room and the Master Bedroom
- An elegant sunken formal Living Room
- A first floor study/guest room with closet space and accessiblity to a full hall bath
- A spacious Family Room with a fireplace and an open layout into the eating Nook and Kitchen
- A private Master Suite with a fireplace and a lavish Master Bath
- Two additonal bedrooms that share a full hall bath

FIRST FLOOR — 1,574 SQ. FT.
SECOND FLOOR — 1,098 SQ. FT.
GARAGE — 522 SQ. FT.

TOTAL LIVING AREA:
2,672 SQ. FT.

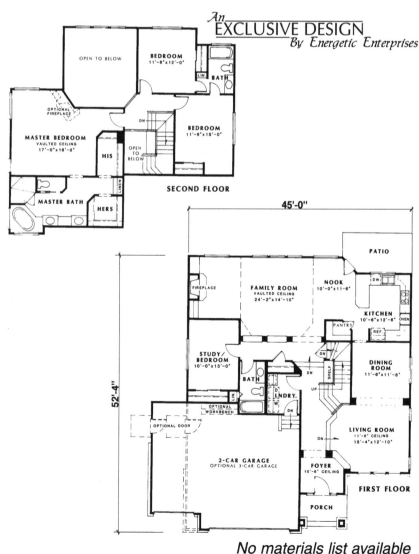

No materials list available

PRICE CODE B

GREAT ROOM HAS VAULTED CEILING

No. 90361

■ This plan features:

— Three bedrooms

— Two full and one half baths

■ A bay window Breakfast area flowing into the charming Kitchen with ample cabinet and counter space

■ A vaulted ceiling in the Great Room with a cozy fireplace

■ A Master Bedroom with a vaulted ceiling and luxurious master Bath enhanced by a platform tub, stall shower, and an oversized walk-in closet

■ Two additional bedrooms that share a full hall bath

FIRST FLOOR — 1,105 SQ. FT.
SECOND FLOOR — 460 SQ. FT.

TOTAL LIVING AREA:
1,565 SQ. FT.

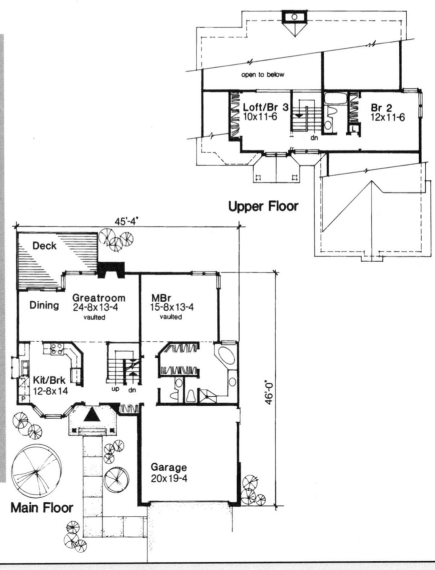

PRICE CODE A

LOTS OF SPACE IN THIS SMALL PACKAGE

No. 90378

■ This plan features:

— Two bedrooms with possible third /Loft

— Two full baths

■ A Living Room with dynamic, soaring angles and a fireplace

■ A first floor Master Suite with full bath and walk in-closet

■ Walk-in closets in all bedrooms

FIRST FLOOR — 878 SQ. FT.
SECOND FLOOR — 405 SQ. FT.

TOTAL LIVING AREA:
1,283 SQ. FT.

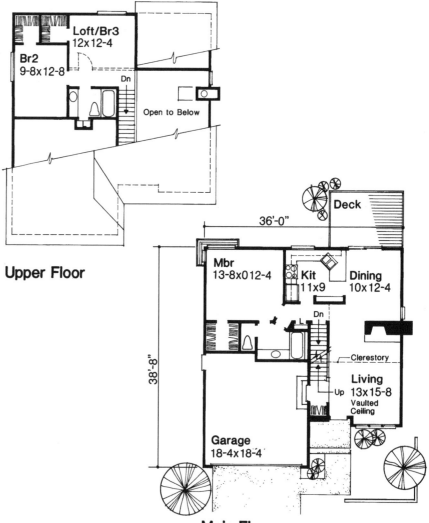

Upper Floor

Loft/Br3
12x12-4

Br2
9-8x12-8

Dn

Open to Below

Deck

36'-0"

Mbr
13-8x012-4

Kit
11x9

Dining
10x12-4

Dn

38'-8"

Clerestory

Living
13x15-8
Vaulted
Ceiling

Up

Garage
18-4x18-4

Main Floor

PRICE CODE C

HOMEY COUNTRY PORCH

No. 24325

■ This plan features:

— Three bedrooms

— Two full and one half baths

■ A spacious Living Room with a cozy fireplace, triple front window and atrium door to Patio

■ A Family Room flowing into the Dining Room and Kitchen creates a comfortable gathering space

■ An efficient Kitchen including a peninsula counter, double sink, walk-in pantry and broom closet

■ A Master Suite with a walk-in closet, private Bath and a built-in audio/video center

■ A Laundry Room ideally located near the bedrooms

■ Two additional bedrooms that share a full hall bath

FIRST FLOOR — 908 SQ. FT.
SECOND FLOOR — 908 SQ. FT.
GARAGE — 462 SQ. FT.

TOTAL LIVING AREA:
1,816 SQ. FT.

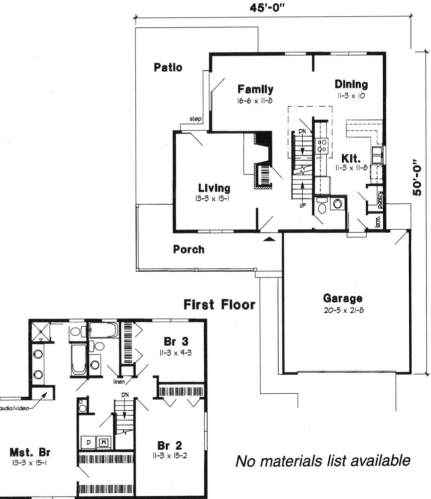

No materials list available

An
EXCLUSIVE DESIGN
By Marshall Associates

PRICE CODE F

STUCCO & STONE GIVE THIS HOUSE CLASS

No. 10540

■ This plan features:

— Four bedrooms

— Two and one half baths

■ A large, majestic foyer flowing into the formal Dining Room

■ A Great Room accented by a wet-bar, a stone fireplace, and access to a spacious deck

■ A spacious Kitchen highlighted by a writing area, work area, and a beamed Breakfast Room

■ A huge Master Bedroom with a dressing room and a separate whirlpool bath

■ A lower level featuring a recreation area and two additional bedrooms

FIRST FLOOR — 2,473 SQ. FT.
LOWER FLOOR — 1,624 SQ. FT.
BASEMENT — 732 SQ. FT.
GARAGE & STORAGE — 686 SQ. FT.

TOTAL LIVING AREA:
4,097 SQ. FT.

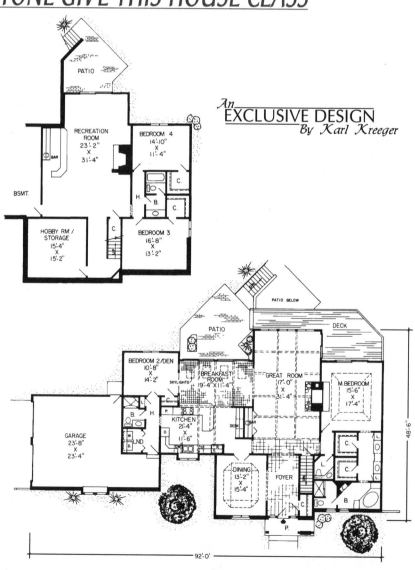

An
EXCLUSIVE DESIGN
By Karl Kreeger

PRICE CODE C

CATHEDRAL AND TRAY CEILINGS ADD INTREST

No. 24601

■ This plan features:

— Three bedrooms

— Two and one half baths

■ A mood enhancing, focal point fireplace and cathedral ceiling in the spacious Living Room

■ A built-in pantry, peninsula counter, double sinks and ample storage in the efficient Kitchen

■ A sunny Eating Nook

■ A tray ceiling that crowns the Master Bedroom

■ A Master Bath that includes an oval tub, double vanity, step-in shower and a compartmented toilet

■ Two additional bedrooms located on the second floor that share a full hall bath

FIRST FLOOR — 1,483 SQ. FT.
SECOND FLOOR — 575 SQ. FT.

**TOTAL LIVING AREA:
2,058 SQ. FT.**

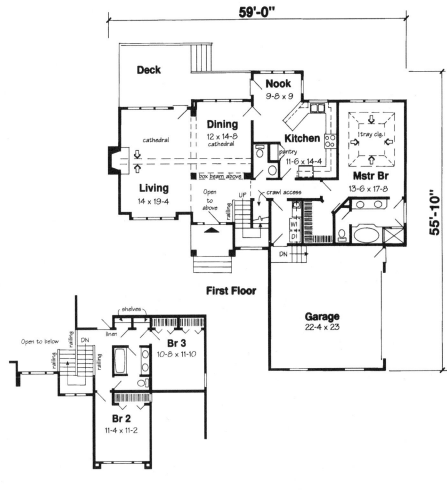

No materials list available

PRICE CODE B

FOUR BEDROOM TWO STORY DESIGN

No. 90358

■ This plan features:

— Three bedrooms

— Two full baths

■ A vaulted ceiling in the Great Room and a fireplace

■ An efficient Kitchen with a peninsula counter and double sink

■ A Family Room with easy access to the wood Deck

■ A Master Bedroom with private bath entrance

■ Convenient laundry facilities outside the Master Bedroom

■ Two additional bedrooms upstairs with walk-in closets and the use of the full hall bath

FIRST FLOOR — 1,062 SQ. FT.
SECOND FLOOR — 469 SQ. FT.

TOTAL LIVING AREA:
1,531 SQ. FT.

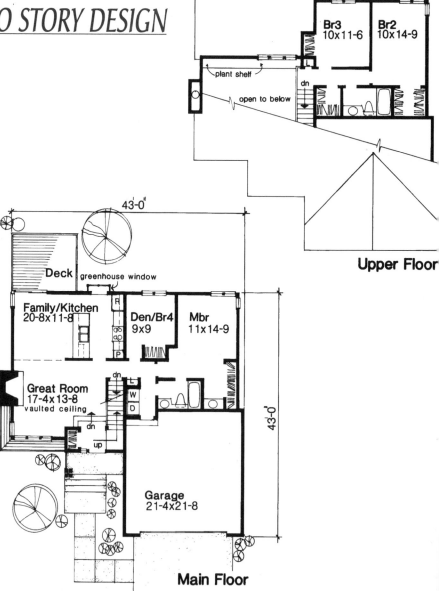

PRICE CODE C

CUSTOMIZED FOR SLOPING VIEW SITE

No. 91343

■ This plan features:

— Three bedrooms

— Two full and one half baths

■ A stone-faced fireplace and vaulted ceiling in the Living Room

■ An island food preparation center with a sink and a Breakfast bar in the Kitchen

■ Sliding glass doors leading from the Dining Room to the adjacent deck

■ A Master Suite with a vaulted ceiling, a sitting room, and a lavish Master Bath with a whirlpool tub, skylights, double vanity, and a walk-in closet

FIRST FLOOR — 1,338 SQ. FT.
SECOND FLOOR — 763 SQ. FT.
LOWER FLOOR — 61 SQ. FT.

TOTAL LIVING AREA:
2,101 SQ. FT.

FIRST FLOOR

SECOND FLOOR

GARAGE
25'-6" X 23'-0"
27'-0" (MAX.)

PRICE CODE D

MASTER SUITE FEATURES PRIVATE DECK

No. 91404

■ This plan features:

— Four bedrooms

— Three full baths

■ A curving stairway surrounded by a two story bay window

■ A sunken Great Room united with the outdoors by three magnificent window walls

■ A bayed formal Dining Room located efficiently close to the Kitchen

■ A well-appointed Kitchen that flows into a sunny eating Nook

■ A Master Bedroom with a private deck, walk-in closet, and a lavish Master Bath

FIRST FLOOR — 1,550 SQ. FT.
SECOND FLOOR — 1,001 SQ. FT.
GARAGE — 750 SQ. FT.

TOTAL LIVING AREA: 2,551 SQ. FT.

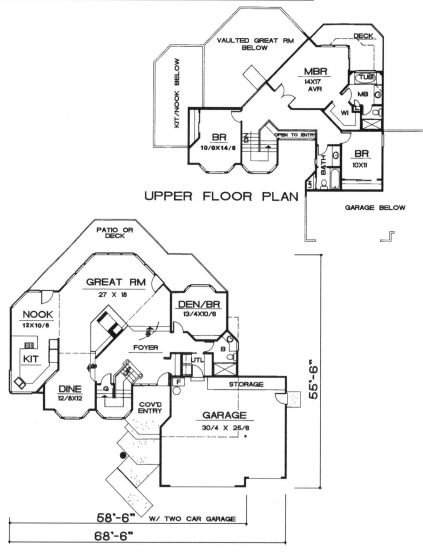

UPPER FLOOR PLAN

MAIN FLOOR PLAN

PRICE CODE A

Balcony Overlooks Living Room Below

No. 90356

■ This plan features:

— Three bedrooms

— Two full and one half baths

■ A vaulted ceiling Living Room with a balcony above and a fireplace

■ An efficient, well-equipped Kitchen with stovetop island and easy flow of traffic into the Dining Room

■ A deck accessible from the Living Room

■ A luxurious Master Suite with a bay window seat, walk-in closet, dressing area, and a private shower

■ Two additional bedrooms that share a full hall bath

FIRST FLOOR — 674 SQ. FT.
SECOND FLOOR — 677 SQ. FT.

TOTAL LIVING AREA:
1,351 SQ. FT.

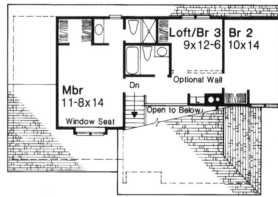

UPPER FLOOR PLAN

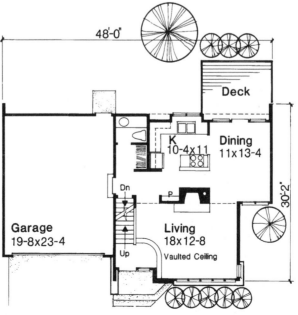

MAIN FLOOR PLAN

PRICE CODE C

LARGE LIVING ROOM WITH FIREPLACE

No. 24600

■ This plan features:

— Four bedrooms

— Two full and one half bath

■ A focal point fireplace in the spacious Living Room

■ An efficient Kitchen, situated between the formal and informal dining areas, that includes a double sink, peninsula counter and built-in pantry

■ A sunny bay window in the Breakfast Nook area

■ A Master Suite that includes a walk-in closet, and compartmented private Master Bath

■ Three additional bedrooms that share a full hall bath

■ A second floor Laundry Center

FIRST FLOOR — 850 SQ. FT.
SECOND FLOOR — 1,090 SQ. FT.
GARAGE — 440 SQ. FT.

**TOTAL LIVING AREA:
1,940 SQ. FT.**

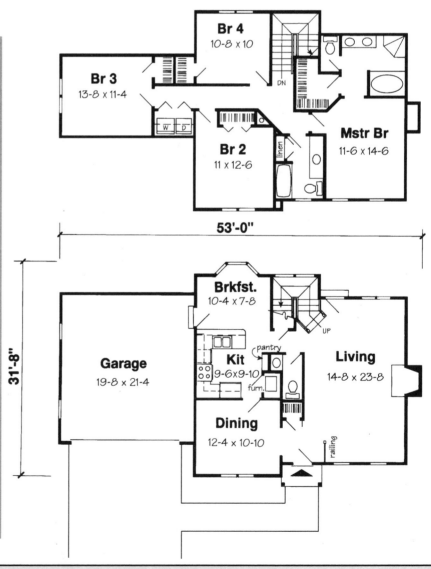

Br 4
10-8 x 10

Br 3
13-8 x 11-4

DN

Mstr Br
11-6 x 14-6

W D

linen

Br 2
11 x 12-6

53'-0"

31'-8"

Brkfst.
10-4 x 7-8

UP

Garage
19-8 x 21-4

Kit
9-6x9-10

pantry

furn.

Living
14-8 x 23-8

Dining
12-4 x 10-10

railing

PRICE CODE F

PALATIAL SPLENDOR

No. 24556

This plan features:

— Five bedrooms

— Two full and one half baths

■ Elaborate detailing around the multi-paned windows and a varied roofline

■ Columned doorways and a split center staircase that add to the elegance of the home

■ A Living Room, with a fireplace, that adjoins the Dining Room

■ A Kitchen that includes a cooktop island and a built-in pantry

■ A sunny Breakfast Room

■ A sunken Family Room with a fireplace and built-in shelves

■ A Master Suite crowned by a pan ceiling and warmed by a two-sided fireplace that can be enjoyed in the Bath as well

FIRST FLOOR — 2,224 SQ. FT.
SECOND FLOOR — 1,841 SQ. FT.

TOTAL LIVING AREA:
4,065 SQ. FT.

No materials list available

An
EXCLUSIVE DESIGN
By Britt J. Willis

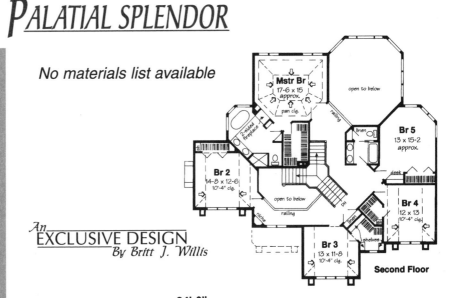

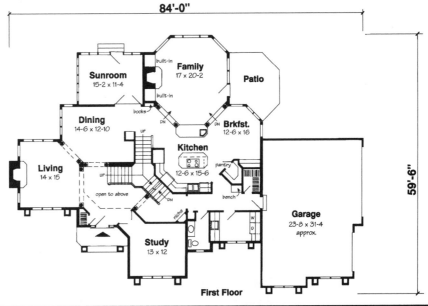

PRICE CODE B

COMPACT DESIGN IMAGES BIGGER HOUSE LOOK

No. 90370

■ This plan features:

— Three bedrooms

— Two full and one half baths

■ An open Entry leading into the Great Room with unique corner windows and a fireplace

■ A Dining Room ideally located between the Great Room and the Kitchen for easy entertaining

■ A Family Room open to the Kitchen and accessing the deck

■ An L-shaped Kitchen with ample counter and cabinet space featuring a Breakfast area with a boxed window

■ A Master Suite with a private bath and a walk-in closet

■ Two additional bedrooms, one a loft, share a full hall bath

FIRST FLOOR — 817 SQ. FT.
SECOND FLOOR — 699 SQ. FT.

TOTAL LIVING AREA:
1,516 SQ. FT.

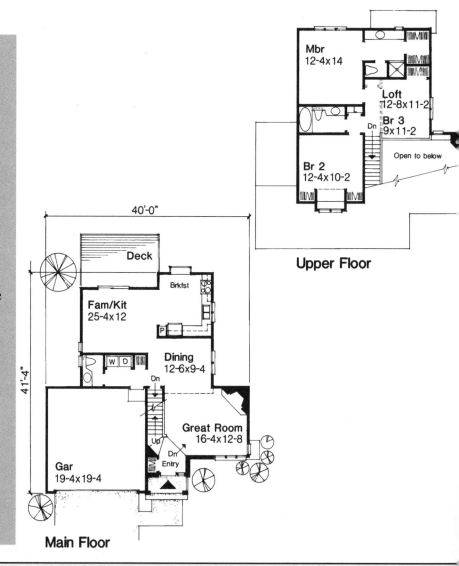

Upper Floor

Main Floor

DESIGN NO. 24268

PRICE CODE D

STATELY ENTRANCE ADDS TO HOME

No. 24268

■ This plan features:

— Three or four bedrooms

— Two full and one half baths

■ A vaulted ceiling in the Living Room adding to its spaciousness

■ A formal Dining Room with easy access to both the Living Room and the Kitchen

■ An efficient Kitchen with double sinks, and ample storage and counter space

■ An informal Eating Nook with a built-in pantry

■ A Family Room with a fireplace

■ A Master Suite with a vaulted ceiling and luxurious Master Bath plus two walk-in closets

■ Two additional bedrooms share a full bath

FIRST FLOOR — 1,115 SQ. FT.
SECOND FLOOR — 1,129 SQ. FT.
BASEMENT — 1,096 SQ. FT.
GARAGE — 415 SQ. FT.

TOTAL LIVING AREA:
2,244 SQ. FT.

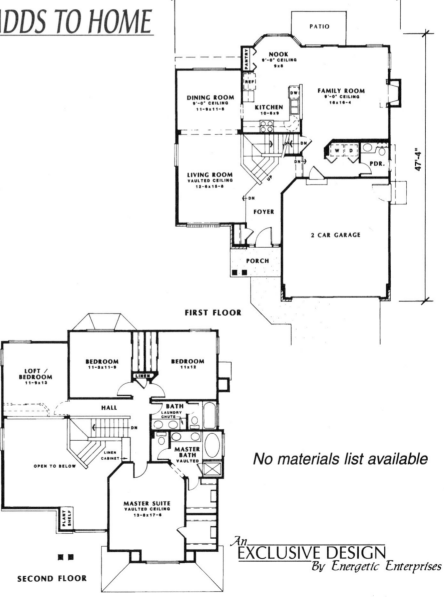

No materials list available

An **EXCLUSIVE DESIGN** *By Energetic Enterprises*

PRICE CODE E

TWO-STORY ENTRY ADDS ELEGANCE

No materials list available

No. 24322

■ This plan features:

— Four bedrooms

— Three full baths

■ A two-story entry with elegant curved staircase

■ Formal Living and Dining Rooms with convenient built-ins

■ A spacious Family Room with direct access to rear yard

■ A well-appointed Kitchen with access to both Dining Room and Breakfast area

■ A lavish Master Suite with a private Master Bath and walk-in closet

■ Three additional bedrooms share a full bath

FIRST FLOOR — 1,499 SQ. FT.
SECOND FLOOR — 1,168 SQ. FT.
GARAGE — 473 SQ. FT.

TOTAL LIVING AREA:
2,667 SQ. FT.

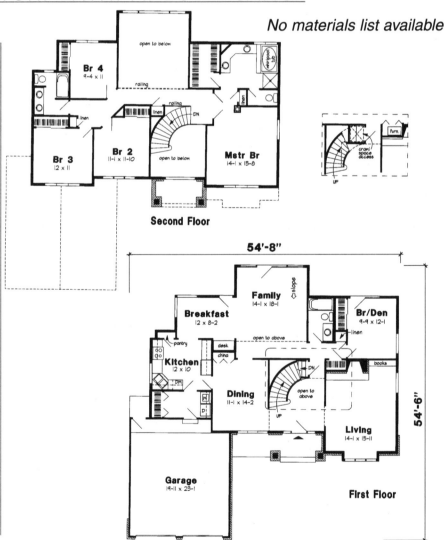

PRICE CODE E

IMPRESSIVE BRICK

An EXCLUSIVE DESIGN
By Britt J. Willis

No. 24550

■ This plan features:

— Four bedrooms

— Two full and one half baths

■ A cathedral ceiling and a two-way fireplace in the Living Room

■ A formal Dining Room accented by a lovely bay window

■ A Family Room with a fireplace and built-in entertainment center

■ An island Kitchen with an atrium sink, walk-in pantry, built-in desk as well as a Utility room and Garage

■ A Master Suite with a vaulted ceiling, walk-in closet, and a Bath with a corner window tub, two vanities and a shower

■ Three additional bedrooms, on second floor, sharing a full bath

FIRST FLOOR — 1,428 SQ. FT.
SECOND FLOOR — 1,248 SQ. FT.

TOTAL LIVING AREA:
2,676 SQ. FT.

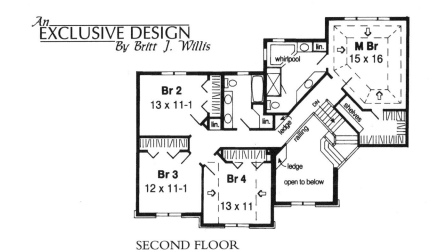

SECOND FLOOR

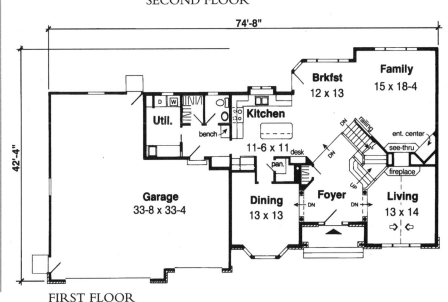

FIRST FLOOR

PRICE CODE D

CONTEMPORARY ANGLES ADD EXTERIOR APPEAL

No. 91804

■ This plan features:

— Four bedrooms

— Three full baths

■ A vaulted, two story ceiling and an open stairway in the Foyer

■ An eleven foot high ceiling in the sunken Living Room, adding volume to the space

■ An efficient, angular Kitchen that is open to the Nook and sunken Family Room

■ A corner fireplace warming the Family Room

■ A phenomenal Master Suite with a walk-in closet, spa tub, step-in shower, and a double vanity

■ Two additional bedrooms that share a full hall bath

■ An optional crawl space or slab foundation — please specify when ordering

FIRST FLOOR — 1,396 SQ. FT.
SECOND FLOOR — 1,034 SQ. FT.

TOTAL LIVING AREA:
2,430 SQ. FT.

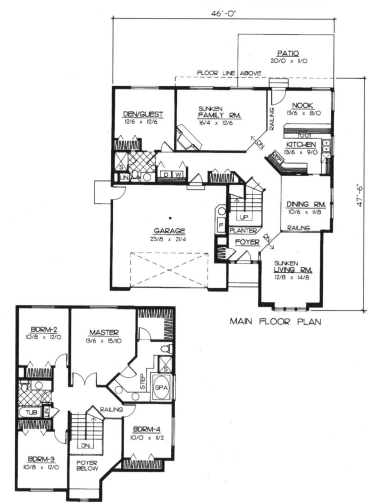

MAIN FLOOR PLAN

UPPER FLOOR PLAN

PRICE CODE E

TRADITIONAL WARMTH WITH A MODERN ACCENT

No. 10638

■ This plan features

— Four bedrooms

— Two and one half baths

■ Recessed ceilings in the Living, Dining and Master Bedrooms

■ Rustic beams, a fireplace and built-in shelves located in the Family Room

■ A Kitchen, with a laundry room close by, adjoins a cozy Breakfast area

■ A Master Suite complete with private bath and bay window sitting nook

FIRST FLOOR — 1,405 SQ. FT.
SECOND FLOOR — 1,364 SQ. FT.
GARAGE — 458 SQ. FT.

**TOTAL LIVING AREA:
2,769 SQ. FT.**

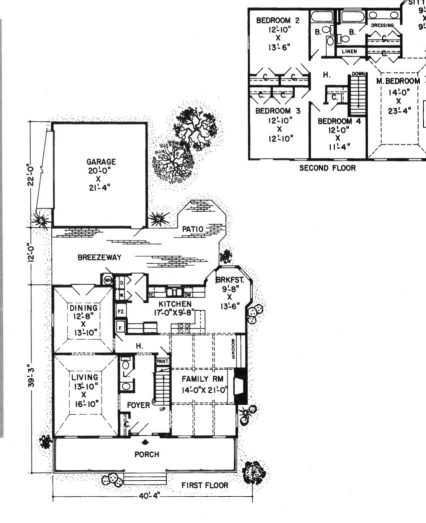

PRICE CODE D

SUN SPACE WARMTH

No. 10495

■ This plan features:

— Four bedrooms

— Three full baths

■ Tile to soak up solar heat in the sun space and also to add a tailored accent to the total home arrangement

■ Air-lock entry conserving warmth in home

■ Master Bedroom with private bath

■ Efficient Kitchen with a space stretching central island for added work space

■ Two additional Bedrooms occupying the second floor, sharing a full Bath

FIRST FLOOR — 1,691 SQ. FT.
SECOND FLOOR — 512 SQ. FT.
GARAGE — 484 SQ. FT.
SUN SPACE — 108 SQ. FT.
BASEMENT — 1,691 SQ. FT.

TOTAL LIVING AREA:
2,311 SQ. FT.

An
EXCLUSIVE DESIGN
By Karl Kreeger

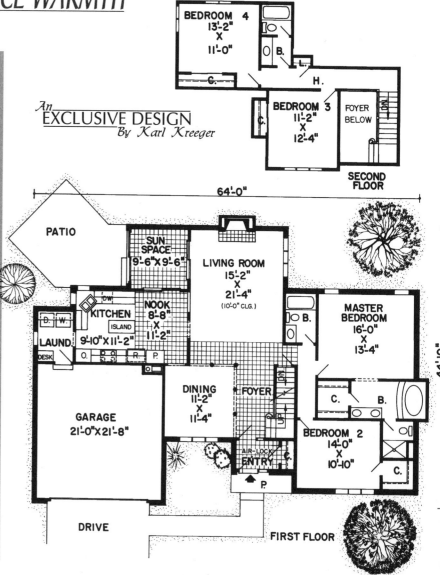

PRICE CODE E

No. 24558

■ This plan features:

— Three bedrooms

— Two full and one half baths

■ Elegant, open Foyer with regal staircase and Library on the right

■ Columned entrance into the Living Room and the Dining Room

■ A well-appointed Kitchen that includes a work island, double sink, built-in desk and a walk-in Pantry

■ A fireplace and sloped ceiling in the Family Room, leads to the multi-windowed Sunroom with more sloped ceilings

■ A luxurious Master Suite equipped with a vaulted ceiling, large walk-in closet, whirlpool tub and a separate shower, plus a double vanity

■ Two additional second floor Bedrooms share a full hall bath

FIRST FLOOR — 1,747 SQ. FT.
SECOND FLOOR — 1,276 SQ. FT.
GARAGE — 687 SQ. FT.
BASEMENT — 1,747 SQ. FT.

TOTAL LIVING AREA:
3,023 SQ. FT.

IMPRESSIVE EXTRAS

An
EXCLUSIVE DESIGN
By Britt J. Willis

Optional Crawl/Slab Plan

No materials list available

Second Floor

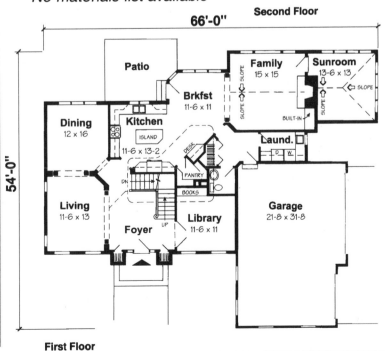

First Floor

PRICE CODE C

FIRST FLOOR MASTER SUITE

No. 24316

■ This plan features:

— Four bedrooms

— Two full and one half baths

■ A formal Living Room, with a distinctive boxed window, stepping down from an open Foyer and formal Dining Room

■ An efficient Kitchen with a corner double sink, bay window area for informal eating and access to the Family Room and Patio

■ Unique corner fireplace in the Family Room serving as a cozy focal point

■ A first floor Master Suite featuring a double closet and a private Bath with a double vanity and a raised window tub

■ Three additional bedrooms on the second floor sharing a hall bath

FIRST FLOOR — 1,400 SQ. FT.
SECOND FLOOR — 540 SQ. FT.

**TOTAL LIVING AREA:
1,940 SQ. FT.**

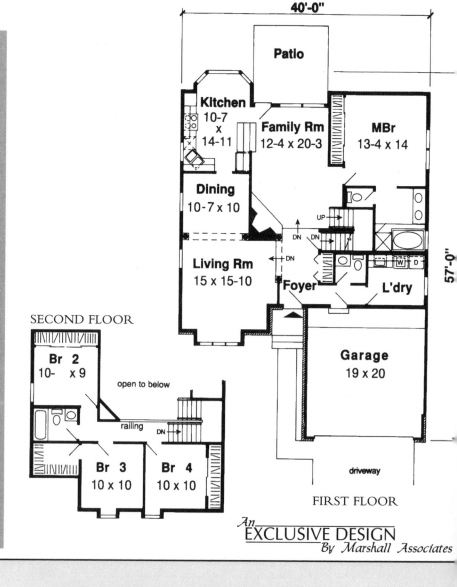

An
EXCLUSIVE DESIGN
By Marshall Associates

An
EXCLUSIVE DESIGN
By Patrick Morabito. A.I.A. Architect

PRICE CODE F

No. 93336

- ◼ This plan features:
- — Four bedrooms
- — Three and a half baths
- ◼ Two high ceiling Entries with landing staircases connecting a Hall/Balcony providing ease in accessing all areas of this expansive home
- ◼ Decorative beams highlighting a huge fireplace and a large bay window in the Family Room
- ◼ A well-equipped Kitchen with a cooktop island/eating bar, a double sink, built-in pantry and desk, and a Dinette with sliding glass doors to the Deck
- ◼ A private and plush Master Suite with an exclusive Screened Porch, dressing area with pocket doors into room size closet, a Bath with a platform, whirlpool tub, and Sitting Room, beyond the Kitchen/Bar alcove, with a corner fireplace and built-in book shelves
- ◼ Three additional bedrooms on the second floor, each with private access to a full bath, and a Bonus Room with many options

EXECUTIVE TREATMENT

FIRST FLOOR — 2,092 SQ. FT.
SECOND FLOOR — 1,934 SQ. FT.
BONUS — 508 SQ. FT.

TOTAL LIVING AREA:
4,026 SQ. FT.

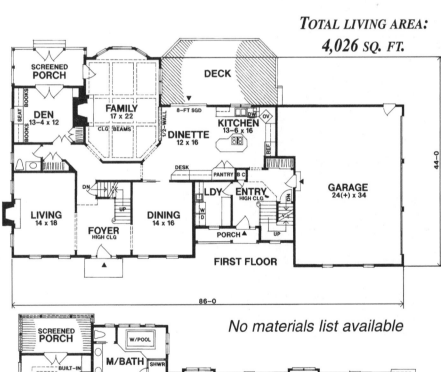

No materials list available

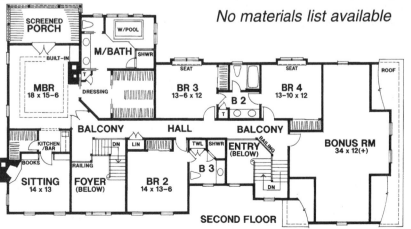

PRICE CODE C

Multi-Level Excitement

No. 20102

■ This plan features:

— Four bedrooms

— Two and a half baths

■ A skylit Breakfast Room with sliders to a rear deck

■ A sunken, fireplaced Living Room

■ An island Kitchen that serves both the formal Dining Room and the Breakfast Room easily

■ A spacious Master Suite with private bath and walk-in closet

■ A third floor containing the fourth Bedroom with a walk-in closet and sloping ceiling

FIRST FLOOR — 1,003 SQ. FT.
SECOND FLOOR — 808 SQ. FT.
THIRD FLOOR — 241 SQ. FT.
BASEMENT — 573 SQ. FT.
GARAGE — 493 SQ. FT.

TOTAL LIVING AREA:
2,052 SQ. FT.

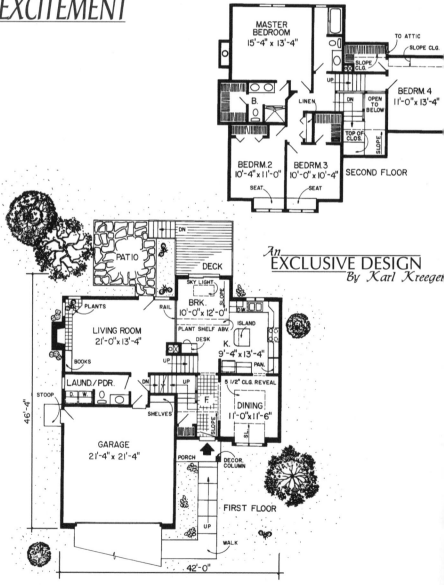

An
EXCLUSIVE DESIGN
By Karl Kreeger

PRICE CODE F

INTELLIGENT PLAN SEPARATES FORMAL FROM FAMILY AREAS

No. 20359

■ This plan features:

— Four bedrooms

— Three and one half baths

■ A sunken Study with large front window illuminating the room

■ A sunken Living Room with a stunning fireplace and opened to the Dining Room

■ An island Kitchen with walk-in pantry, built-in desk and sky-lit Breakfast room

■ A Family Room made spacious by a vaulted ceiling and cozy by a corner fireplace

■ A Master Suite with a tray ceiling, private deck, walk-in closet and private Master Bath

■ A Guest Room with a private full bath

■ Two additional bedrooms that have shared access to the full hall bath with double vanities

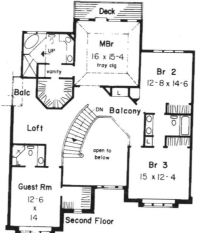

FIRST FLOOR — 2,516 SQ. FT.
SECOND FLOOR — 1,602 SQ. FT.
BASEMENT — 2,516 SQ. FT.
GARAGE — 822 SQ. FT.

TOTAL LIVING AREA:
4,118 SQ. FT.

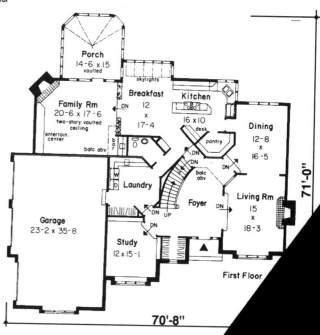

PRICE CODE F

HIGH IMPACT TWO STORY DESIGN

No. 99373

■ This plan features:

— Four bedrooms

— Three and one half baths

■ A high impact two story, double door transom Entry

■ A two story Family Room with a wall consisting of a fireplace and windows

■ A spacious Master Suite with unique curved glass block behind the tub in the Master Bath and a semi-circular window wall with see-through fireplace in sitting area

■ A gourmet Kitchen and Breakfast area opening to a Lanai

■ A Guest Suite with private deck and walk-in closet

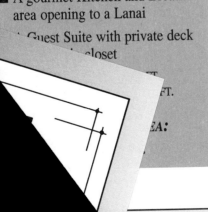

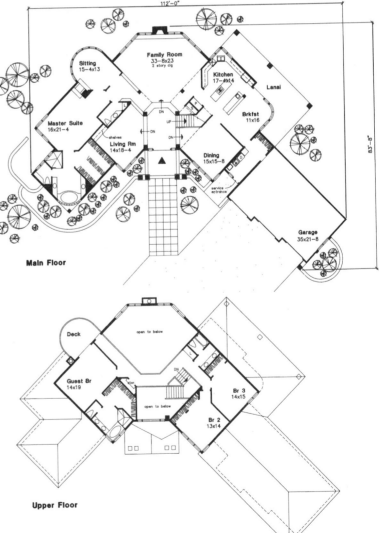

Main Floor

Upper Floor

PRICE CODE D

TRADITIONAL ELEMENTS

No. 91900

- This plan features:
- — Three bedrooms
- — Two full and one half baths

- A vaulted ceiling in the elegant Dining Room

- A see-through fireplace in the Great Room and Kitchen

- A roomy Kitchen with a step-in pantry, separate ovens, built-in desk, and sit-down snack bar

- A gazebo Breakfast area

- A Master Suite with a vaulted ceiling, large walk-in closet and a private Bath

- A dramatic, sky-lit staircase leading to two additional bedrooms and a full bath

FIRST FLOOR — 1,855 SQ. FT.
SECOND FLOOR — 530 SQ. FT.

TOTAL LIVING AREA:
2,385 SQ. FT.

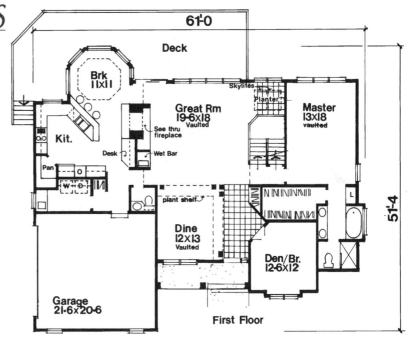

61'-0

Deck

Brk
11x11

Kit.

Great Rm
19-6x18
Vaulted

Skylites
Planter

Master
13x18
vaulted

See thru
fireplace

Desk

Wet Bar

Pan

W D

plant shelf

Dine
12x13
Vaulted

Den/Br.
12-6x12

Garage
21-6x20-6

51'-4

First Floor

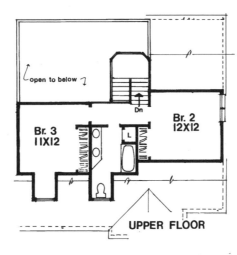

open to below

Dn

Br. 2
12x12

Br. 3
11x12

L

UPPER FLOOR

No materials list available

PRICE CODE E

WINDOWS HIGHLIGHT THIS SPACIOUS HOME

No. 90118

- This plan features:
  - Four or five bedrooms
  - Two and one half baths
- Double windows in the Living Room and the formal Dining Room
- A bay window off the Kitchen's dining area
- A fireplace with built-in bookshelves in the spacious Family Room
- A Master Suite with a private Master Bath and his-n-her closets
- A mudroom entrance with a half-bath
- A basement foundation only

FIRST FLOOR — 1,392 SQ. FT.
SECOND FLOOR — 1,282 SQ. FT.

TOTAL LIVING AREA: 2,674 SQ. FT.

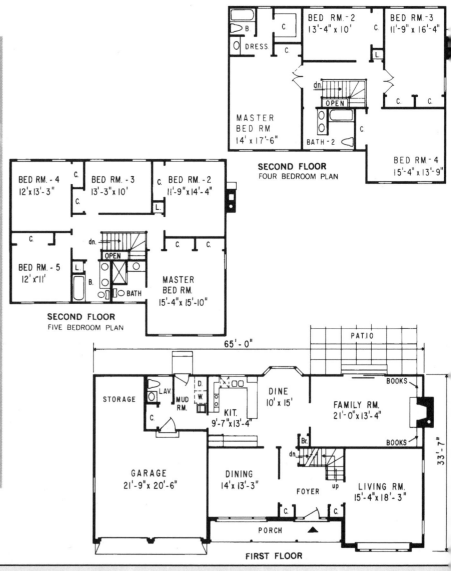

SECOND FLOOR
FOUR BEDROOM PLAN

SECOND FLOOR
FIVE BEDROOM PLAN

FIRST FLOOR

PRICE CODE B

DESIGN IS IDEAL FOR A SMALL LOT

No. 34800

■ This plan features:

— Three bedrooms

— Two and one half baths

■ Individual dressing areas adjacent to an upstairs bath

■ A large Master Bedroom including a walk-in closet

■ An inviting two-story foyer

■ A Kitchen including a pantry, space for a dinette set, and direct access to a rear deck

FIRST FLOOR — 1,187 SQ. FT.
SECOND FLOOR — 597 SQ. FT.
BASEMENT — 1,169 SQ. FT.
GARAGE — 484 SQ. FT.

TOTAL LIVING AREA: 1,784 SQ. FT.

An EXCLUSIVE DESIGN *By Karl Kreeger*

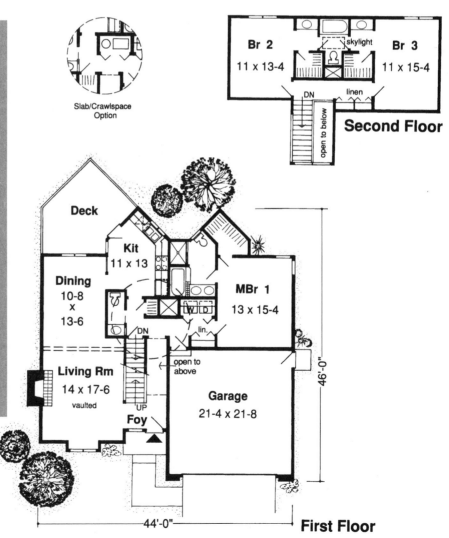

Slab/Crawlspace Option

Second Floor

Br 2
11 x 13-4

skylight

Br 3
11 x 15-4

DN   linen   open to below

First Floor

Deck

Kit
11 x 13

Dining
10-8 x 13-6

MBr 1
13 x 15-4

W D   lin.

DN

open to above

Living Rm
14 x 17-6
vaulted

UP

Foy

Garage
21-4 x 21-8

46'-0"

44'-0"

PRICE CODE D

COMFORTABLE FAMILY HOME LEAVES ROOM TO GROW

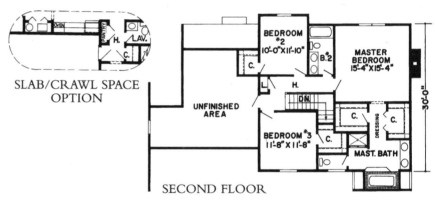

SLAB/CRAWL SPACE
OPTION

SECOND FLOOR

No. 34827

- This plan features:
— Three bedrooms
— Two and one half baths
- Formal Living and Dining Rooms off the central foyer for ease in entertaining
- A Family Room with a large fireplace adjoining the Breakfast area with a bay window
- A short hall leading past the powder room, linking the formal Dining Room with the Kitchen
- Each bedroom containing a walk-in closet
- A Master Suite including both a raised tub and a step-in shower

FIRST FLOOR — 1,212 SQ. FT.
SECOND FLOOR — 1,030 SQ. FT.
BASEMENT — 1,212 SQ. FT.
GARAGE — 521 SQ. FT.

TOTAL LIVING AREA:
2,242 SQ. FT.

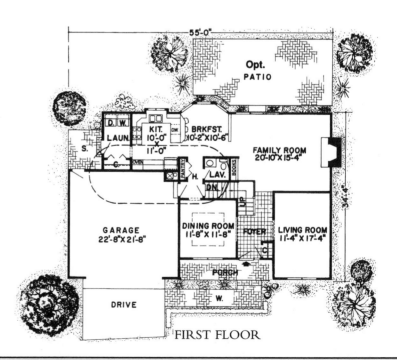

FIRST FLOOR

PRICE CODE C

BAY WINDOWS ADD LIGHT & SPACE

No. 34851

■ This plan features:

— Three bedrooms

— Two full and one half baths

■ A sloped-ceiling Living/Dining Room combination that is brightened by abundant windows

■ An expansive Family Room with a fireplace and access to the deck

■ An efficient, well-appointed island Kitchen with a built-in pantry and laundry facilities that serves both the Breakfast area and the formal Dining Room

■ A Master Suite with a sloped ceiling, private Master Bath, and a walk-in closet

■ Two additional bedrooms that share a full hall bath

FIRST FLOOR — 1,056 SQ. FT.
SECOND FLOOR — 874 SQ. FT.
BASEMENT — 1,023 SQ. FT.
GARAGE — 430 SQ. FT.

TOTAL LIVING AREA:
1,930 SQ. FT.

Slab/Crawlspace Option

Second Floor

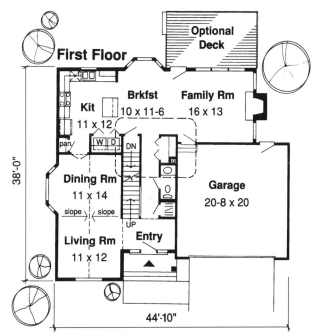

First Floor

PRICE CODE A

CONTEMPORARY EXTERIORS

No. 90327

■ This plan features:

— Three bedrooms

— Two full baths

■ A vaulted ceiling and front corner windows enhancing the Living Room

■ A clerestory accenting the open design of the Dining Room and Kitchen

■ A U-shaped Kitchen with a corner double sink and peninsula counter, plus all the amenities

■ A secluded Master Bedroom with a walk-in closet and a large, compartmented bath

■ Two additional bedrooms that share the full hall bath

FIRST FLOOR — 846 SQ. FT.
SECOND FLOOR — 400 SQ. FT.
BASEMENT — 846 SQ. FT.
GARAGE — 400 SQ. FT.

**TOTAL LIVING AREA:
1,246 SQ. FT.**

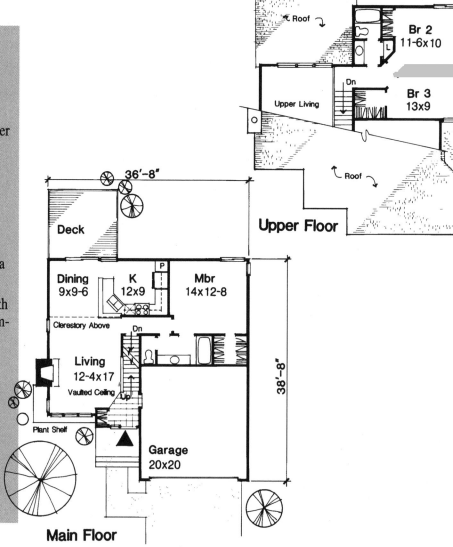

PRICE CODE E

*I*MPRESSIVE TWO STORY FOYER

No. 24650

■ This plan features:

— Four bedrooms

— Two full and one half baths

■ A two story Foyer with an angled staircase

■ An open layout between the formal Living Room and the formal Dining Room

■ A well-appointed, island Kitchen equipped with a double sink, a walk-in pantry and ample cabinet and counter space

■ An expansive Family Room enhanced by a cozy fireplace and a bumped out window

■ A luxurious Master Suite with Bath and two walk-in closets

■ Three additional bedrooms that share a double vanity hall bath

FIRST FLOOR — 1,435 SQ. FT.
SECOND FLOOR — 1,462 SQ.FT.
BONUS ROOM — 347 SQ. FT.
GARAGE — 616 SQ. FT.

**TOTAL LIVING AREA:
2,897 SQ. FT.**

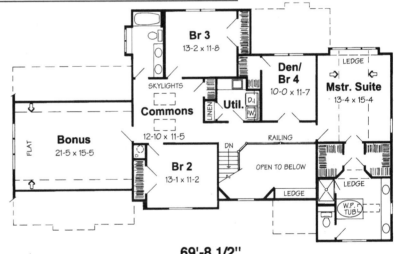

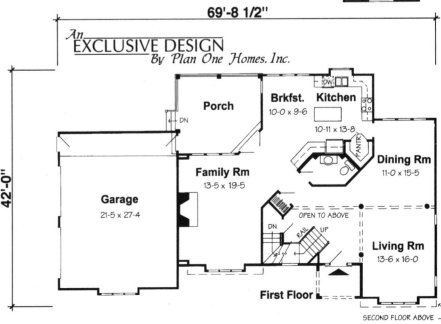

An
EXCLUSIVE DESIGN
By Plan One Homes, Inc.

PRICE CODE F

GARDEN ROOM ADDS WARMTH

No. 28018

■ This plan features:

— Three bedrooms

— Two full and one half baths

■ A unique Garden Room as the hub of activity for living areas

■ A fireplace adding a cozy touch to the Living Room and the adjoining formal Dining Room

■ An expansive Kitchen has a built-in pantry area and food preparation island making it the gourmet's preference

■ A private Master Suite includes a room-sized, walk-in closet and full Bath with an atrium tub

■ An upper level containing two bedrooms, a full bath, a studio and storage area

FIRST FLOOR — 2,527 SQ. FT.
SECOND FLOOR — 1,115 SQ. FT.
GARAGE, LAVATORY, WORKSHOP — 884 SQ. FT.

TOTAL LIVING AREA :
3,642 SQ. FT.

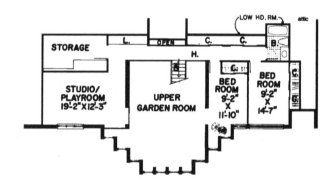

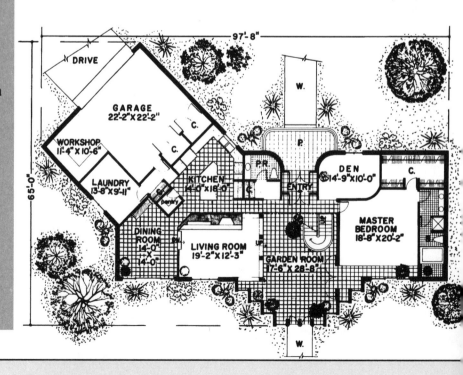

PRICE CODE D

A MODERN PLAN WITH A FARMHOUSE FLAVOR

No. 90201

- ■ This plan features:
- — Four bedrooms
- — Two full and one half baths
- ■ A sprawling covered porch
- ■ A cozy Family Room warmed by a fireplace with a raised hearth
- ■ A formal Dining Room with a large bay window
- ■ A handy Kitchen with built-ins including an eating bar
- ■ A Master Bedroom equipped with a dressing room, two closets and a private bath

FIRST FLOOR — 1,370 SQ. FT.
SECOND FLOOR — 969 SQ. FT.

**TOTAL LIVING AREA:
2,339 SQ. FT.**

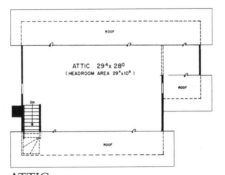

ATTIC

SECOND FLOOR

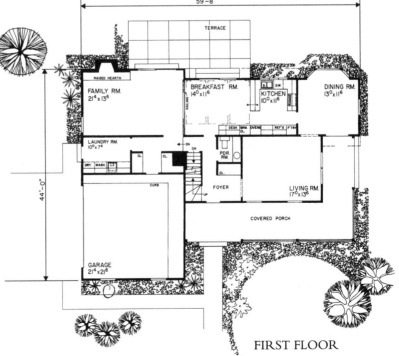

FIRST FLOOR

PRICE CODE F

PRIVATE COURT WITH HOT TUB

SECOND FLOOR PLAN

An
EXCLUSIVE DESIGN
By Karl Kreeger

No. 10534

■ This plan features:

— Four bedrooms

— Three and one half baths

■ A private court adjoining the Master Suite which includes a hot tub

■ A cozy Library which opens onto the two-story foyer through French doors

■ A Morning Room with built-ins, a bar with wine storage, and a sun porch

FIRST FLOOR — 2,486 SQ. FT.
SECOND FLOOR — 954 SQ. FT.
BASEMENT — 2,486 SQ. FT.
GARAGE — 576 SQ. FT.

TOTAL LIVING AREA:
3,440 SQ. FT.

FIRST FLOOR PLAN

PRICE CODE B

COUNTRY STYLE CHARMER

No. 91903

■ This plan features:

— Three bedrooms

— Two full and one half baths

■ A classical symmetry and gracious front porch

■ Formal areas zoned towards the front of the house

■ A large Family Room with fireplace

■ A winder staircase located off the Family Room

■ A Master Bedroom with double vanities, separate glass shower and tub, and a built-in entertainment center

FIRST FLOOR — 910 SQ. FT.
SECOND FLOOR — 769 SQ. FT.
BASEMENT — 890 SQ. FT.

**TOTAL LIVING AREA:
1,679 SQ. FT.**

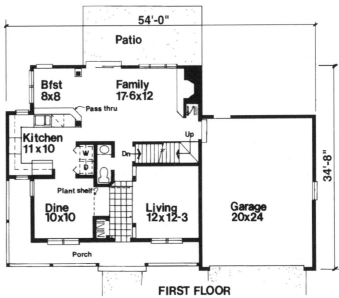

54'-0"

Patio

Bfst 8x8

Family 17·6x12

Pass thru

Kitchen 11 x 10

Up

Dn

34'-8"

Plant shelf

Dine 10x10

Living 12x12-3

Garage 20x24

Porch

FIRST FLOOR

Mbr 14 x 12

Tv

L

Dn

Br 2 10x11·6

Open to below

Br 3 12 x10

SECOND FLOOR

PRICE CODE C

PORCH ADORNS ELEGANT BAY

No. 20093

■ This plan features:

— Three bedrooms

— Two and one half baths

■ A Master Suite with a romantic bay window and full Bath

■ Bedrooms with huge closets and use of the full hall bath

■ A roomy island Kitchen with a modern, efficient layout

■ A Formal Dining Room with a recessed decorative ceiling

■ Sloping skylit ceilings illuminating the fireplaced Living Room

■ A rear Deck accessible from both the Kitchen and the Living Room

FIRST FLOOR — 1,027 SQ. FT.
SECOND FLOOR — 974 SQ. FT.
GARAGE — 476 SQ. FT.

TOTAL LIVING AREA:
2,001 SQ. FT.

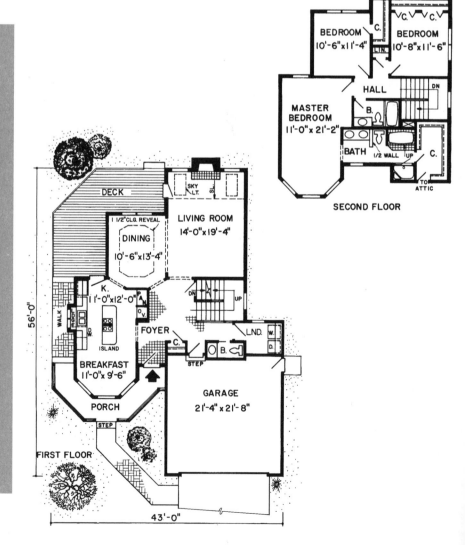

PRICE CODE C

EXTERIOR HIGHLIGHTED BY MANY DECKS

No. 90629

- This plan features:
— Three bedrooms
— Three full and one half baths
- All rooms with outdoor decks
- A Living Room with a heat-circulating fireplace
- A Kitchen with ample counter and cabinet space and easy access to the Dining Room and outdoor dining area
- A Master Bedroom with a heat-circulating fireplace, plush Master Bath and a walk-in closet
- A basement foundation only

FIRST FLOOR — 1,001 SQ. FT.
SECOND FLOOR — 712 SQ. FT.
LOWER FLOOR — 463 SQ. FT.

TOTAL LIVING AREA:
2,176 SQ. FT.

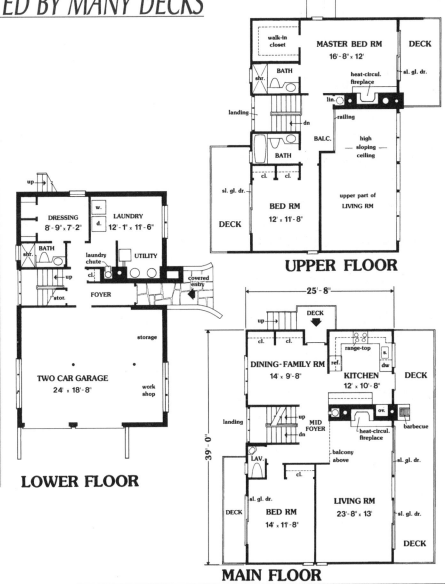

LOWER FLOOR

UPPER FLOOR

MAIN FLOOR

PRICE CODE E

PERFECT FOR PARTIES

No. 10663

■ This plan features:

— Three bedrooms

— Three and one half baths

■ Two bedroom suites, with two full baths, adjoining a sitting room on the second floor

■ A vaulted Family Room with a fireplace and a bay window in the Living Room

■ An elegant Dining Room with floor-to-ceiling windows and a nearby Study

■ A Nook nestled between the Kitchen and the utility room

FIRST FLOOR — 2,310 SQ. FT.
SECOND FLOOR — 866 SQ. FT.
GARAGE — 679 SQ. FT.

TOTAL LIVING AREA:
3,176 SQ. FT.

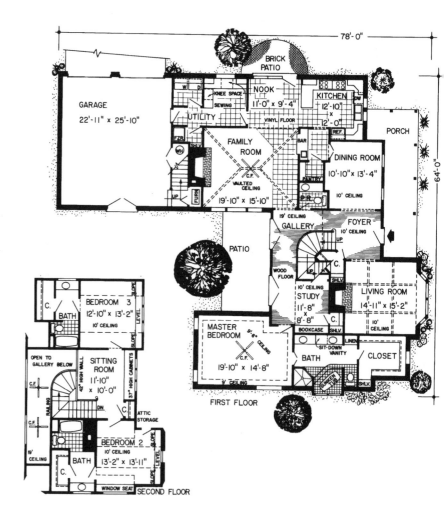

PRICE CODE A

LARGE FRONT PORCH ADDS A COUNTRY TOUCH

No. 34601

■ This plan features:

— Three bedrooms

— Two full baths

■ A country-styled front porch

■ Vaulted ceiling in the Living Room which includes a fireplace

■ An efficient Kitchen with double sinks and peninsula counter that may double as an eating bar

■ Two first floor bedrooms with ample closet space

■ A second floor Master Suite with sloped ceiling, walk-in closet and private master Bath

FIRST FLOOR — 1,007 SQ. FT.
SECOND FLOOR — 408 SQ. FT.

TOTAL LIVING AREA:
1,415 SQ. FT.

Alternate Foundation Plan

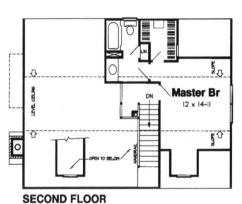

SECOND FLOOR

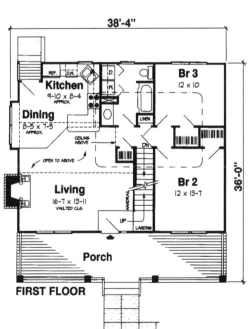

FIRST FLOOR

PRICE CODE C

STREETSIDE APPEAL

No. 20160

■ This plan features:

— Three bedrooms

— Two full and one half baths

■ An elegant Living and Dining Room combination that is divided by columns

■ A Family/Hearth Room with a two-way fireplace to the Breakfast room

■ A well-appointed Kitchen with built-in pantry, peninsula counter and double corner sink

■ A Master Suite with decorative ceiling, walk-in closet and private bath

■ Two additional bedrooms that share a full hall bath

FIRST FLOOR — 1,590 SQ. FT.
SECOND FLOOR — 567 SQ. FT.
BASEMENT — 1,576 SQ. FT.
GARAGE — 456 SQ. FT.

TOTAL LIVING AREA:
2,157 SQ. FT.

An
EXCLUSIVE DESIGN
By Karl Kreeger

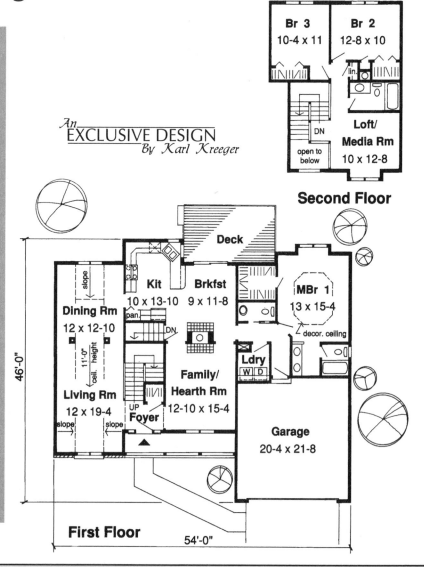

PRICE CODE D

COLONIAL HOME WITH ALL THE TRADITIONAL COMFORTS

No. 34705

- ■ This plan features:
- — Four bedrooms
- — Two and one half baths
- ■ A formal Living Room and Dining Room flanking a spacious entry
- ■ Family areas flowing together into an open space at the rear of the home
- ■ An island Kitchen with a built-in pantry centrally located for easy service to the Dining Room and Breakfast area
- ■ A Master Suite including large closets and double vanities in the bath

FIRST FLOOR — 1,090 SQ. FT.
SECOND FLOOR — 1,134 SQ. FT.
BASEMENT — 1,090 SQ. FT.
GARAGE — 576 SQ. FT.

TOTAL LIVING AREA:
2,224 SQ. FT.

Second Floor

Br 4
11-4 x 10-8

MBr 1
13-8 x 15-6

Br 2
11-8 x 16

Br 3
11-4 x 10-8

Slab/Crawlspace
Option

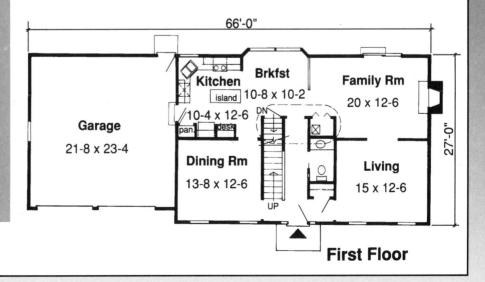

First Floor

66'-0"

Garage
21-8 x 23-4

Kitchen
island
10-4 x 12-6

Brkfst
10-8 x 10-2

Family Rm
20 x 12-6

pan.   desk

Dining Rm
13-8 x 12-6

Living
15 x 12-6

27'-0"

PRICE CODE B

COMPACT DREAM HOUSE

No. 90245

- This plan features:
- — Three bedrooms
- — Two and one half baths
- A central entry flanked by a cozy Study and sunny formal Living Room
- Two fireplaces to help with heating bills
- A Kitchen featuring a triple window with built-in seating and a beamed ceiling

FIRST FLOOR — 1,020 SQ. FT.
SECOND FLOOR — 777 SQ. FT.

**TOTAL LIVING AREA:
1,797 SQ. FT.**

SECOND FLOOR

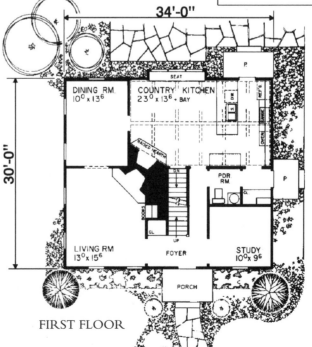

FIRST FLOOR

PRICE CODE D

COMPACT, YET ELEGANT

No. 34926

■ This plan features:

— Three bedrooms

— Two and one half baths

■ An angular plan giving each room an interesting shape

■ A wrap-around veranda

■ An entry foyer leading through the Living Room and Parlor

■ A Dining Room with a hexagonal recessed ceiling

■ A sunny Breakfast room off the island Kitchen

■ A Master Suite with a bump-out window, walk-in closet, and double sinks in the private bath

FIRST FLOOR — 1,409 SQ. FT.
SECOND FLOOR — 1,116 SQ. FT.
BASEMENT — 1,409 SQ. FT.
GARAGE — 483 SQ. FT.

TOTAL LIVING AREA:
2,525 SQ. FT.

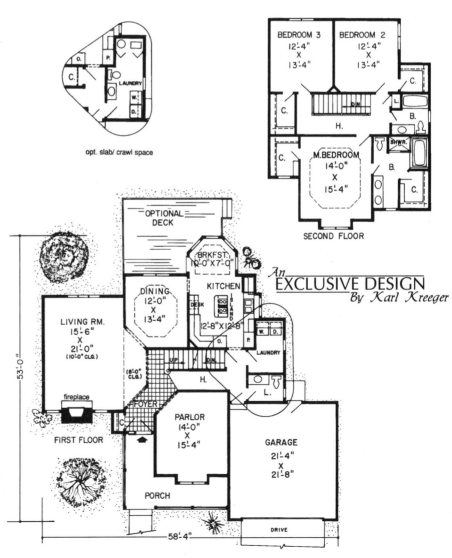

opt. slab/ crawl space

An EXCLUSIVE DESIGN
By Karl Kreeger

PRICE CODE A

GOOD THINGS COME IN SMALL PACKAGES

No. 90264

■ This plan features:

— Three bedrooms

— Two and one half baths

■ A bonus space over the Garage

■ An entry opening to a fireplaced Living Room

■ A Dining Room overlooking the backyard

■ A Kitchen spacious enough for informal family meals

FIRST FLOOR — 624 SQ. FT.
SECOND FLOOR — 624 SQ. FT.

TOTAL LIVING AREA:
1,248 SQ. FT.

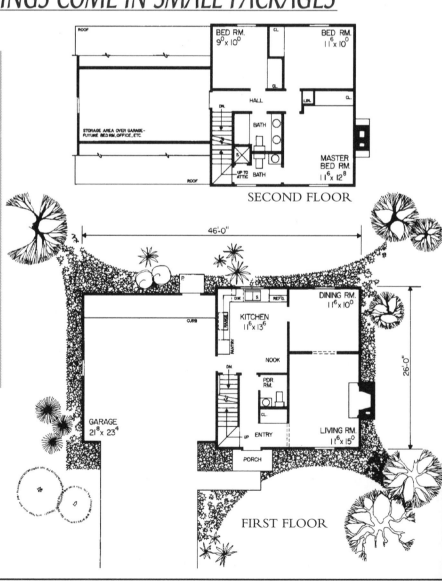

SECOND FLOOR

FIRST FLOOR

PRICE CODE D

SPIRAL STAIRS LEAD TO LOFT

No. 90127

■ This plan features:

— Four bedrooms

— Two full baths

■ A large eat-in Kitchen easily serving the formal Dining Room or Great Room

■ A cathedral ceiling and cozy fireplace in the Great Room with sliding glass doors leading to the patio

■ A Master Bedroom with a large master Bath and two walk-in closets

■ Three additional bedrooms sharing a full hall bath

■ An optional basement or crawl space foundation — please specify when ordering

FIRST FLOOR — 2,093 SQ. FT.

LOFT AREA — 326 SQ. FT.

TOTAL LIVING AREA:
2,419 SQ. FT.

LOFT AREA

BASEMENT GARAGE
FOR HILLSIDE LOT

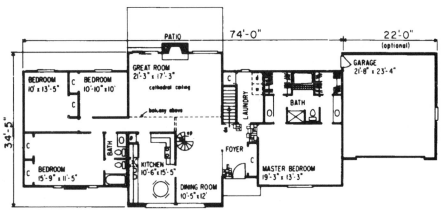

FIRST FLOOR WITH BASEMENT

PRICE CODE D

WARM WELCOME UPON ENTERING

No. 92013

■ This plan features:

— Three bedrooms

— Two full and one half baths

■ A large, island Kitchen with a built-in pantry, built-in desk and a double sink

■ A vaulted ceiling in the Sun Room

■ A tray ceiling in the formal Dining Room with easy access to the Kitchen

■ A fireplace and a built-in wetbar in the informal Family Room

■ A vaulted ceiling in the Master Suite which is equipped with his -n-her walk-in closets and a private full Bath

■ A barrel vaulted ceiling in the front bedroom

■ A convenient second floor Laundry Room

FIRST FLOOR — 1,336 SQ. FT.
SECOND FLOOR — 1,015 SQ. FT.
BASEMENT — 1,336 SQ. FT.
GARAGE — 496 SQ. FT.

TOTAL LIVING AREA:
2,351 SQ. FT.

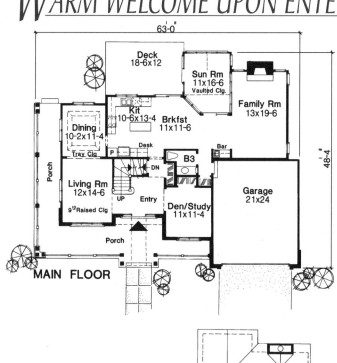

MAIN FLOOR

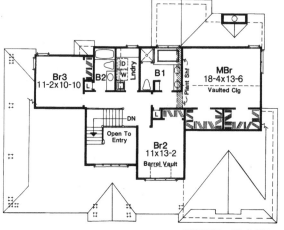

UPPER FLOOR

PRICE CODE E

FAMILY PREFERRED FEATURES

BEDROOM 3
11'-4"
X
13'-4"

B.   C.

GREAT ROOM
BELOW

H.

DN.

LOFT

CEDAR
CLOSET

BOOKS

FOYER
BELOW

BEDROOM 2
11'-10"
X
13'-0"

SKYLIGHT TO
M.BATH BELOW

No. 10568

■ This plan features:

— Three bedrooms

— Two and one half baths

■ An energy-efficient foyer leading into a Great Room with a large fireplace

■ A Master Bedroom with its own private deck, and a bath area with a two-way shower

■ An efficient Kitchen with a large Breakfast Nook

FIRST FLOOR — 2,167 SQ. FT.
SECOND FLOOR — 755 SQ. FT.
BASEMENT — 2,224 SQ. FT.
GARAGE — 1,020 SQ. FT.

TOTAL LIVING AREA:
2,922 SQ. FT.

An
EXCLUSIVE DESIGN
By Karl Kreeger

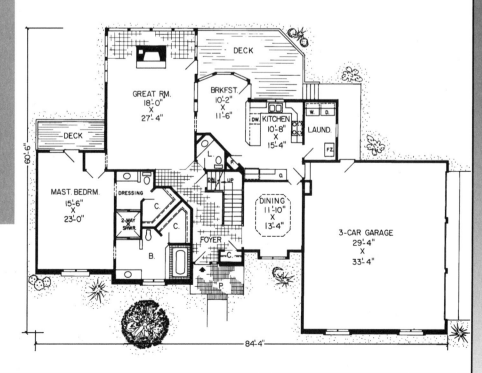

DECK

GREAT RM.
18'-0"
X
27'-4"

BRKFST.
10'-2"
X
11'-6"

KITCHEN
10'-8"
X
15'-4"

DW.   W. D.

LAUND.

FZ

DECK

MAST. BEDRM.
15'-6"
X
23'-0"

DRESSING

C.

2-WAY
SHWR

C.

DN.   UP

DINING
11'-10"
X
13'-4"

FOYER

3-CAR GARAGE
29'-4"
X
33'-4"

B.

C.

P

60'-6"

84'-4"

PRICE CODE D

MASTER BEDROOM ON FIRST LEVEL

No. 90142

■ This plan features:

— Four bedrooms

— Two full and one half baths

■ A first floor Master Bedroom equipped with a walk-in closet and large bath area with a skylight over the tub

■ A large bay window allowing lots of natural light in the Living Room

■ Built-in bookshelves and a fireplace in the Family Room

■ An abundance of cabinet space and a pantry in the Kitchen

■ Three additional bedrooms that share a full hall bath

■ An optional basement or crawl space foundation — please specify when ordering

FIRST FLOOR — 1,633 SQ. FT.
SECOND FLOOR — 727 SQ. FT.

**TOTAL LIVING AREA:
2,360 SQ. FT.**

36'-0"

BEDROOM 13'-4"x13'   B

BEDROOM 11'-4"x10'-4"

c.   c.   c.

ATTIC

BEDROOM 12'-8"x10'-6"

SECOND FLOOR

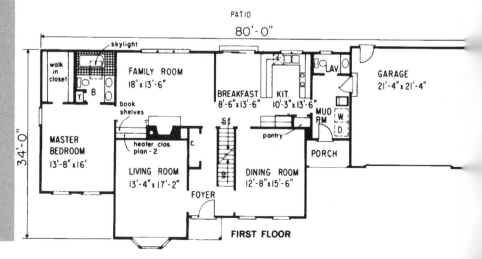

PATIO

80'-0"

walk in closet!   skylight

FAMILY ROOM 18'x13'-6"

BREAKFAST 8'-6"x13'-6"   KIT. 10'-3"x13'-6"   LAV.

GARAGE 21'-4" x 21'-4"

book shelves

T   B

pantry

MUD RM   W D

MASTER BEDROOM 13'-8"x16'

heater clos. plan - 2   c.

34'-0"

PORCH

LIVING ROOM 13'-4"x17'-2"

DINING ROOM 12'-8"x15'-6"

FOYER

FIRST FLOOR

PRICE CODE C

TOWER STIMULATES INTEREST

No. 34049

■ This plan features:

— Four bedrooms

— Three full baths

■ Sloping ceilings and lofty open spaces

■ A rustic, fireplaced Living Room with sloped ceilings to enhance the atmosphere

■ A Master Suite with vaulted ceilings, walk-in closet, dressing area and Master Bath

■ Two upstairs bedrooms sharing a full bath

FIRST FLOOR — 1,496 SQ. FT.
SECOND FLOOR — 520 SQ. FT.
GARAGE — 424 SQ. FT.

TOTAL LIVING AREA:
2,016 SQ. FT.

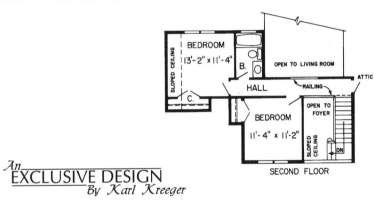

SECOND FLOOR

An
EXCLUSIVE DESIGN
By Karl Kreeger

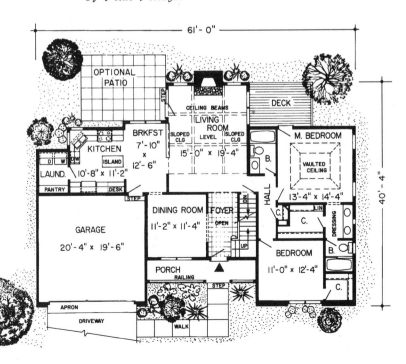

PRICE CODE E

No. 20196

- ■ This plan features:
- — Four bedrooms
- — Three full baths
- ■ A bay window that enhances the Living Room with natural light
- ■ A decorative ceiling accentuating the formal Dining Room
- ■ A Breakfast room with an incredible shape
- ■ An island Kitchen with an efficient layout and in close proximity to both the formal Dining Room and the informal Breakfast Room
- ■ A spacious Family Room that is warmed by a cozy fireplace
- ■ A fantastic Master Suite with a decorative ceiling, private Master Bath and a large walk-in closet
- ■ Three additional bedrooms, with walk-in closets, that share a full hall bath

FIRST FLOOR — 1,273 SQ. FT.
SECOND FLOOR — 1,477 SQ. FT.
BASEMENT — 974 SQ. FT.
GARAGE — 852 SQ. FT.

TOTAL LIVING AREA:
2,750 SQ. FT.

GORGEOUS AND LIVABLE

An EXCLUSIVE DESIGN
By Karl Kreeger

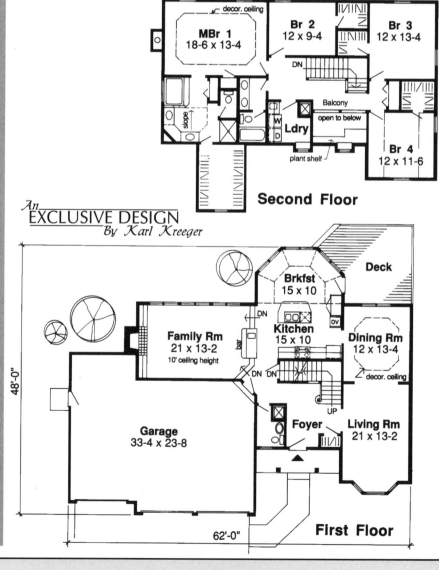

PRICE CODE F

NO WASTED SPACE

No. 10686

■ This plan features:

— Four bedrooms

— Two and one half baths

■ An open staircase leading to the bedrooms and dividing the space between the vaulted Living and Dining Rooms

■ A wide family area including the Kitchen, Dinette and Family Room complete with built-in bar, bookcases, and fireplace

■ A Master Bedroom with a vaulted ceiling, spacious closets and Jacuzzi

FIRST FLOOR — 1,786 SQ. FT.
SECOND FLOOR — 1,490 SQ. FT.
BASEMENT — 1,773 SQ. FT.
GARAGE — 579 SQ. FT.

**TOTAL LIVING AREA:
3,276 SQ. FT.**

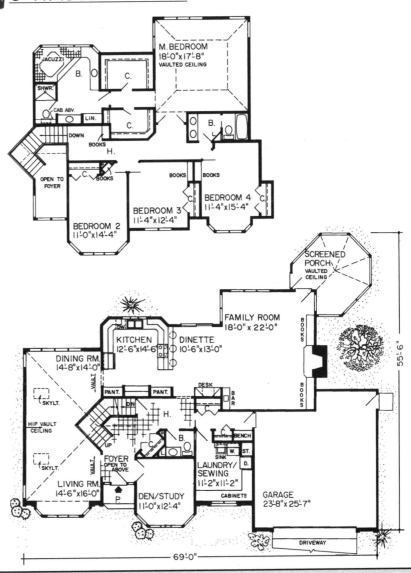

PRICE CODE F

SINGULAR HOME PRACTICAL TO BUILD

No. 9950

■ This plan features:

— Five bedrooms

— Two and one half baths

■ A Living Room with exposed beams and a cathedral ceiling, encircled by a deck

■ An immense Family Room opening to a patio with a built-in barbecue

■ A boat storage area on the lower level along with a Den, bedroom and bath equipped with a shower

FIRST FLOOR — 1,672 SQ. FT.
LOWER LEVEL — 1,672 SQ. FT.
GARAGE — 484 SQ. FT.

TOTAL LIVING AREA:
3,344 SQ. FT.

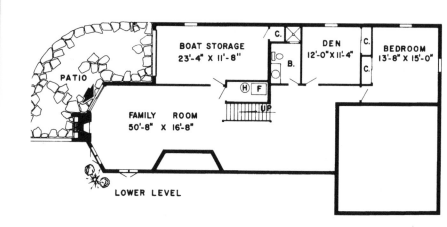

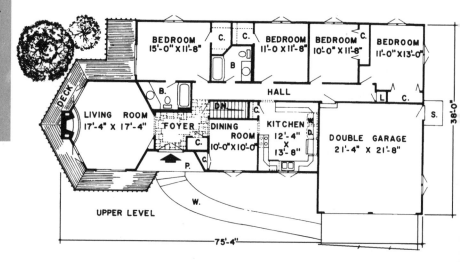

PRICE CODE D

RICH CLASSIC LINES

No. 91901

■ This plan features:

— Four bedrooms

— Three full and one half baths

■ A two story Foyer flooded by light through a half-round transom

■ A vaulted ceiling in the Great Room that continues into the Master Suite

■ A corner fireplace in the Great Room with French doors to the Breakfast/Kitchen area

■ A center island in the Kitchen with an angled sink and a built-in desk and pantry

■ A tray ceiling and recessed hutch area in the formal Dining Room

■ A Master Suite with a walk-in closet, a whirlpool tub, and a double sink vanity

FIRST FLOOR — 1,496 SQ. FT.
SECOND FLOOR — 716 SQ. FT.
BASEMENT — 1,420 SQ. FT.
GARAGE — 460 SQ. FT.

TOTAL LIVING AREA: 2,212 SQ. FT.

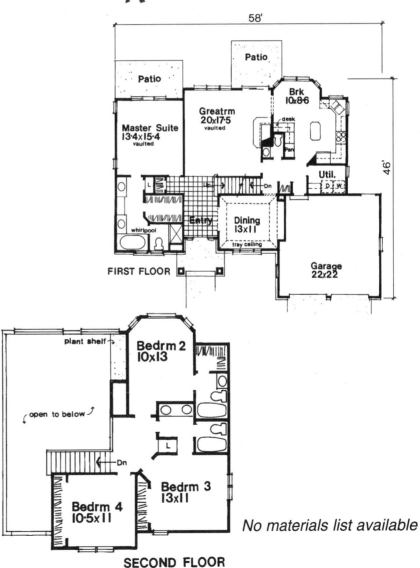

No materials list available

PRICE CODE C

FAMILY FAVORITE

No. 20146

■ This plan features:

— Three bedrooms

— Two full and one half baths

■ A sky-lit breakfast bay

■ A Dining Room with recessed ceilings

■ A Master Suite featuring a double vanity bath and walk-in closet

FIRST FLOOR — 1,352 SQ. FT.
SECOND FLOOR — 736 SQ. FT.
BASEMENT — 1,340 SQ. FT.
GARAGE — 490 SQ. FT.

**TOTAL LIVING AREA:
2,088 SQ. FT.**

An
EXCLUSIVE DESIGN
By Karl Kreeger

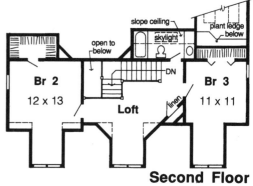

Second Floor

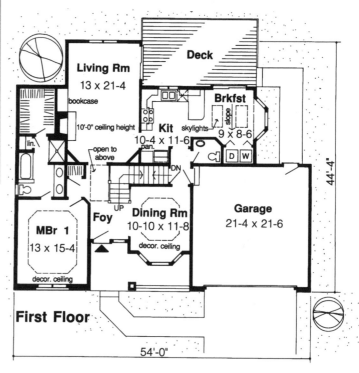

First Floor

PRICE CODE B

COMPACT COMFORT

No. 10787

- This plan features:
  - — Three bedrooms
  - — Two and one half baths
- Soaring ceilings and a wall of stacked windows
- A formal Dining Room perfect for entertaining
- A Kitchen/Family Room combination with a cozy fireplace
- An efficient Kitchen layout
- Three bedrooms upstairs and two full baths, including the luxury bath in the Master Bedroom

FIRST FLOOR — 1,064 SQ. FT.
SECOND FLOOR — 708 SQ. FT.
BASEMENT — 1,064 SQ. FT.
GARAGE — 576 SQ. FT.

TOTAL LIVING AREA:
1,772 SQ. FT.

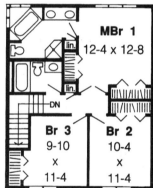

MBr 1
12-4 x 12-8

Br 3
9-10
x
11-4

Br 2
10-4
x
11-4

DN

lin.

lin.

Second Floor

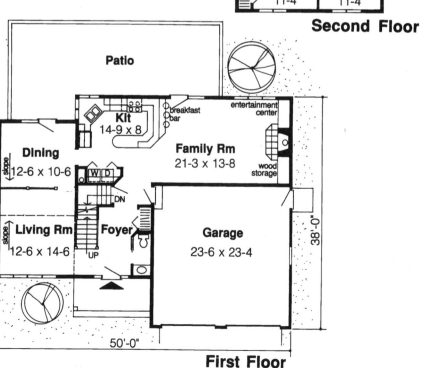

Patio

breakfast bar

Kit
14-9 x 8

entertainment center

Family Rm
21-3 x 13-8

wood storage

Dining
12-6 x 10-6

slope

W D

DN

slope

Living Rm
12-6 x 14-6

Foyer

UP

Garage
23-6 x 23-4

38'-0"

50'-0"

First Floor

PRICE CODE D

DESIGNED WITH TODAY'S ACTIVE FAMILY IN MIND

No. 24323

■ This plan features:

— Three or four bedrooms

— Three full baths

■ An open layout between the Kitchen, Breakfast Bay and Family Room

■ An island Kitchen with more than ample counter and storage space, a double sink, built-in pantry and an eating bar peninsula counter

■ A fireplace in the Family Room which has direct access to the rear yard

■ A vaulted ceiling adding a touch of elegance to the Dining Room

■ A luxurious Master Suite with a lavish, private Master Bath

■ Two additional bedrooms that share a full hall bath

FIRST FLOOR — 1,420 SQ. FT.
SECOND FLOOR — 1,080 SQ. FT.
GARAGE — 477 SQ. FT.

TOTAL LIVING AREA:
2,500 SQ. FT.

An
EXCLUSIVE DESIGN
By Marshall Associates

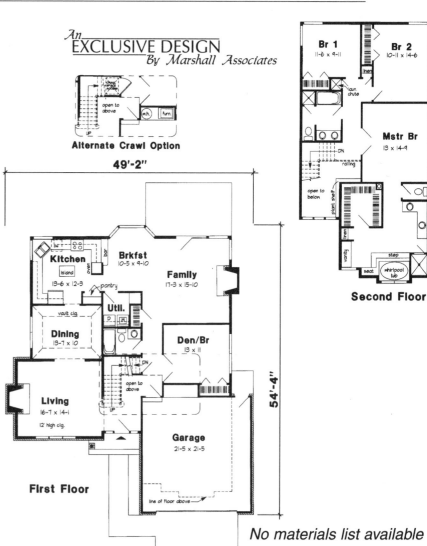

No materials list available

PRICE CODE A

APPEAL EVERYONE WANTS

No. 92016

■ This plan features:

— Three bedrooms

— Two and one half baths

■ Repeating front gables, shuttered windows, and wrap-around front porch

■ A large Family/Kitchen opening to a screened porch and private side deck

■ A Master Bedroom with private Bath and one wall of closet space

■ Second floor laundry facilities

FIRST FLOOR — 760 SQ. FT.
SECOND FLOOR — 728 SQ. FT.
BASEMENT — 768 SQ. FT.

TOTAL LIVING AREA:
1,488 SQ. FT.

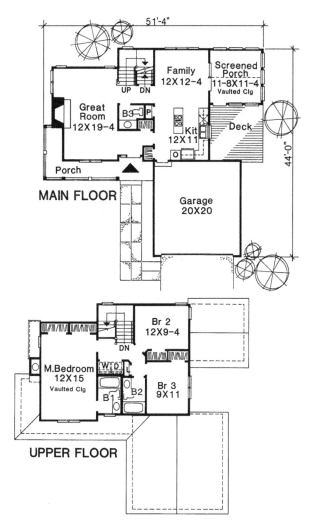

MAIN FLOOR

51'-4"

Family
12X12-4

Screened Porch
11-8X11-4
Vaulted Clg

UP DN

Great Room
12X19-4

B3 P

Kit
12X11

Deck

Porch

Garage
20X20

44'-0"

UPPER FLOOR

Br 2
12X9-4

DN

M.Bedroom
12X15
Vaulted Clg

W/D

Br 3
9X11

B1 B2

PRICE CODE B

EXCELLENT CHOICE FOR THE FIRST TIME BUYER

No. 91055

■ This plan features:

— Three bedrooms

— Two and a half baths

■ A friendly, covered Porch sheltering the front entrance

■ A formal Living Room with an expansive floor-to-ceiling triple window flowing into a formal Dining Room

■ A comfortable Family Room with a sliding glass door to backyard, a Utility Closet with washer and dryer and a access to the Kitchen

■ An efficient Kitchen with a peninsula counter/snackbar on the Family Room side and adjacent to the Dining Room for ease in serving

■ A cozy Master Bedroom with a recessed dormer window, an oversized, walk-in closet and a private Bath

■ Two additional bedrooms, on the second floor, sharing a full hall bath and a Playroom that could be a fourth bedroom

FIRST FLOOR — 805 SQ. FT.
SECOND FLOOR — 961 SQ. FT.
GARAGE — 540 SQ. FT.

TOTAL LIVING AREA:
1,766 SQ. FT.

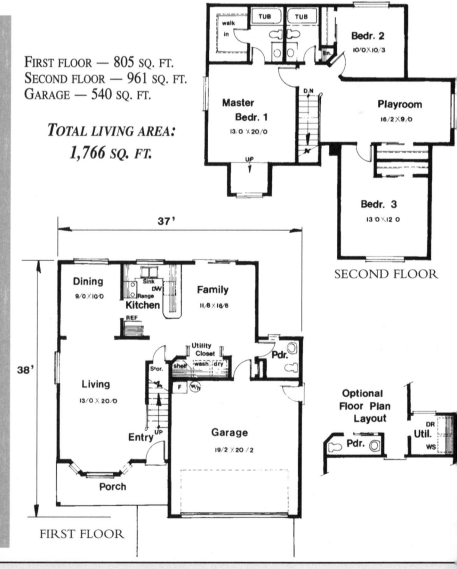

SECOND FLOOR

FIRST FLOOR

PRICE CODE C

TRADITION WITH A TWIST

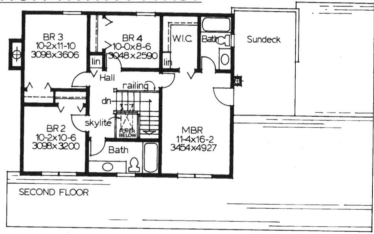

SECOND FLOOR

An
EXCLUSIVE DESIGN
By Westhome Planners, Ltd.

No. 90933

■ This plan features:

— Four bedrooms

— Two full and one half baths

■ A sky-lit foyer

■ A sunken Family Room warmed by a fireplace and separated by a railing from the Breakfast Nook

■ A well-appointed Kitchen which serves either the informal Breakfast Nook or the formal Dining Room with efficiency

■ A Master Suite with a walk-in closet, full bath and a private, hidden sun deck

FIRST FLOOR — 1,104 SQ. FT.
SECOND FLOOR — 845 SQ. FT.
GARAGE & WORKSHOP — 538 SQ. FT.
BASEMENT — 1,098 SQ. FT.
WIDTH — 55'-0"
DEPTH — 32'-0"

TOTAL LIVING AREA:
1,949 SQ. FT.

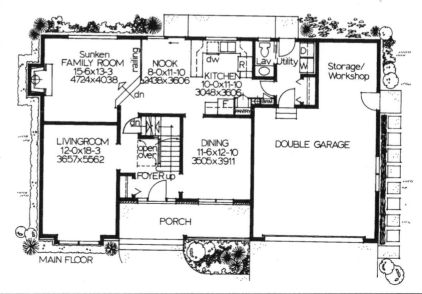

MAIN FLOOR

PRICE CODE F

TRADITIONAL ELEGANCE

No. 92504

■ This plan features:

— Four bedrooms

— Three and one half baths

■ A elegant entrance leading into a two story Foyer with an impressive staircase highlighted by a curved window

■ Floor to ceiling windows in both the formal Living and Dining Rooms

■ A spacious Den with a hearth fireplace, built-in book shelves, a wetbar and a wall of windows viewing the backyard

■ A large, efficient Kitchen, equipped with lots of counter and storage space, a bright Breakfast area, and access to the Dining Room, Utility Room, walk-in pantry and Garage

■ A grand Master Suite with decorative ceilings, a private Porch, an elaborate Bath and two walk-in closets

■ Three additional bedrooms on the second floor with walk-in closets, sharing adjoining, full baths and a ideal Children's Den

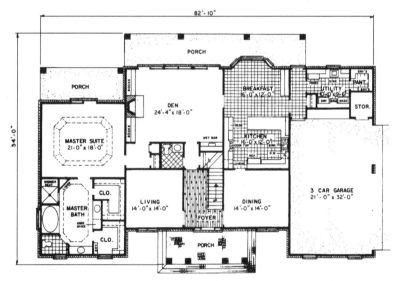

FIRST FLOOR PLAN

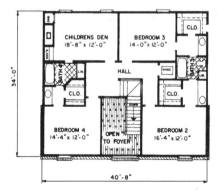

SECOND FLOOR PLAN

FIRST FLOOR — 2,533 SQ. FT.
SECOND FLOOR — 1,260 SQ. FT.
GARAGE — 714 SQ. FT.

TOTAL LIVING AREA:
3,813 SQ. FT.

PRICE CODE D

EXPANSIVE TWO-STORY FOYER

No. 10588

- ■ This plan features:
- — Four bedrooms
- — Two and one half baths
- ■ A peninsula dividing the Kitchen from the Breakfast Nook
- ■ A Family Room with a fireplace just off the Breakfast area
- ■ A foyer linking the Living and Dining Rooms

FIRST FLOOR — 1,450 SQ. FT.
SECOND FLOOR — 1,082 SQ. FT.
BASEMENT — 1,340 SQ. FT.
GARAGE — 572 SQ. FT.

**TOTAL LIVING AREA:
2,532 SQ. FT.**

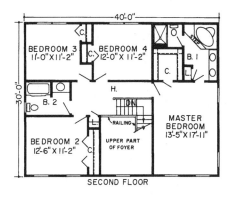

SECOND FLOOR

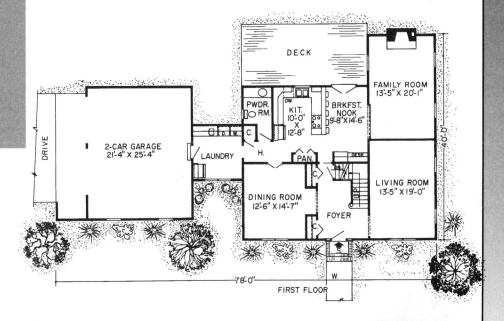

FIRST FLOOR

PRICE CODE E

ROOM TO GROW

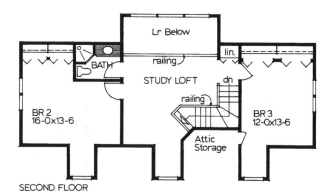

SECOND FLOOR

No. 90838

■ This plan features:

— Three bedrooms

— Three full baths

■ A corner gas fireplace in the spacious Living Room

■ A Master Suite including a private Bath with a whirlpool tub, separate shower and a double vanity

■ An island Kitchen that is well-equipped to efficiently serve both formal Dining Room and informal Nook

■ Two additional bedrooms sharing a full bath on the second floor

FIRST FLOOR — 1,837 SQ. FT.
SECOND FLOOR — 848 SQ. FT.
BASEMENT — 1,803 SQ. FT.
BONUS ROOM(OVER GARAGE) — 288 SQ. FT.

TOTAL LIVING AREA:
2,685 SQ. FT.

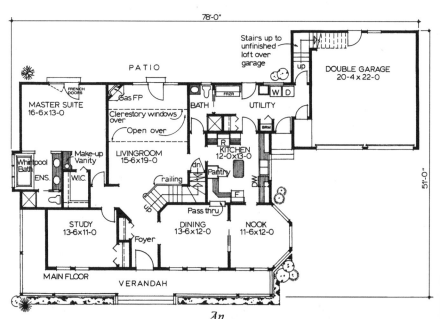

An
EXCLUSIVE DESIGN
By Westhome Planners, Ltd.

PRICE CODE B

ADAPT THIS COLONIAL TO YOUR LIFESTYLE

No. 90671

- This plan features:
— Four bedrooms
— Two full baths
- A Living Room with a beam ceiling and a fireplace
- An eat-in Kitchen efficiently serving the formal Dining Room
- A Master Bedroom with his and her closets
- Two upstairs bedrooms sharing a split bath

FIRST FLOOR — 1,056 SQ. FT.
SECOND FLOOR — 531 SQ. FT.

TOTAL LIVING AREA:
1,587 SQ. FT.

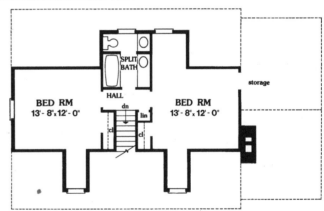

SECOND FLOOR

FIRST FLOOR

PRICE CODE C

COUNTRY FARMHOUSE

No. 90639

- This plan features:
- — Three bedrooms
- — Three full baths
- An old-fashioned Porch surrounding this Saltbox design with two convenient entrances
- A central Foyer with a curved staircase opening to a Sunken Living Room with a heat-circulating fireplace
- A formal Dining Room with a sliding glass door to the Terrace and separated from Living Room by a railing
- A comfortable Family Room with a built-in entertainment center is conveniently located near the Mudroom and Foyer
- An efficient, U-shaped Kitchen serving both the Dining Room and Dinette with ease
- An expansive Master Suite with two closets, a dressing area, and a private Bath highlighted by skylights
- Two additional, roomy bedrooms sharing a full hall bath

FIRST FLOOR — 1,238 SQ. FT.
SECOND FLOOR — 797 SQ. FT.
BASEMENT — 1,159 SQ. FT.
GARAGE — 439 SQ. FT.

TOTAL LIVING AREA:
2,035 SQ. FT.

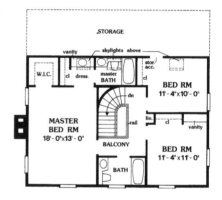

SECOND FLOOR

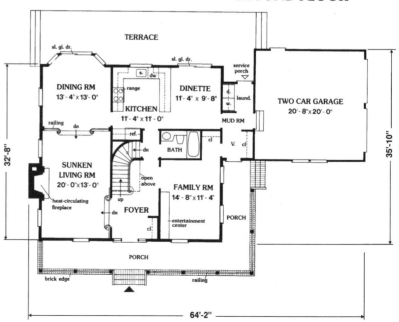

FIRST FLOOR

PRICE CODE E

COMFORTABLE OUTDOOR AND INDOOR LIVING

No. 91319

■ This plan features:

— Three bedrooms

— Three full baths

■ A wall of windows taking full advantage of the front view

■ An open stairway to the upstairs study and the Master Bedroom

■ A master bedroom with a private master bath and a walk-in wardrobe

■ An efficient Kitchen including a breakfast bar that opens into the Dining Area

■ A formal Living Room with a vaulted ceiling and a stone fireplace

FIRST FLOOR — 1,306 SQ. FT.
SECOND FLOOR — 598 SQ. FT.
LOWER FLOOR(NOT SHOWN) — 1,288 SQ. FT.

TOTAL LIVING AREA:
3,192 SQ. FT.

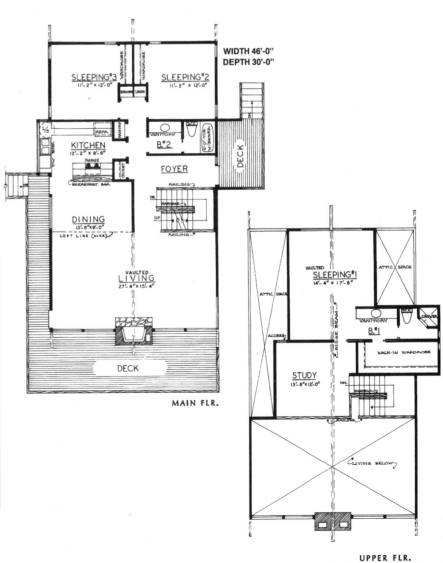

WIDTH 46'-0"
DEPTH 30'-0"

MAIN FLR.

UPPER FLR.

PRICE CODE F

FOYER WELCOMES GUESTS

No. 10501

■ This plan features:

— Four bedrooms

— Three full and one half baths

■ A massive welcoming foyer which steps right into the Great Room

■ A Great Room enlarged by a wrap-around deck and highlighted by a fireplace, built-in bookcases, and a wet bar

■ A Kitchen with a built-in desk, octagonal morning room, and central island

FIRST FLOOR — 2,419 SQ. FT.
SECOND FLOOR — 926 SQ. FT.
BASEMENT — 2,419 SQ. FT.
GARAGE — 615 SQ. FT.

TOTAL LIVING AREA: 3,345 SQ. FT.

SECOND FLOOR

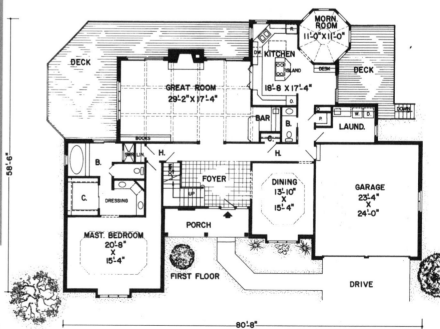

FIRST FLOOR

An
EXCLUSIVE DESIGN
By Karl Kreeger

PRICE CODE F

TWO STORY DAYLIGHT BASEMENT DESIGN

No. 92111

■ This plan features:

— Four bedrooms

— Four full and one half baths

■ A secluded Study with corner window

■ An exceptional Family Room with an elegant corner fireplace

■ An island Kitchen with a double sink, walk-in pantry, ample cabinet and cupboard space and an eating Nook area

■ A Master Suite with a private Master Bath and large walk-in closet

■ Two second floor bedrooms that share a full bath and a third bedroom with a private bath

■ A Recreation Room with a wet-bar, private bath, luxurious hot tub and an angled vanity

FIRST FLOOR — 1,888 SQ. FT.
SECOND FLOOR — 1,613 SQ. FT.
FINISHED BASEMENT — 1,365 SQ. FT.
SHOP — 543 SQ. FT.
GARAGE — 955 SQ. FT.

TOTAL LIVING AREA:
4,866 SQ. FT.

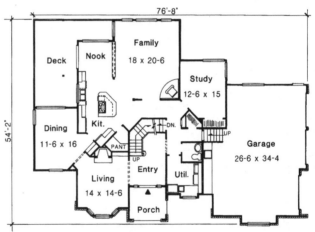

First Floor

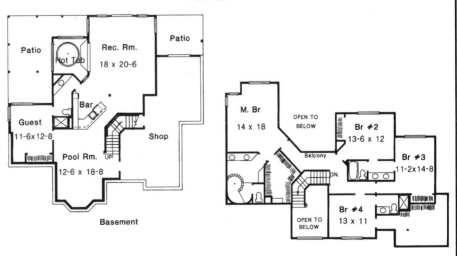

Basement

Second Floor

PRICE CODE B

FARMHOUSE FLAVOR

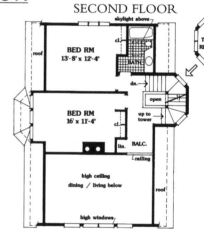

SECOND FLOOR

No. 90685

■ This plan features:

— Three bedrooms

— Two full baths

■ An octagonal stair tower

■ A Foyer opening to a Living and Dining Room combination, enhanced by a striking glass wall

■ A heat-circulating fireplace adding welcome warmth

■ A galley-style Kitchen including a large pantry, snack bar, and laundry area

■ A Master Suite with a private deck overlooking the backyard

FIRST FLOOR — 1,073 SQ. FT.
SECOND FLOOR — 604 SQ. FT.
RETREAT TOWER — 93 SQ. FT.
GARAGE — 428 SQ. FT.

**TOTAL LIVING AREA:
1,770 SQ. FT.**

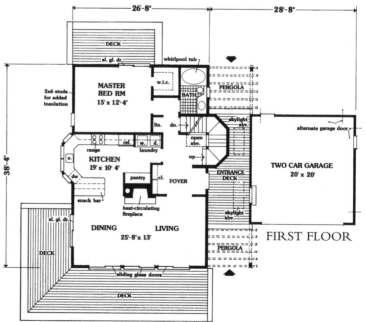

FIRST FLOOR

PRICE CODE B

A-FRAME UPDATE

An **EXCLUSIVE DESIGN**
By Westhome Planners, Ltd.

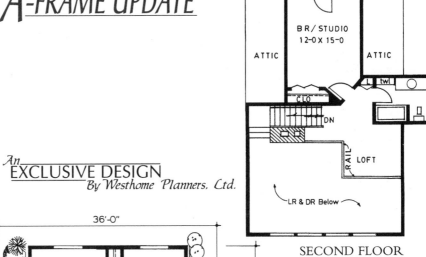

SECOND FLOOR

No. 90844

■ This plan features:

— Three bedrooms

— Two full and one half baths

■ A wrap-around deck adding outdoor living space

■ Two-story glass walls in the Dining Room and Living Room

■ A Master Bedroom with a private half-bath

■ An open loft with an expansive bedroom having its own private deck and full bath

FIRST FLOOR — 1,086 SQ. FT.
SECOND FLOOR — 466 SQ. FT.
BASEMENT — 1,080 SQ. FT.

TOTAL LIVING AREA:
1,552 SQ. FT.

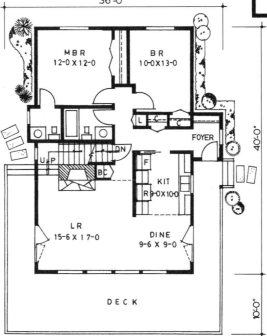

FIRST FLOOR

PRICE CODE D

GINGERBREAD CHARM

No. 10690

- This plan features:
- — Three bedrooms
- — Two and one half baths
- A wrap-around porch and rear deck adding lots of outdoor living space
- A formal Parlor and Dining Room just off the central entry
- A Family Room with a fireplace
- A Master Suite complete with a five-sided sitting nook, walk-in closets and a sunken tub

FIRST FLOOR — 1,260 SQ. FT.
SECOND FLOOR — 1,021 SQ. FT.
BASEMENT — 1,186 SQ. FT.
GARAGE — 840 SQ. FT.

**TOTAL LIVING AREA:
2,281 SQ. FT.**

FIRST FLOOR

SECOND FLOOR

PRICE CODE B

BRIGHT AND TRULY BEAUTIFUL

No. 91008

■ This plan features:

— Three bedrooms

— Two and a half baths

■ A fireplaced Living Room that flows into the Dining Room for easy entertaining

■ A Master Suite with a private Master Bath and walk-in closet

■ A bay windowed Kitchen with an informal Nook eating area

■ An optional basement or crawl space foundation — please specify when ordering

FIRST FLOOR — 1,153 SQ. FT.
SECOND FLOOR — 493 SQ. FT.

TOTAL LIVING AREA: 1,646 SQ. FT.

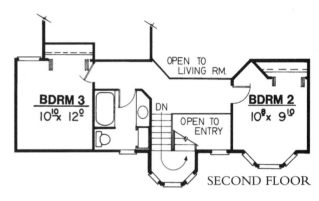

OPEN TO LIVING RM.

BDRM 3
10^{10} x 12^{0}

DN

OPEN TO ENTRY

BDRM 2
10^{8} x 9^{10}

SECOND FLOOR

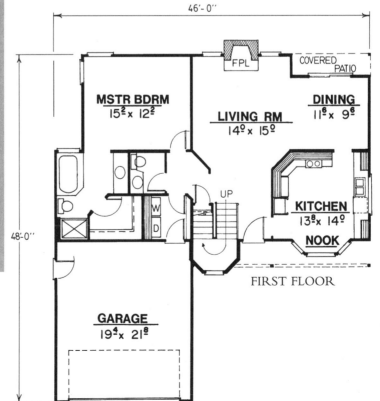

46'-0"

FPL

COVERED PATIO

MSTR BDRM
15^{2} x 12^{2}

LIVING RM
14^{0} x 15^{0}

DINING
11^{6} x 9^{6}

W
D

UP

KITCHEN
13^{8} x 14^{0}

NOOK

48'-0"

FIRST FLOOR

GARAGE
19^{4} x 21^{8}

PRICE CODE B

GREAT TRAFFIC PATTERN HIGHLIGHTS HOME

No. 90901

■ This plan features:

— Three bedrooms

— Two full and one half baths

■ A sheltered entry leading to the two-story foyer

■ An island Kitchen with a convenient pass-through to the formal Dining Room

■ A cozy Living Room brightened by a bay window

■ A lovely Master Suite with a sitting area, walk-in closet and private bath

FIRST FLOOR — 940 SQ. FT.
SECOND FLOOR — 823 SQ. FT.
BASEMENT — 940 SQ. FT.
GARAGE — 440 SQ. FT.

TOTAL LIVING AREA:
1,763 SQ. FT.

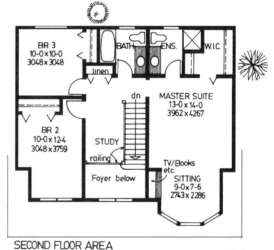

SECOND FLOOR AREA

BR 3
10-0 x 10-0
3048 x 3048

BATH   ENS.   W.I.C.

linen

MASTER SUITE
13-0 x 14-0
3962 x 4267

dn

BR 2
10-0 x 12-4
3048 x 3759

STUDY

railing

Foyer below

TV/Books etc.

SITTING
9-0 x 7-6
2743 x 2286

An
EXCLUSIVE DESIGN
By Westhome Planners, Ltd.

DOUBLE GARAGE
19-6 x 21-0
5943 x 6400

Lav.

NOOK
7-4 x 12-4
2235 x 3759

KITCHEN
7-6 x 12-4
2286 x 3759

FAMILY ROOM
13-0 x 12-4
3962 x 3759

PATIO

D W   F

BUFFET

Pass-thru

PANTRY BRM

dn

DINING
10-0 x 12-4
3048 x 3759

FOYER
open over

up

LIVINGROOM
13-0 x 17-10
3962 x 5435

If built with optional single garage width will be 46'-0"

PORCH

MAIN FLOOR AREA

WIDTH: 54'-0"
DEPTH: 33'-0"

PRICE CODE C

MASTER SUITE WITH PRIVATE DECK

No. 91411

■ This plan features:

— Four bedrooms

— Two and one half baths

■ A sunken Living Room, formal Dining Room, and island Kitchen enjoying an expansive view of the patio and backyard

■ A fireplaced Living Room keeping the house toasty after the sun goes down

■ Skylights brightening the balcony and Master Bath

FIRST FLOOR — 1,249 SQ. FT.
SECOND FLOOR — 890 SQ. FT.
GARAGE — 462 SQ. FT.

TOTAL LIVING AREA:
2,139 SQ. FT.

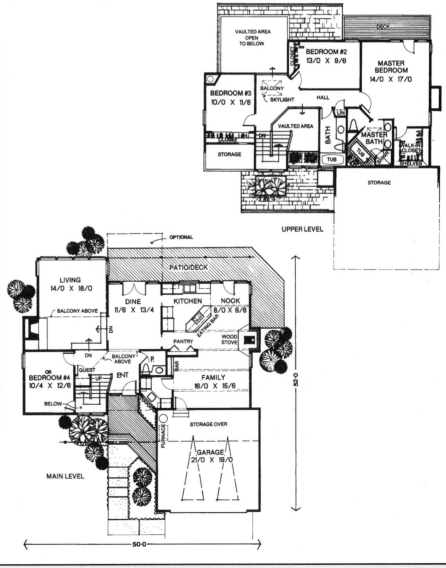

PRICE CODE F

MODERN TUDOR IS HARD TO RESIST

No. 10737

■ This plan features:

— Four bedrooms

— Three and one half baths

■ A seven-sided Breakfast room, an island Kitchen adjoining the Formal Dining Room

■ A beamed Family Room with private Study

■ A Master Suite complete with sauna, whirlpool, double vanity and fireplace

FIRST FLOOR — 2,457 SQ. FT.
SECOND FLOOR — 1,047 SQ. FT.
BASEMENT — 2,457 SQ. FT.
GARAGE — 837 SQ. FT.
SUN ROOM — 213 SQ. FT.

**TOTAL LIVING AREA:
3,504 SQ. FT.**

An
EXCLUSIVE DESIGN
By Karl Kreeger

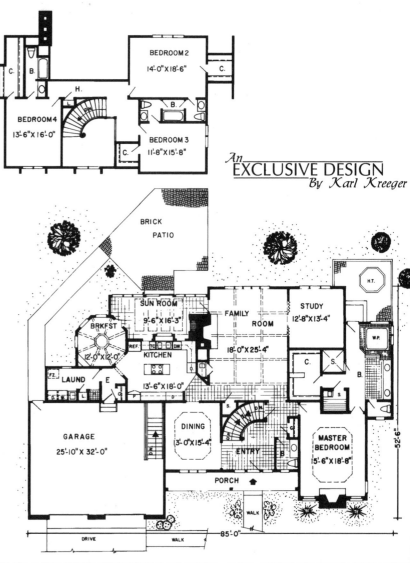

PRICE CODE C

GREAT FOR EMPTY NESTERS OR FAMILIES WITH TEENS

No. 92608

This plan features:

— Three bedrooms

— Two full and one half baths

Decorative brick, arched windows and unique hip roof on the outside and a two story Foyer with an open staircase, balcony and dormer window

A grand sunken Great Room with a cathedral ceiling, built-in entertainment center and a stone fireplace

Dramatic views from the octagon-shaped, formal Dining Room

An outstanding Kitchen with a central work island, built-in pantry, an abundance of counter and cabinet space, a pass-thru to Dining Room and a bright, bay windowed Breakfast area

A first floor, private Master Suite with walk-in closet, and a plush Bath with double vanity, oversized shower and raised, corner window tub

On the second floor, three additional bedrooms sharing a full hall bath and a Bonus Room

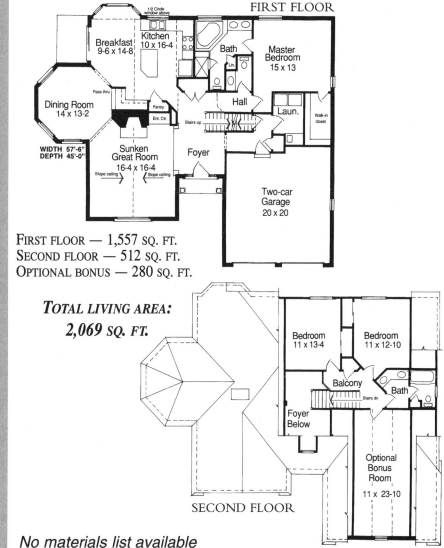

FIRST FLOOR — 1,557 SQ. FT.
SECOND FLOOR — 512 SQ. FT.
OPTIONAL BONUS — 280 SQ. FT.

TOTAL LIVING AREA: 2,069 SQ. FT.

No materials list available

PRICE CODE C

*E*NERGY-SAVING CAPE

No. 90696

■ This plan features:

— Four bedrooms

— Two full baths

■ A large Living Room with an exposed wood beam ceiling, heat-circulating fireplace and a bay window

■ A sunny Dining and Family Room enlarged by a bay window with sliding glass doors to a rear deck

■ A country Kitchen with generous cabinet and counter space

■ A first floor Master Bedroom with his-n-her closets

■ Two additional upstairs bedrooms with sitting areas and skylights

FIRST FLOOR — 1,298 SQ. FT.
SECOND FLOOR — 542 SQ. FT.

TOTAL LIVING AREA:
1,840 SQ. FT.

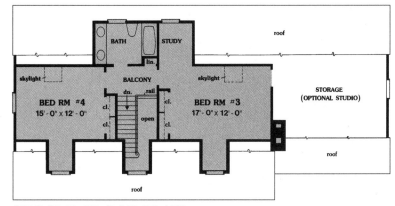

SECOND FLOOR PLAN

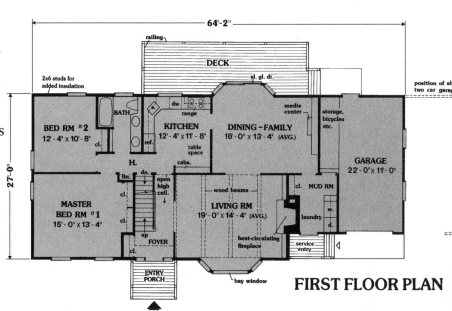

FIRST FLOOR PLAN

PRICE CODE C

UPDATED VICTORIAN

No. 91053

■ This plan features:

— Three bedrooms

— Two and a half baths

■ A classic Victorian exterior design accented by a wonderful turret room and second floor covered porch above a sweeping veranda

■ A spacious formal Living Room leading into a formal Dining Room for ease in entertaining

■ An efficient, U-shaped Kitchen with loads of counter space and a peninsula snackbar, opens to an eating Nook and Family Room for informal gatherings and activities

■ An elegant Master Suite with a unique, octagon Sitting area, a private Porch, an oversized, walk-in closet and private Bath with a double vanity and a window tub

■ Two additional bedrooms with ample closets sharing a full hall bath

FIRST FLOOR — 1,150 SQ. FT.
SECOND FLOOR — 949 SQ. FT.
GARAGE — 484 SQ. FT.

TOTAL LIVING AREA:
2,099 SQ. FT.

SECOND FLOOR

BEDRM • 2
13/10 x 10/0

BEDRM • 3
13/10 x 10/0

LINEN

MASTER BEDROOM
15/0 x 14/0 AVG.

W·I·C

B • 3

DN

SITTING

M • B

FRENCH

36" RAILING

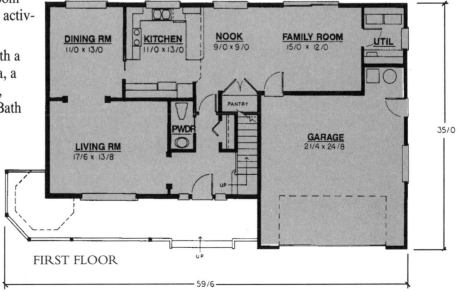

FIRST FLOOR

DINING RM
11/0 x 13/0

KITCHEN
11/0 x13/0

NOOK
9/0 x 9/0

FAMILY ROOM
15/0 x 12/0

UTIL

PANTRY

PWDR

LIVING RM
17/6 x 13/8

GARAGE
21/4 x 24/8

UP

UP

35/0

59/6

PRICE CODE F

*C*ONTEMPORARY *GRANDEUR*

No. 92115

■ This plan features:

— Three bedrooms

— Three full baths

■ Elegant brickwork leads to a unique front Porch and impressive, grandiose Foyer with a curved staircase

■ A sunken, fireplaced Living Room with spacious views

■ An island kitchen, surrounded by cabinets, a walk-in pantry, with a sunny Nook that opens up to the wrap-around bi-level deck

■ Oversized, private Master Bedroom Suite complete with a private deck, fireplace, spa, double windows, and an enormous walk-in closet

■ Downstairs, the large fireplaced Rec Room features a full second kitchen/bar with pantry and wine storage room

■ Two full-sized Bedrooms with large, airy windows and a complete bathroom finish off the lower level

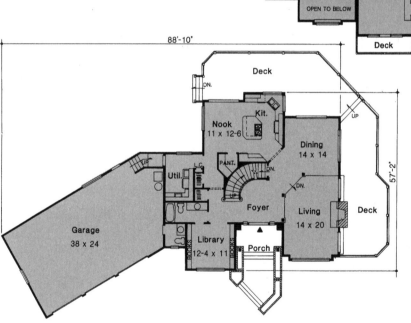

FIRST FLOOR — 1,587 SQ. FT.
SECOND FLOOR — 905 SQ. FT.
BASEMENT FLOOR — 1,289 SQ. F
GARAGE — THREE-CAR

TOTAL LIVING AREA:
3,781 SQ. FT.

PRICE CODE F

*L*UXURY IS ALWAYS POPULAR

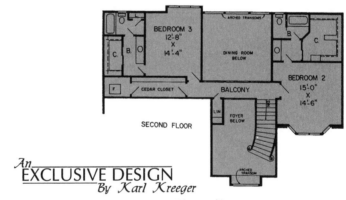

No. 10531

■ This plan features:

— Three bedrooms

— Three full and one half bath

■ A sunken Great Room, a spectacular Breakfast Nook, and a bridge-like balcony on the second floor

■ A Master Suite highlighted by two huge walk-in closets, a five-piece bath, and a sitting room with bay window

■ A Great Room accented by a bar, fireplace, and built-in cabinets for the television and stereo

■ Cathedral ceilings in the Dining Room and foyer

FIRST FLOOR — 2,579 SQ. FT.
SECOND FLOOR — 997 SQ. FT.
BASEMENT — 2,579 SQ. FT.
GARAGE & STORAGE — 1,001 SQ. FT.

TOTAL LIVING AREA:
3,576 SQ. FT.

An
EXCLUSIVE DESIGN
By Karl Kreeger

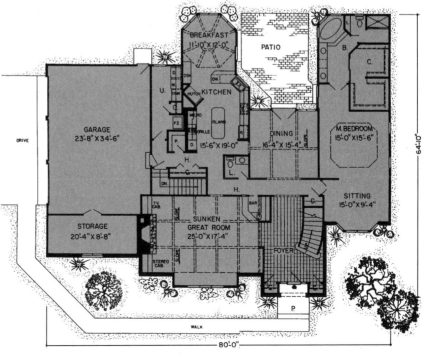

PRICE CODE C

*C*IRCULAR STAIRCASE MAKES A STUNNING IMPRESSION

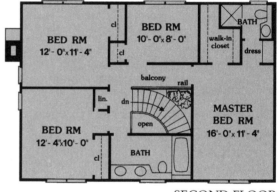

SECOND FLOOR

No. 90663

■ This plan features:

— Four bedrooms

— Two full baths

■ A sunny well-equipped Kitchen efficiently located near the Dinette and formal Dining Room

■ A spacious fireplaced Family Room

■ A bow window dressing up the Living Room and making it seem larger

■ A Master Suite with a walk-in closet and private Master Bath

FIRST FLOOR — 1,119 SQ. FT.
SECOND FLOOR — 837 SQ. FT.
BASEMENT — 1,080 SQ. FT.

TOTAL LIVING AREA:
1,956 SQ. FT.

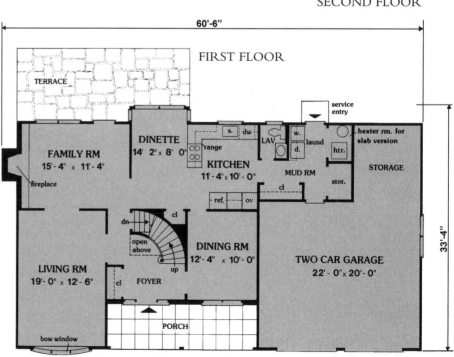

PRICE CODE C

FAMILY FAVORITE

No. 90690

■ This plan features:

— Five bedrooms

— Two full baths

■ An efficient Kitchen with a peninsula counter opening into the Family Room

■ A cozy bay window seat in the formal Dining Room

■ A first floor Master Bedroom with an adjoining private bath including double vanities

■ A heat-circulating fireplace in the Living Room which has sliding glass doors to the Terrace

■ Three bedrooms located on the second floor that share a full Bath

FIRST FLOOR — 1,407 SQ. FT.
SECOND FLOOR — 675 SQ. FT.

TOTAL LIVING AREA:
2,082 SQ. FT.

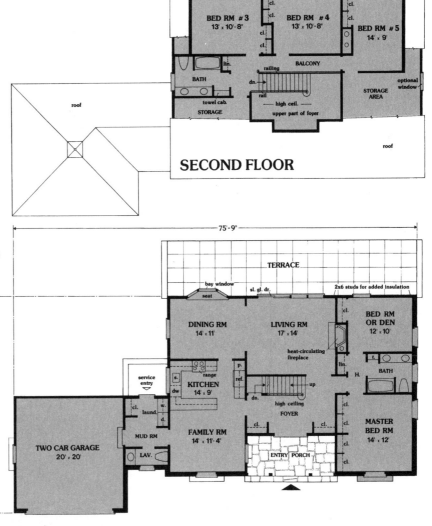

PRICE CODE F

No. 92505

■ This plan features:

— Four bedrooms

— Three and a half baths

■ A unique facade created by arched windows, a copper roof over the two story bay, and a detailed mixture of stucco and stone

■ Elegant columns rising up two floors through the balcony providing an unusual entrance to a expansive, two story Den

■ This wonderful Den with highlights such as; a two-story fireplace that is framed by sliding doors leading to a covered Porch, and a wall of built-ins including a wetbar, cabinets and shelves

■ A vaulted ceiling adding a spacious feeling to the gourmet Kitchen that also includes a cooktop snackbar, a built-in pantry, and a separate Breakfast area

■ A cozy, private Sitting area with a vaulted ceiling providing quiet moments in the Master Suite

■ A Master Bath with his-n-her walk-in closets, separate vanities and linen closets, an over-sized shower and a whirlpool tub

STUCCO & BRICK UNITE

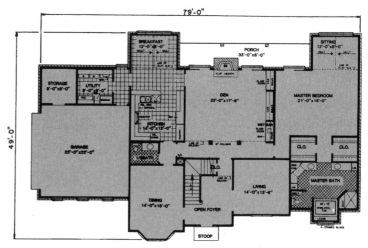

FIRST FLOOR PLAN

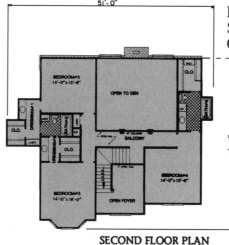

SECOND FLOOR PLAN

FIRST FLOOR — 2,442 SQ. FT.
SECOND FLOOR — 1,062 SQ. FT.
GARAGE — 565 SQ. FT.

TOTAL LIVING AREA:
3,504 SQ. FT.

PRICE CODE F

ARCHES DOMINATE FACADE

No. 10666

■ This plan features:

— Five bedrooms

— Three and one half baths

■ A window wall and French doors linking the in-ground pool

■ A wetbar with wine storage and built-in bookcases in the Living Room

■ A Library on the second floor with space for the largest book collections

■ Dressing rooms and adjoining baths in all the bedrooms

FIRST FLOOR — 3,625 SQ. FT.
SECOND FLOOR — 937 SQ. FT.
GARAGE — 636 SQ. FT.

TOTAL LIVING AREA:
4,562 SQ. FT.

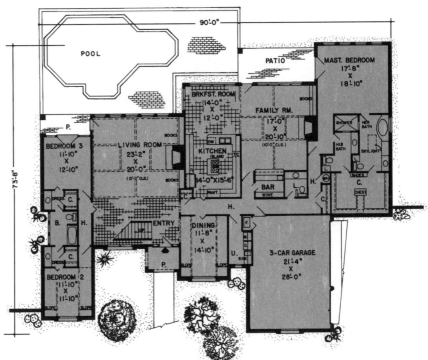

PRICE CODE D

DISTINCTIVE BAY WINDOWS

No. 24551

■ This plan features:

— Four bedrooms

— Two full and one half baths

■ Distinctive windows and a raised Foyer

■ A Family Room, adjacent to the Living Room, has a fireplace and triple window view of outdoors

■ An island Kitchen with lots of counter and storage space extending into a bright Breakfast area and adjoining the Dining Room, laundry area and Garage

■ A Master Suite with a dramatic cathedral ceiling, walk-in closet and a unusual bay window Bath featuring an atrium, whirlpool tub

■ Three additional bedrooms with ample closet space having easy access to a full hall bath

FIRST FLOOR — 1,324 SQ. FT.
SECOND FLOOR — 1,216 SQ. FT.

TOTAL LIVING AREA:
2,540 SQ. FT.

An
EXCLUSIVE DESIGN
By Britt J. Willis

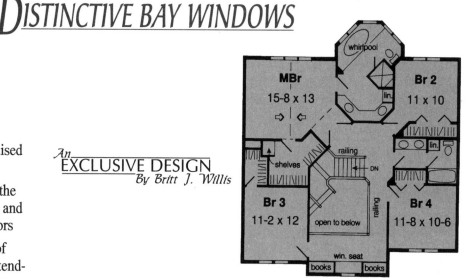

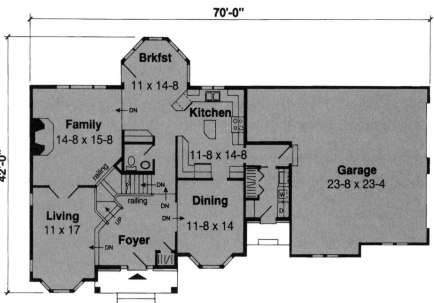

PRICE CODE F

SPECIAL ROOMS HIGHLIGHT DESIGN

No. 10492

This plan features:

— Three/four bedrooms

— Three full baths

A Television Room, Den, Family Room and an upstairs Sitting Room for many individual activities

A well-equipped Kitchen with double bay windows, separate dining Nook, and adjoining the formal Dining Room

A fireplace warming the Sitting Room adjacent to the spacious Master Suite

A private Deck and Master Bath complete with Roman tub and room-size, walk-in closet enhance the Master Suite

Two smaller bedrooms connecting to a walk-through, full bath

FIRST FLOOR — 2,409 SQ. FT.
SECOND FLOOR — 2,032 SQ. FT.
GARAGE — 690 SQ. FT.

TOTAL LIVING AREA:
4,441 SQ. FT.

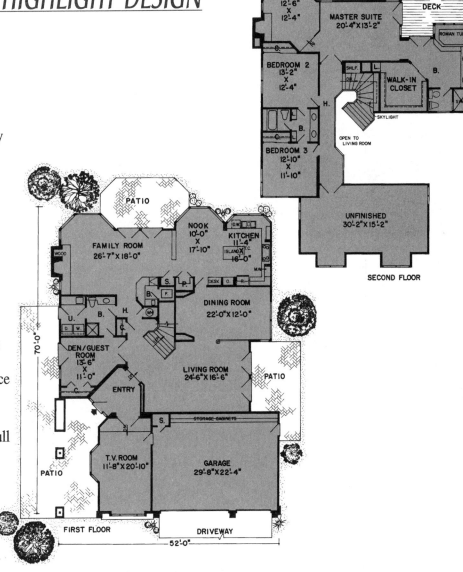

PRICE CODE B

CONTEMPORARY HEIGHT

No. 10675

- This plan features:

— Three bedrooms

— Two and one half baths

- Vertical siding and stacked windows combine to create a soaring facade

- Sloping ceilings, bump-out windows, and an open staircase uniting the foyer, Living Room and formal Dining Room

- A Family Room with a large fireplace flanking the Breakfast nook and a rear deck

- A full bath serving two ample bedrooms

- A luxurious Master Suite including a skylit bath, walk-in closet, and double vanities

FIRST FLOOR — 969 SQ. FT.
SECOND FLOOR — 714 SQ. FT.
BASEMENT — 969 SQ. FT.
GARAGE — 484 SQ. FT.

**TOTAL LIVING AREA:
1,683 SQ. FT.**

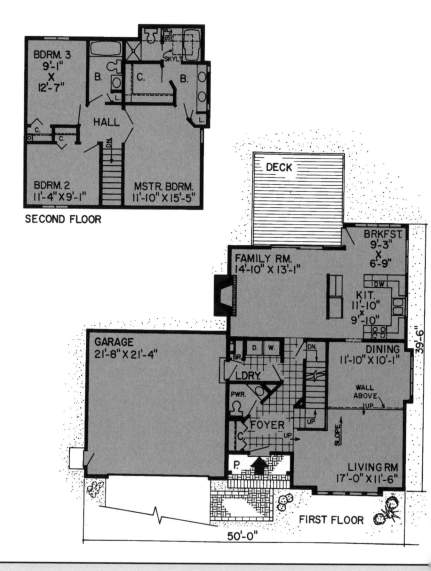

PRICE CODE C

Skylit Breakfast Room with Plant Shelf Above

No. 20128

■ This plan features:

— Three bedrooms

— Two full baths

■ A Kitchen with range peninsula that separates the Kitchen from a sunny, sky-lit Breakfast Nook

■ A fireplaced Living Room which adjoins the formal Dining Room

■ A Master Suite with his-n-her walk-in closets and a private bath

FIRST FLOOR — 942 SQ. FT.
SECOND FLOOR — 895 SQ. FT.
BASEMENT — 942 SQ. FT.
GARAGE — 484 SQ. FT.

TOTAL LIVING AREA:
1,837 SQ. FT.

An
EXCLUSIVE DESIGN
By Karl Kreeger

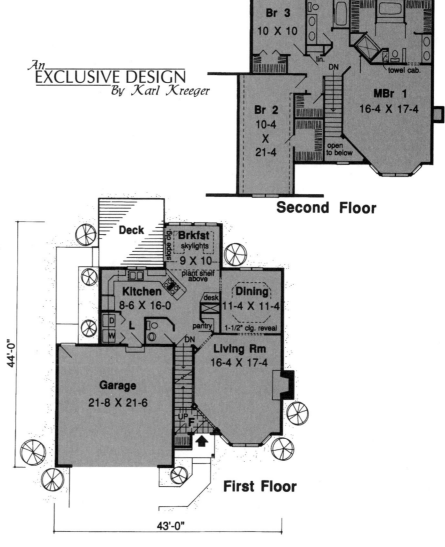

PRICE CODE E

VAULTED SUNKEN LIVING ROOM

An
EXCLUSIVE DESIGN
By Westhome Planners, Ltd.

No. 90941

■ This plan features:

— Four bedrooms

— Two full and one half baths

■ A dramatic, sunken Living Room with a vaulted ceiling, fireplace, and glass walls to enjoy the view

■ A well-appointed, Kitchen with a peninsula counter and direct access to the Family Room, Dining Room or the sun deck

■ A Master Suite with a walk-in closet and a private full bath

■ A Family Room with direct access to the rear sun deck

FIRST FLOOR — 1,464 SQ. FT.
BASEMENT FLOOR— 1,182 SQ. FT.
GARAGE — 418 SQ. FT.

TOTAL LIVING AREA:
2,646 SQ. FT.

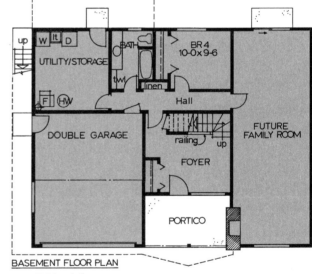

BASEMENT FLOOR PLAN

WIDTH=48'-0"
DEPTH=39'-0"

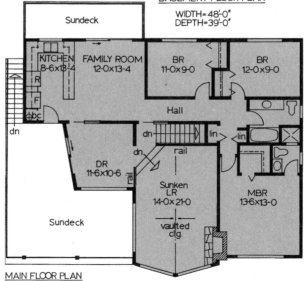

MAIN FLOOR PLAN

PRICE CODE B

A TOUCH OF VICTORIAN

An
EXCLUSIVE DESIGN
By Greg Stafford

No. 24611

■ This plan features:

— Three bedrooms

— Two full and one half baths

■ A cozy fireplace enhancing the Living Room

■ A formal Dining Room that can easily view and enjoy the Living Room's fireplace, adding ambience to entertaining

■ A efficient, well-appointed, U-shaped Kitchen

■ A sunny Breakfast Nook that views the rear yard

■ A second floor Master Suite with a sloped ceiling, private bath and a walk-in closet

■ Two additional bedrooms that share a full hall bath

FIRST FLOOR — 857 SQ. FT.
SECOND FLOOR — 829 SQ. FT.
GARAGE — 484 SQ. FT.
PORCH — 120 SQ. FT.

TOTAL LIVING AREA:
1,686 SQ. FT.

No materials list available

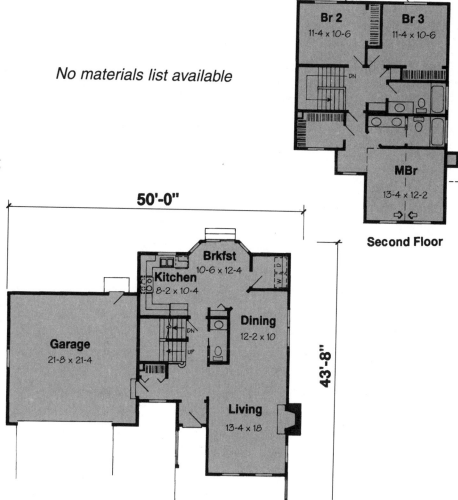

Second Floor

First Floor

PRICE CODE D

MASTER SUITE CROWNS PLAN

No. 91650

■ This plan features:

— Three bedrooms

— Two full and one half baths

■ A stately vaulted ceiling in the foyer accented by a winding staircase

■ A bright bay window and a fireplace enhancing the Living Room

■ A cook-top island Kitchen with corner double sinks, and a built-in pantry

■ A Family Room with a fireplace and direct access to the rear yard

■ An extensive Master Suite with a decorative ceiling, full bath and a walk-in closet

■ Two additional bedrooms that share a full hall bath

FIRST FLOOR — 1,288 SQ. FT.
SECOND FLOOR — 1,094 SQ. FT.
BONUS ROOM — 255 SQ. FT.

TOTAL LIVING AREA:
2,382 SQ. FT.

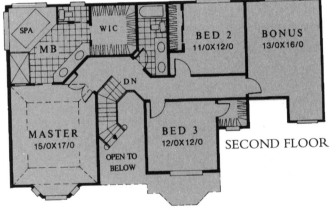

SECOND FLOOR

No materials list available

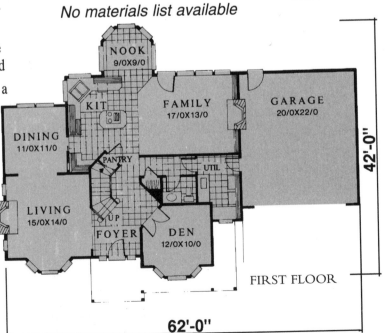

FIRST FLOOR

62'-0"

42'-0"

PRICE CODE B

FORMAL BALANCE

No. 91502

■ This plan features:

— Three bedrooms

— Two full and one half baths

■ A two story foyer crowned by a towering palladium window

■ A formal Living Room that flows into the formal Dining Room for ease in entertaining

■ A cozy Family Room with a brick hearth fireplace

■ An angular Kitchen with a peninsula counter, a built-in pantry and a sunny eating Nook

■ A magnificent Master Suite with a garden spa, double vanities and a walk-in closet

■ Two additional bedrooms sharing a sky-lit full bath

FIRST FLOOR — 935 SQ. FT.
SECOND FLOOR — 772 SQ. FT.
BONUS ROOM — 177 SQ. FT.

TOTAL LIVING AREA:
1,707 SQ. FT.

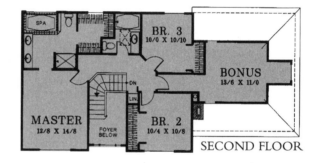

SECOND FLOOR

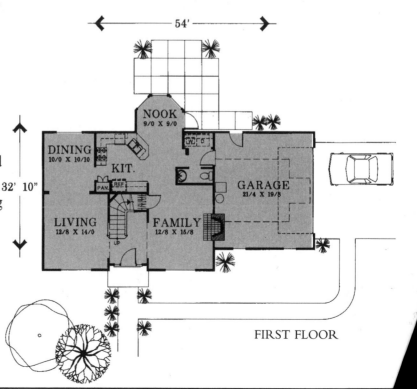

FIRST FLOOR

PRICE CODE F

FIREPLACES ADD WARMTH

No. 10779

■ This plan features:

— Three bedrooms

— Three full and one half bath

■ A balcony giving a sweeping view of the vaulted Great Room, the two-story foyer, and the bi-level Master Suite

■ A sunken formal Dining Room

■ A country Kitchen with a cook top island and a greenhouse window for growing herbs

■ A book-lined Study next to the Living Room

■ A Master Suite with ample closet space, double vanities, and a large fireplace

OOR — 2,962 SQ. FT.
OOR — 1,883 SQ. FT.
— 2,962 SQ. FT.
0 SQ. FT.

VING AREA:

SQ. FT.

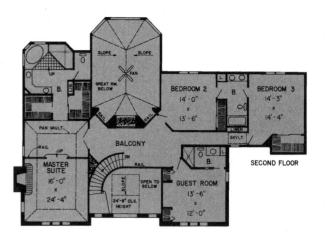

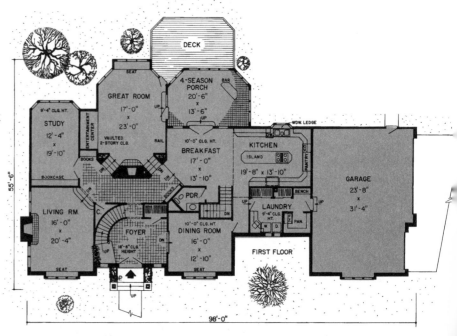

PRICE CODE B

TRADITION WITH A HINT OF DRAMA

No. 92609

■ This plan features:

— Three bedrooms

— Two and one half baths

■ A 12′ high Entry with transom and sidelights, multiple gables and a box window

■ A sunken Great Room with a fireplace and access to a rear Porch

■ A Breakfast Bay and Kitchen flowing into each other and accessing a rear Porch

■ A Master Bedroom with a tray ceiling, walk-in closet and a private Master Bath

FIRST FLOOR — 960 SQ. FT.
SECOND FLOOR — 808 SQ. FT.

TOTAL LIVING AREA: 1,768 SQ. FT.

PRICE CODE A

VACATION PLAN HAS WELL ORGANIZED LAYOUT

No. 91033

- This plan features:
- — Two bedrooms
- — Two full baths
- A two-story Living Room and Dining Room with a handsome stone fireplace
- A well-appointed Kitchen with a peninsula counter
- A Master Suite with a walk-in closet and private Master Bath
- A large utility room with laundry facilities
- An optional basement or crawl space foundation — please specify when ordering

...OR — 952 SQ. FT.
...OR — 297 SQ. FT.

...*ING AREA:*

...*Q. FT.*

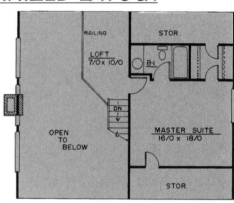

UPPER FLOOR

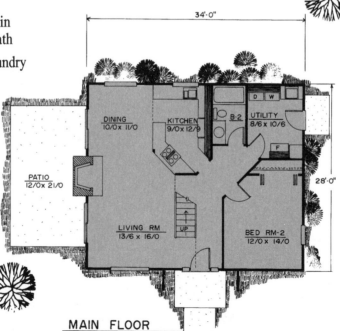

MAIN FLOOR

PRICE CODE B

LARGE FRONT WINDOW PROVIDES NATURAL LIGHT

No. 91514

■ This plan features:

— Three bedrooms

— Two full and one half bathS

■ An outstanding, two-story Great Room with an unusual floor-to-ceiling, corner front window and cozy, hearth fireplace

■ A formal Dining Room opening from the Great Room makes entertaining easy

■ An efficient Kitchen with a work island, pantry, a corner, double sink opening to the Great Room, and a bright, bay window eating Nook

■ A quiet, Master Suite with a vaulted ceiling and a plush Bath with a double vanity, spa tub and walk-in closet

■ On the second floor, two additional bedrooms share a full hall bath and a Bonus area that can be used to suit your needs

FIRST FLOOR — 1,230 SQ. FT.
SECOND FLOOR — 477 SQ. FT.

TOTAL LIVING AREA:
1,707 SQ. FT.

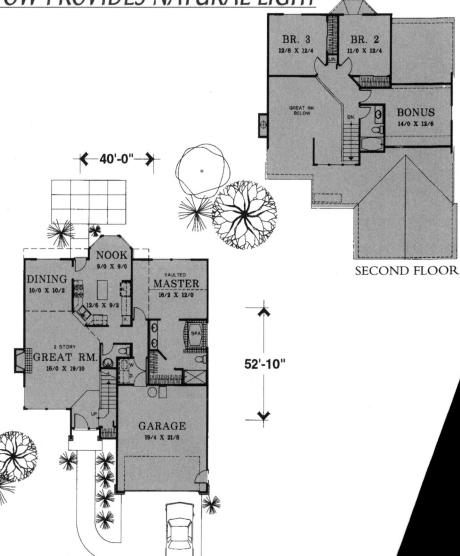

SECOND FLOOR

FIRST FLOOR

PRICE CODE E

GABLE AND GLASS GRACE FACADE

No. 91640

■ This plan features:

— Four bedrooms

— Two full and one half baths

■ A Sun Room that opens directly into the Family Room

■ A modern wrap-around Kitchen with a central island

■ A large front window in the formal Living Room which flows directly into the formal Dining Room

■ A spacious Master Suite with a huge walk-in closet and private Master Bath

■ Three additional bedrooms served by full hall bath

FLOOR — 1,540 SQ. FT.

FLOOR — 1,178 SQ. FT.

OM — 222 SQ. FT.

VING AREA:

. FT.

No materials list available

An
EXCLUSIVE DESIGN
By Mark Stewart

UPPER FLOOR

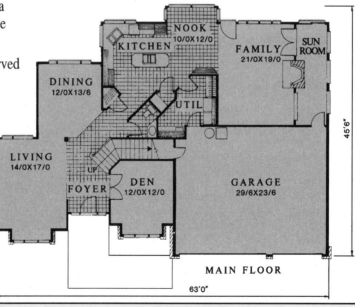

MAIN FLOOR

PRICE CODE C

ATTRACTIVE MODERN DESIGN

An
EXCLUSIVE DESIGN
By Mark Stewart

No. 91655

■ This plan features:

— Three bedrooms

— Two full and one half baths

■ A coved ceiling and a five-sectioned window in the formal Living Room

■ A well-appointed Kitchen with convenient access to both the formal Dining Room and the informal eating Nook

■ A Family Room with direct access to the patio and a lovely fireplace

■ A coved ceiling in the Master Suite including a full private bath with all the amenities

■ Two additional bedrooms served by a full, double-vanity hall bath

FIRST FLOOR — 1,173 SQ. FT.
SECOND FLOOR — 823 SQ. FT.
BONUS ROOM — 204 SQ. FT.

TOTAL LIVING AREA:
1,996 SQ. FT.

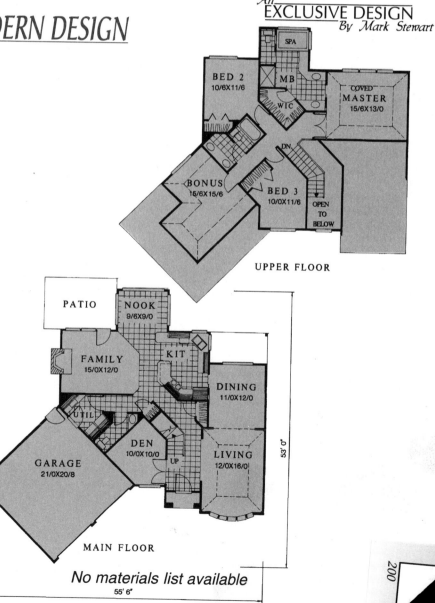

No materials list available

200

PRICE CODE B

COMPACT CLASSIC

No. 91413

■ This plan features:

— Three bedrooms

— Two full and one half baths

■ A spacious Family Room with a cozy fireplace and direct access to the patio

■ A well-appointed Kitchen with an eating bar peninsula, double sink and sunny eating Nook

■ A formal Living Room and Dining Room located at the front of the house

■ A Master Suite equipped with a walk-in closet, a double vanity and a full Master Bath

FIRST FLOOR — 963 SQ. FT.
SECOND FLOOR — 774 SQ. FT.

TOTAL LIVING AREA:
1,737 SQ. FT.

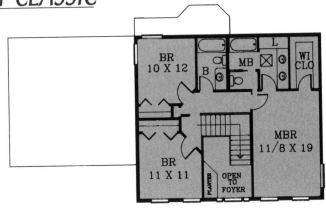

SECOND FLOOR PLAN

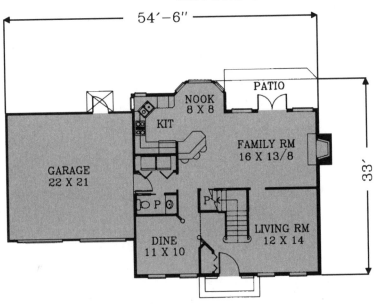

FIRST FLOOR PLAN

PRICE CODE F

STUCCO DESIGN IS TRULY A MASTERPIECE

No. 91613

■ This plan features:

— Three bedrooms

— Three full baths

■ A cozy Den with an adjoining full bath and French doors

■ A coved ceiling in both the Living and Dining Rooms

■ An efficient, cook-top island Kitchen with more than ample counter and storage space

■ A glass-walled eating Nook

■ A built-in wetbar and a fire-place in the Family Room

■ An enchanting Master Suite with a private sitting room, fabulous spa bath and a walk-in closet

FIRST FLOOR — 2,268 SQ. FT.
SECOND FLOOR — 1,484 SQ. FT.
BONUS ROOM — 300 SQ. FT.

TOTAL LIVING AREA: 3,752 SQ. FT.

An
EXCLUSIVE DESIGN
By Mark Stewart

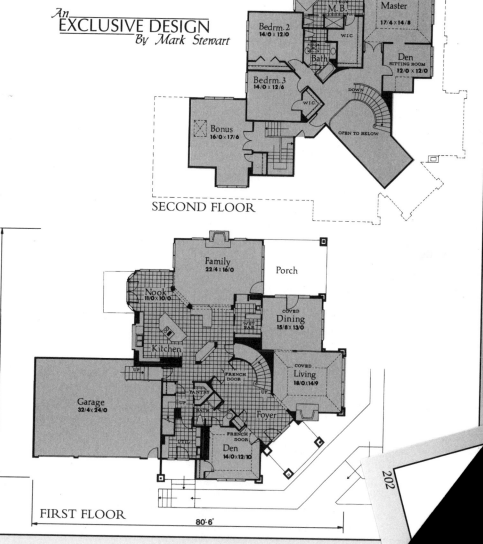

SECOND FLOOR

FIRST FLOOR

PRICE CODE F

BRIDGE OVER FOYER INTRODUCES UNIQUE FEATURES

No. 10535

■ This plan features:

— Four bedrooms

— Two full and two half baths

■ A dramatic two-story foyer opening into a Great Room with a cathedral ceiling

■ A Great Room with a cozy fire-place framed by a bookcase

■ A foyer flanked by a Parlor and the formal Dining Room

■ A spacious Kitchen complete with an octagonal Breakfast nook tucked into a bank of windows

■ A first floor Master Bedroom including a quaint but roomy sitting room

FIRST FLOOR — 2,335 SQ. FT.
SECOND FLOOR — 1,157 SQ. FT.
BASEMENT — 2,281 SQ. FT.
GARAGE — 862 SQ. FT.

TOTAL LIVING AREA:
3,492 SQ. FT.

An
EXCLUSIVE DESIGN
By Karl Kreeger

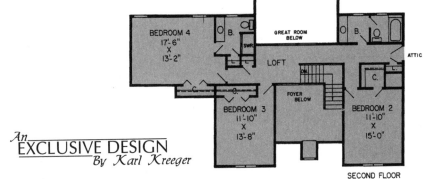

SECOND FLOOR

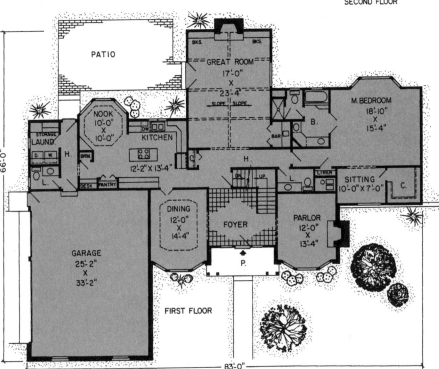

FIRST FLOOR

PRICE CODE E

No. 92613

■ This plan features:

— Three bedrooms

— Two full and two half baths

■ A classic design with decorative stucco, keystone arches and boxed windows surrounding a broad, pillar entrance into a spacious Foyer

■ A sloped ceiling in the Great Room accenting a wall of windows, a great hearth fireplace and an entertainment center nestled in the corner

■ An elegant formal Dining Room with a tray ceiling highlighting the decorative, boxed window

■ An efficient, island Kitchen opening to the Patio through atrium door and a spacious Breakfast Room as well as Laundry area and Garage

■ A private wing, featuring the Master Bedroom Suite with a luxurious Bath, an over-sized walk-in closet, two vanities and a raised, corner window tub

■ A second floor with two additional bedrooms sharing a full hall bath and a Bonus Room for future expansion

*C*LASSIC EUROPEAN STYLING

FIRST FLOOR — 2,192 SQ. FT.
SECOND FLOOR — 325 SQ. FT.

TOTAL LIVING AREA:
2,846 SQ. FT.

No materials list available

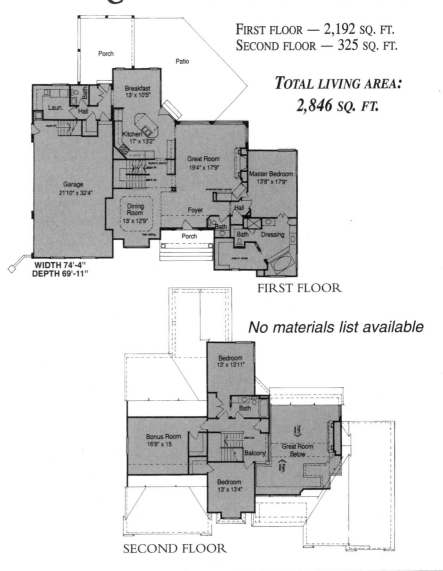

FIRST FLOOR

SECOND FLOOR

PRICE CODE D

No. 91424

- This plan features:
- — Three bedrooms
- — Two full and one half baths
- A dramatic vaulted entry
- An arched floor-to-ceiling window, a vaulted ceiling, and a fireplace in the Living Room
- A formal Dining Room adjoining the Living Room
- An open layout between the Kitchen, eating Nook and the Family Room making for a spacious atmosphere
- A peninsula counter in the efficient Kitchen
- Direct access to the patio from the Family Room which also has a fireplace
- A Master Suite with a vaulted ceiling, walk-in closet and private Master Bath

FIRST FLOOR — 1,290 SQ. FT.
SECOND FLOOR — 932 SQ. FT.
BONUS ROOM — 228 SQ. FT.

TOTAL LIVING AREA:
2,222 SQ. FT.

INFINITE POSSIBILITIES

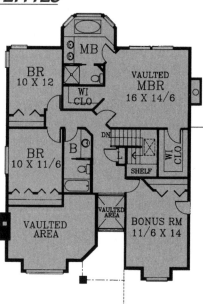

UPPER FLOOR PLAN

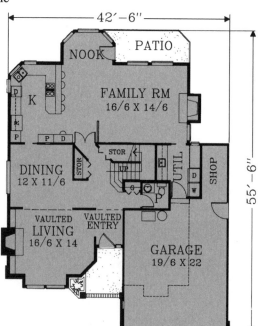

FIRST FLOOR PLAN

PRICE CODE E

Spacious Design Appeals To All

No. 91630

■ This plan features:

— Five bedrooms

— Four full baths

■ A Living Room with a fireplace that is separated by columns from the Dining Room

■ A wide-open layout between the Kitchen, Nook and Family Room

■ A Den accessible to a bath with a shower, making it a perfect guest room

■ A luxurious Master Suite with a spa tub and a walk-in closet

■ Two additional full baths serving the four additional bedrooms

FIRST FLOOR — 1,452 SQ. FT.
SECOND FLOOR — 1,431 SQ. FT.
BONUS ROOM — 316 SQ. FT.

TOTAL LIVING AREA: 2,883 SQ. FT.

An
EXCLUSIVE DESIGN
By Mark Stewart

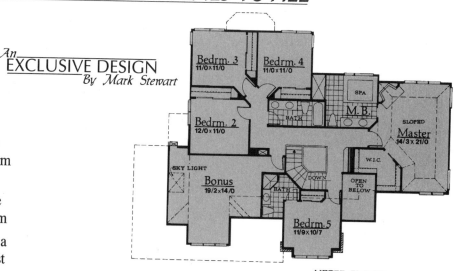

UPPER FLOOR

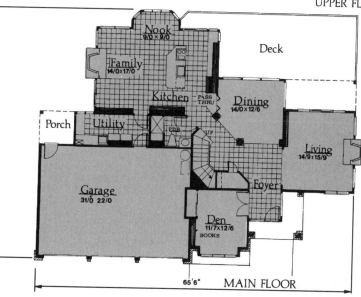

MAIN FLOOR

PRICE CODE C

No. 91669

■ This plan features:

— Three bedrooms

— Two full and one half bath

■ A stone and decorative stucco exterior with unusual windows leading into a tile floor Entry and a landing staircase

■ A vaulted ceiling in the Living Room accenting a triple front window and warm, hearth fireplace

■ A quiet Den with double door and large front window could double as a home office

■ A formal Dining Room flowing from the Living Room and directly accessing the backyard and the Kitchen

■ An efficient Kitchen with a cooktop island, corner double sink, and recessed, eating Nook defined by a tile floor

■ An ideal Family Room with a second fireplace and a wall of windows to view the backyard

■ A double door and a coved ceiling in the Master Suite creating a special area also with a private Bath equipped with a recessed spa tub

WITH ROOM TO EXPAND

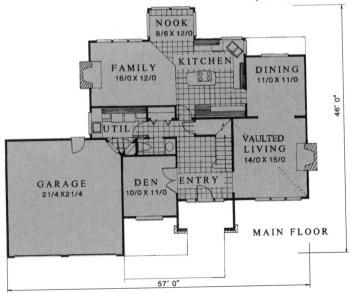

UPPER FLOOR

SPA

BED 2
11/0 X 11/10

COVED
MASTER
15/6 X 14/3

BONUS
12/0 X 16/0

BED 3
10/0 X 11/0

FIRST FLOOR — 1,200 SQ. FT.
SECOND FLOOR — 917 SQ. FT.
BONUS — 230 SQ. FT.
GARAGE — 484 SQ. FT.

TOTAL LIVING AREA :
2,117 SQ. FT.

An EXCLUSIVE DESIGN
By Mark Stewart

NOOK
8/6 X 12/0

KITCHEN

FAMILY
16/0 X 12/0

DINING
11/0 X 11/0

UTIL

VAULTED
LIVING
14/0 X 15/0

GARAGE
21/4 X 21/4

DEN
10/0 X 11/0

ENTRY

46' 0"

MAIN FLOOR

57' 0"

No materials list available

PRICE CODE D

No. 91672

■ This plan features:

— Four bedrooms

— Three full and one half baths

■ A elegant covered entrance leading into a Great Hall with direct access to all living areas

■ A unusually shaped Living Room accented by magnificent front windows, a vaulted ceiling and a warm, hearth fireplace

■ A formal Dining Room with a built-in alcove flowing from the Living Room into the Kitchen

■ An efficient Kitchen equipped with a cooktop island/snack-bar, a corner window sink and a bright eating Nook leading to backyard

■ A private Master Suite with a tray ceiling highlighted by a bay window and leading to a lavish Bath with a spa tub and double vanity

■ A secondary bedroom on the first floor with a built-in desk could double as a den

An **EXCLUSIVE DESIGN** *By Mark Stewart*

UNIQUE CEILING TREATMENT

■ On the second floor, two additional bedrooms with walk-in closets sharing a full hall bath and a huge Bonus Room

FIRST FLOOR — 1,928 SQ. FT.
SECOND FLOOR — 504 SQ. FT.
BONUS — 335 SQ. FT.

TOTAL LIVING AREA:
2,432 SQ. FT.

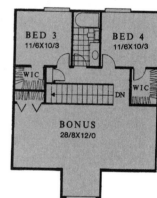

UPPER FLOOR

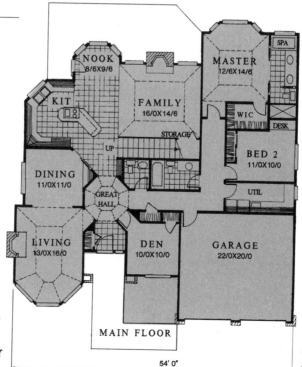

MAIN FLOOR

PRICE CODE D

DESIGNED FOR TODAY'S BUSY LIFESTYLE

No. 91512

■ This plan features:

— Three bedrooms

— Two full and one half baths

■ Open lay-out between the Kitchen, Family Room and Eating Nook giving a feeling of spaciousness

■ A fireplace in both the Family Room and the Living Room

■ An efficient Kitchen that easily accesses the Eating Nook as well as the Formal Dining Room

■ A large multi-panned window provides view of the front yard from the Den

■ A Master Suite with decorative ceiling, large walk-in closet and private Master Bath

■ Two additional bedrooms that share a full hall bath

FIRST FLOOR — 1,408 SQ. FT.
SECOND FLOOR — 1,024 SQ. FT.

TOTAL LIVING AREA:
2,432 SQ. FT.

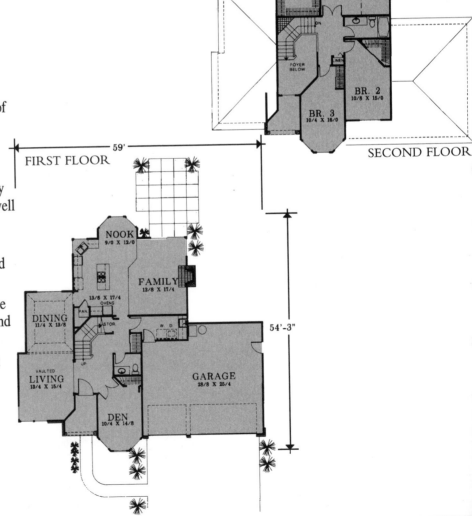

PRICE CODE C

SPACIOUS KITCHEN COMPLETES SPECIAL DESIGN

No. 91654

■ This plan features:

— Three or four bedrooms

— Two or three full baths and one half bath

■ A picture window and fireplace accentuating the Living Room

■ An island Kitchen with a built-in pantry, corner double sink, built-in desk and a sunny eating Nook

■ A spacious Family Room with a cozy fireplace and direct access to the deck

A Master Suite with a decorative ceiling, walk-in closet, and a private Master Bath

Two (optional three) additional bedrooms with easy access to a full hall bath

FIRST FLOOR — 1,233 SQ. FT.
SECOND FLOOR — 902 SQ. FT.
BONUS ROOM — 168 SQ. FT.

TOTAL LIVING AREA: 2,135 SQ. FT.

OPTIONAL UPPER FLOOR

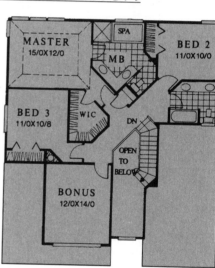

UPPER FLOOR

No materials list available

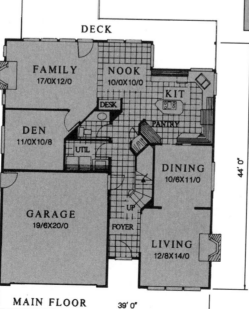

MAIN FLOOR   39' 0"

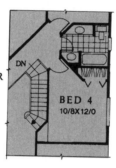

An EXCLUSIVE DESIGN *By Mark Ster*

209

PRICE CODE C

VAULTED VIEWS

No. 91416

■ This plan features:

— Three bedrooms

— Two full baths

■ An expansive, two-story Great Room and full-length deck beyond atrium doors

■ A Kitchen, with rangetop island, flowing into the Dining Room; which has access to the deck

■ A vaulted ceiling in the Master Suite, which includes two walk-in closets, a private Master Bath with garden tub and double vanities

FIRST FLOOR — 1,450 SQ. FT.
SECOND FLOOR — 650 SQ. FT.
BONUS ROOM — 220 SQ. FT.

**TOTAL LIVING AREA:
2,100 SQ. FT.**

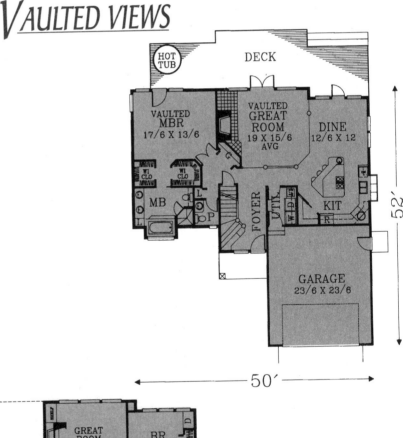

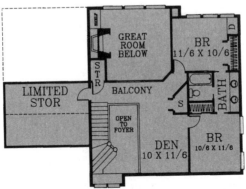

PRICE CODE A

SPECTACULAR VIEWS FROM A HILL OR ANYWHERE

No. 91026

■ This plan features:

— Two bedrooms

— Two full baths

■ Sweeping panels of glass and a wood stove, creating atmosphere for the Great Room

■ An open plan that draws the Kitchen into the warmth of the Great Room's wood stove

■ A sleeping loft that has a full bath all to itself

■ A basement foundation only

FIRST FLOOR — 988 SQ. FT.
SECOND FLOOR — 366 SQ. FT.
BASEMENT — 988 SQ. FT.

TOTAL LIVING AREA:
1,354 SQ. FT.

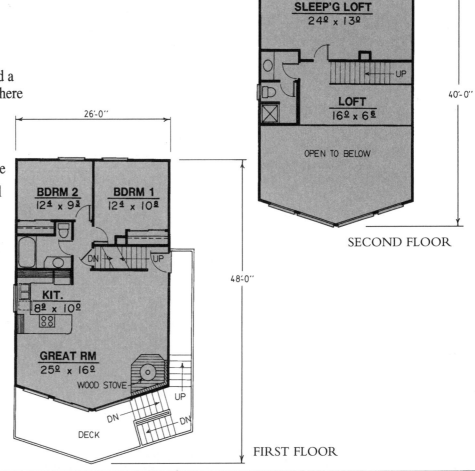

SECOND FLOOR

FIRST FLOOR

PRICE CODE E

ANGULAR ELEGANCE

No. 91509

■ This plan features:

— Three bedrooms

— Two full and one half baths

■ A unique Living Room with a vaulted ceiling and columns separating it from the formal Dining Room

■ A wide-open arrangement between the Family Room, Nook and island Kitchen

■ A fireplace in both the Family Room and the Living Room

■ A skylight and double vanities in the full hall bath

■ A Master Suite with a walk-in closet, garden spa tub, and bay window

FIRST FLOOR — 1,675 SQ. FT.
SECOND FLOOR — 1,032 SQ. FT.
BONUS ROOM — 450 SQ. FT.

TOTAL LIVING AREA:
2,707 SQ. FT.

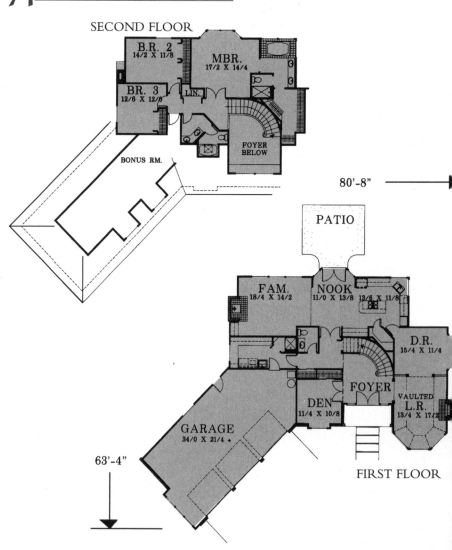

PRICE CODE E

DOUBLE DECKS ADORN MASTER SUITE

No. 91022

■ This plan features:

— Three bedrooms

— Two full and one half baths

■ Abundant windows, indoor planters and three decks uniting every room with the outdoors

■ An efficient Kitchen with direct access to the Nook and the formal Dining Room

■ A wood stove warming the spacious Family Room

■ A secluded Master Suite with private deck, Den and Master Bath

■ An optional basement, slab or crawl space foundation — please specify when ordering

FIRST FLOOR — 1,985 SQ. FT.
SECOND FLOOR — 715 SQ. FT.

TOTAL LIVING AREA:
2,700 SQ. FT.

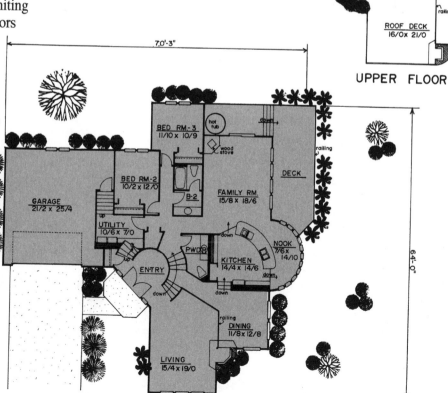

UPPER FLOOR

MAIN FLOOR

PRICE CODE E

ENJOY THE BACKYARD VIEWS

No. 10550

■ This plan features:

— Four bedrooms

— Three full and two half baths

■ Recessed ceilings in the Dining Room and Master Bedroom

■ A sun porch off the Breakfast Nook

■ Two full baths and two convenient baths located on the second floor

■ A full Basement foundation

FIRST FLOOR — 2,069 SQ. FT.
SECOND FLOOR — 821 SQ. FT.
BASEMENT — 2,045 SQ. FT.
GARAGE — 562 SQ. FT.

TOTAL LIVING AREA: 2,890 SQ. FT.

An EXCLUSIVE DESIGN
By Karl Kreeger

PRICE CODE C

SUNKEN GREAT ROOM IS ONE OF THE MANY HIGHLIGHTS

No. 92610

■ This plan features:

— Three bedrooms

— Two full and one half baths

■ An arched front entrance framed by a decorative stone and brick exterior, and a unique turret room

■ A sunken Great Room, centrally located, with a huge, hearth fireplace, an atrium door to the Deck, and leading directly into the Kitchen

■ An efficient, island Kitchen with a double window, corner sink, ample counter and cabinet space, and a bright bay windowed Breakfast area

■ A formal Dining Room with an expansive, bay window and pocket doors for elegant entertaining

■ A quiet wing for the Master Bedroom suite with a sloped ceiling and a plush Bath with a corner window raised tub, double vanity and a large walk-in closet

■ Two additional bedrooms on the second floor sharing a full bath with a double vanity

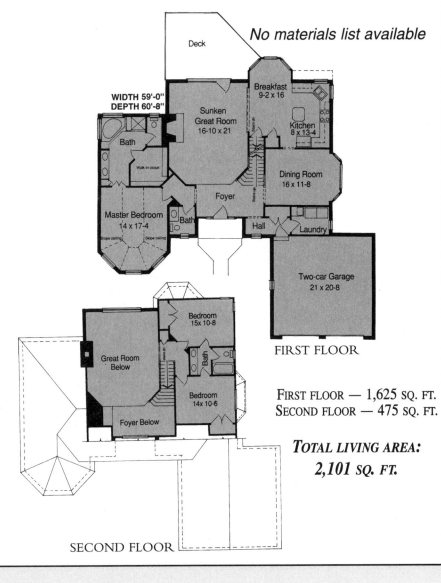

No materials list available

FIRST FLOOR

FIRST FLOOR — 1,625 SQ. FT.
SECOND FLOOR — 475 SQ. FT.

TOTAL LIVING AREA:
2,101 SQ. FT.

SECOND FLOOR

PRICE CODE D

STATELY MANOR

An **EXCLUSIVE DESIGN**
By Westhome Planners, Ltd.

No. 90966

- ■ This plan features:
- — Three bedrooms
- — Two full and one half baths
- ■ A porch serving as a grand entrance
- ■ A very spacious Foyer with an open staircase and lots of angles
- ■ A beautiful Kitchen equipped with a cook top island and a full bay window wall that includes a roomy Breakfast Nook
- ■ A Living Room with a vaulted ceiling that flows into the Dining Room for ease in entertaining
- ■ A grand Master Suite equipped with a walk-in closet and five-piece private bath

FIRST FLOOR — 1,383 SQ. FT.
SECOND FLOOR — 997 SQ. FT.
BASEMENT — 1,374 SQ. FT.
GARAGE — 420 SQ. FT.
WIDTH — 54'-0"
DEPTH — 47'-0"

TOTAL LIVING AREA:
2,380 SQ. FT.

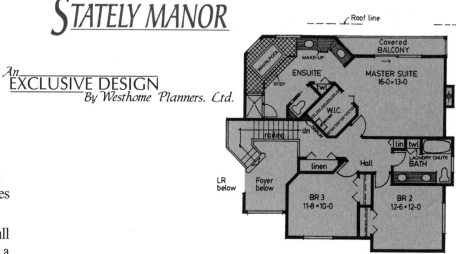

SECOND FLOOR

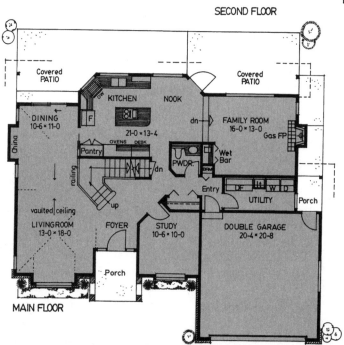

MAIN FLOOR

PRICE CODE D

Two-Story Arched Window Makes Dramatic Statement

No. 91412

■ This plan features:

— Three bedrooms

— Two full and one half baths

■ A spacious Family Room/Kitchen combination

■ A sunken Living Room with a warm and cozy fireplace

■ An impressive Dining Room with a vaulted ceiling in close proximity to the Kitchen

■ A Master Suite with a walk-in closet, a double-vanity bath, and a private deck

FIRST FLOOR — 1,416 SQ. FT.
SECOND FLOOR — 1,056 SQ. FT.
GARAGE — 504 SQ. FT. OR
729 WITH OPTION

**TOTAL LIVING AREA:
2,472 SQ. FT.**

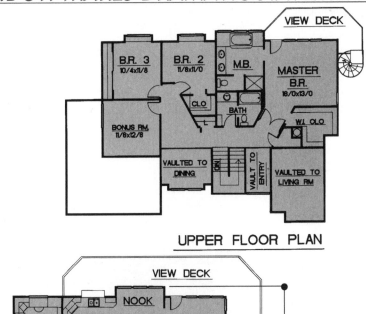

UPPER FLOOR PLAN

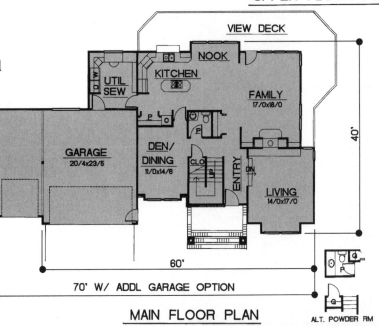

MAIN FLOOR PLAN

PRICE CODE B

MASTER RETREAT CROWNS SPACIOUS HOME

No. 19422

■ This plan features:

— Two bedrooms

— Two full baths

■ An open Foyer leading into a two-story Living Room

■ A unique four-sided fireplace separating the Living Room, Dining area and Kitchen

■ A well-equipped Kitchen featuring a cooktop island, a walk-in pantry and easy access to the Dining area and Laundry room

■ A three-season Screened Porch and Deck

■ A private Master Suite on the second floor offering a cozy, dormer window seat, private balcony, and window tub in the spacious Bath

FIRST FLOOR — 1,290 SQ. FT.
SECOND FLOOR — 405 SQ. FT.
SCREENED PORCH — 152 SQ. FT.
GARAGE — 513 SQ. FT.

TOTAL LIVING AREA:
1,695 SQ. FT.

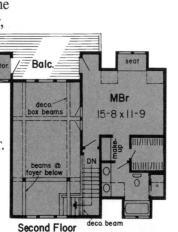
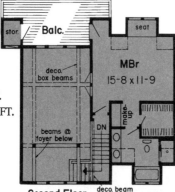

No. 19491

■ This plan features:

— Three bedrooms

— Two full baths

■ A Sheltered Porch leading into a bright two-story Living Room with skylights and windows above and a warm hearth fireplace below

■ An efficient U-shaped kitchen adjoining the Deck, Garage, and Dining Room with a convenient pass-through

■ A secluded Master Suite on the second floor with a private Deck, a room-sized closet and full Bath

■ Two additional bedrooms located on the first floor adjacent to a full Bath with laundry center

FIRST FLOOR — 920 SQ. FT.
SECOND FLOOR — 300 SQ. FT.
GARAGE — 583 SQ. FT.

**TOTAL LIVING AREA:
1,220 SQ. FT.**

HIGH IMPACT IN A SMALL PACKAGE

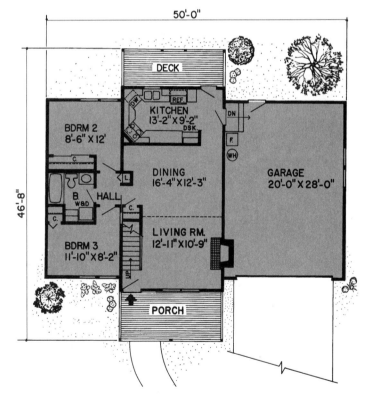

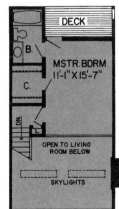

PRICE CODE C

No. 92612

■ This plan features:

— Three bedrooms

— Two full and one half baths

■ A dramatic facade created by a natural stone chimney framed by decorative windows and pillar entrance leading into an open Foyer below a balcony and a wonderful transom window

■ A two-story, sunken Great Room with a 12′ ceiling accenting the large, stone fireplace framed by curved floor-to-ceiling windows

■ A formal Dining Room steps from the Great Room and the Kitchen with a pass-thru and a wall of windows to backyard

■ A efficient, U-shaped Kitchen with a built-in pantry, a peninsula counter/snackbar and bright, glassed Breakfast area with atrium door to the Deck

■ A plush Master Bedroom Suite with a large walk-in closet and a private Bath with a double vanity and corner window tub

■ Two additional bedrooms, on the second floor, sharing a full bath with a double vanity

HIGHLY LIVABLE WITH A TOUCH OF DRAMA

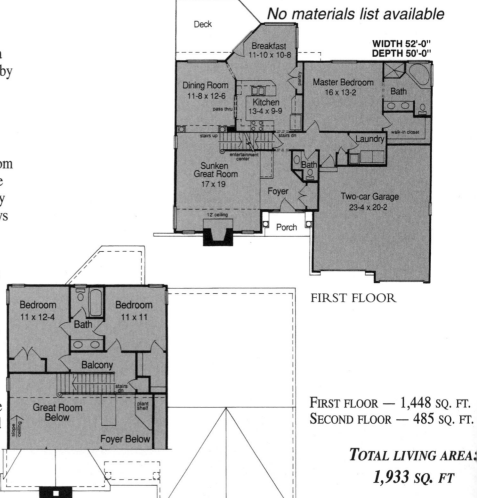

No materials list available

WIDTH 52'-0"
DEPTH 50'-0"

FIRST FLOOR

SECOND FLOOR

FIRST FLOOR — 1,448 SQ. FT.
SECOND FLOOR — 485 SQ. FT.

TOTAL LIVING AREA:
1,933 SQ. FT

PRICE CODE E

DESIGNED FOR PRIVACY

No. 10657

- This plan features:
- — Three bedrooms
- — Two and one half baths
- A Kitchen with a cooking island that opens to a Morning Room accessible to a deck and sunroom with a hot tub
- A Master Suite including a room-sized closet, double vanity and skylit tub with separate shower
- Ample room throughout, including the Living Room with a fireplace and the formal Dining Room with recessed ceilings

FIRST FLOOR — 1,838 SQ. FT.
SECOND FLOOR — 798 SQ. FT.
BASEMENT — 1,831 SQ. FT.
GARAGE — 800 SQ. FT.

TOTAL LIVING AREA:
2,636 SQ. FT.

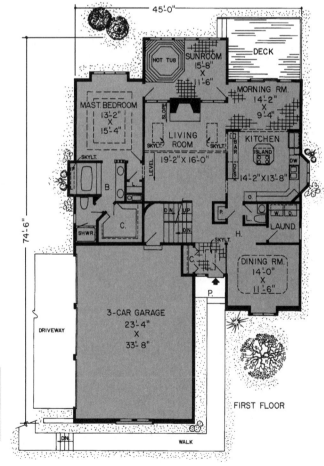

FIRST FLOOR

SECOND FLOOR

An
EXCLUSIVE DESIGN
By Karl Kreeger

PRICE CODE D

CLAPBOARD CLASSIC

No. 91503

■ This plan features:

— Three bedrooms

— Two full and one half baths

■ A cozy Parlor with a fireplace and direct access to the formal Dining Room

■ A bay window adding natural light to the formal Dining Room

■ A sunny Kitchen with a corner window over a double sink, built-in desk, and a bright eating Nook

■ A Family Room opening off the eating Nook with a lovely fireplace

■ A fabulous Master Suite with a garden spa tub, double vanities and a huge walk-in closet

FIRST FLOOR — 1,285 SQ. FT.
SECOND FLOOR — 1,100 SQ. FT.
BONUS ROOM — 238 SQ. FT.

**TOTAL LIVING AREA:
2,385 SQ. FT.**

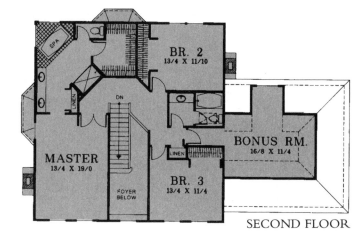

SECOND FLOOR

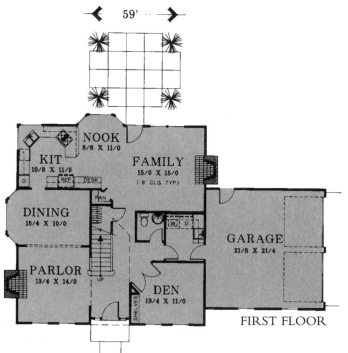

FIRST FLOOR

PRICE CODE C

MANY WINDOWS ADD EYE APPEAL

No. 91638

■ This plan features:

— Three bedrooms (with optional fourth)

— Three full baths

■ A fireplaced Family Room and Living Room

■ An efficient Kitchen with an adjoining eating Nook and easy access to the formal Dining Room

■ A coved ceiling Master Bedroom with a private bath and a walk-in closet

FIRST FLOOR — 1,181 SQ. FT.
SECOND FLOOR — 918 SQ. FT.
BONUS ROOM — 242 SQ. FT.

TOTAL LIVING AREA: 2,099 SQ. FT.

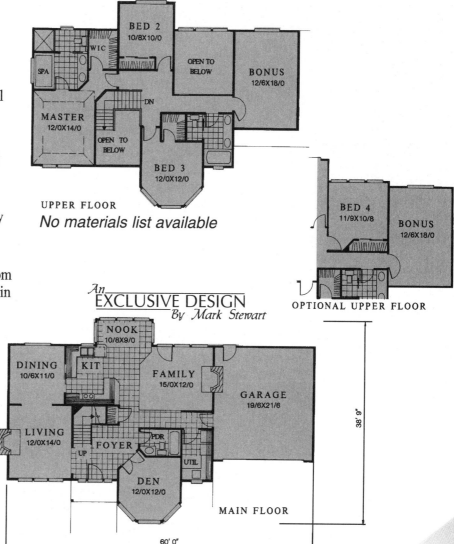

No materials list available

An
EXCLUSIVE DESIGN
By Mark Stewart

OPTIONAL UPPER FLOOR

An EXCLUSIVE DESIGN
By Patrick Morabito, A.I.A. Architect

PRICE CODE F

No. 93334

- ■ This plan features:
- — Four bedrooms
- — Three full and one half baths
- ■ An unusual Living Room featuring a half-circle of windows topped by a stepped ceiling, and French doors into a Sun Room for elegant entertaining
- ■ An informal Family Room, with a massive fireplace, convenient built-ins, and a wall of windows, opening to Dinette/Kitchen area
- ■ An island Kitchen with an abundance of counter space, a double sink, built-in desk and a sky-lit Dinette area leading to the formal Dining Room with a walk-in pantry in between
- ■ A luxurious Master Suite with a tray ceiling and a private Bath featuring a whirlpool, corner window tub, double vanity and an extra large walk-in closet
- ■ On the second floor, three additional bedrooms, each with private access to a full bath, and a Bonus Room with many options

FIRST FLOOR — 1,970 SQ. FT.
SECOND FLOOR — 1,638 SQ. FT.
BONUS ROOM — 587 SQ. FT.

ATTRACTIVE ALL AROUND

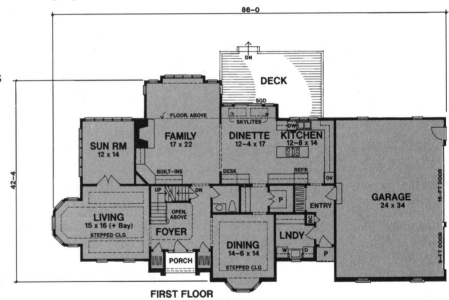

FIRST FLOOR

TOTAL LIVING AREA:
3,608 SQ. FT.

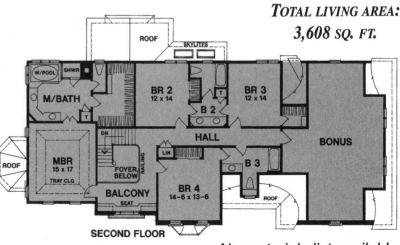

SECOND FLOOR

No materials list available

PRICE CODE B

COUNTRY CLASSIC FULL OF CHARACTER

No. 90397

This plan features:

— Three bedrooms

— Two full and one half baths

A fireplace dividing the vaulted ceiling Living Room and Dining Room

An efficiently designed country Kitchen with a corner sink overlooking the deck and family sitting area

A vaulted ceiling Master Suite with a double-vanity, bath, and a walk-in closet

FIRST FLOOR — 834 SQ. FT.
SECOND FLOOR — 722 SQ. FT.

TOTAL LIVING AREA:
1,556 SQ. FT.

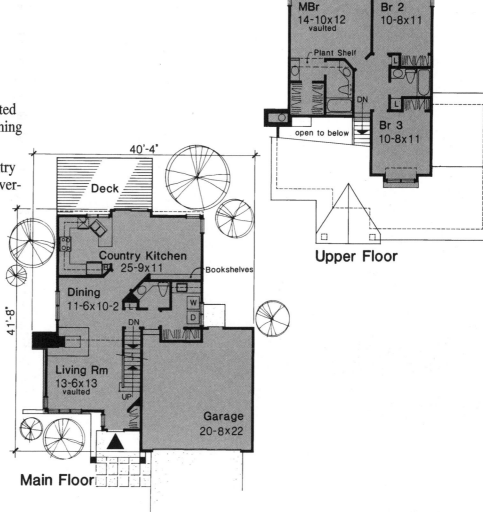

Upper Floor

MBr 14-10x12 vaulted

Br 2 10-8x11

Plant Shelf

open to below

Br 3 10-8x11

Main Floor

40'-4"

41'-8"

Deck

Country Kitchen 25-9x11

Bookshelves

Dining 11-6x10-2

Living Rm 13-6x13 vaulted

Garage 20-8x22

PRICE CODE C

CONTEMPORARY WITH A COZY FRONT PORCH

No. 20219

An
EXCLUSIVE DESIGN
By Karl Kreeger

- This plan features:

— Four bedrooms

— Two full and one half baths

- A welcoming front porch

- A Foyer that opens to a balcony above, giving a first impression of spaciousness

- A Living Room and Dining Room that flow into each other, allowing for ease in entertaining

- An efficient, well-appointed Kitchen that is equipped with a peninsula counter that doubles as an eating bar

- A Breakfast Area that has easy access to a wood deck and a view of the fireplace in the Family Room

- A Master Suite that includes a pan ceiling, private Master Bath and walk-in closet

- Three additional bedrooms that share a full hall bath

Alternate
Foundation Plan

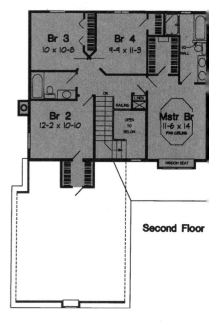

Second Floor

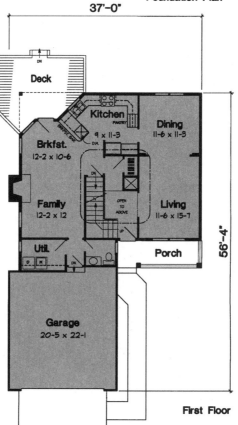

First Floor

FIRST FLOOR — 1,028 SQ. FT.
SECOND FLOOR — 1,013 SQ. FT.
BASEMENT — 1,019 SQ. FT.
GARAGE — 479 SQ. FT.

TOTAL LIVING AREA:
2,041 SQ. FT.

No materials list available

DESIGN NO. 92614

PRICE CODE E

No. 92614

■ This plan features:

— Four bedrooms

— Three full and one half baths

■ A two story entrance with an open Foyer leading to a spacious, open, sunken Great Room with a hearth fireplace framed by built-in book shelves

■ A formal Dining Room accented with columns and custom moldings and adjacent to the Butler's Pantry for easy entertaining

■ A U-shaped, efficient Kitchen with double corner sink, walk-in pantry and snackbar counter opening to the expansive Breakfast area and Hearth Room

■ A cozy Hearth Room providing an informal gathering place with easy access to the outdoors and the Kitchen

■ A private Master Suite including a bright, bay window Sitting Area, tray ceiling, and Bath with a large walk-in closet, two vanities and a corner, atrium tub

■ Three additional bedrooms on the second floor, two sharing a connecting bath, and the third with a private bath

SPACIOUS STYLE AND ELEGANCE

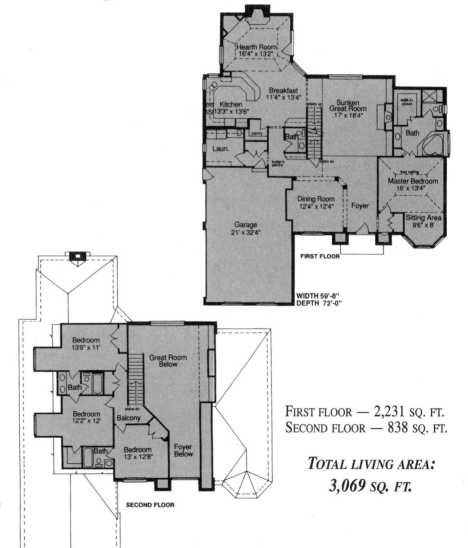

FIRST FLOOR — 2,231 SQ. FT.
SECOND FLOOR — 838 SQ. FT.

TOTAL LIVING AREA:
3,069 SQ. FT.

No materials list available

PRICE CODE D

No. 90413

■ This plan features:

— Three bedrooms

— Two full and one half baths

■ A sunken Family Room with a cathedral ceiling and a massive stone fireplace

■ Two front bedrooms having ample closet space and sharing a unique bath-and-a-half arrangement

■ A Master Bedroom with a walk-in closet and compartmentalized bath with double vanity and linen closet

■ A U-shaped Kitchen, well-equipped and efficient, serving the Breakfast Nook and the formal Dining Room with ease

■ A second floor with a large Studio

■ An optional basement, slab or crawl space foundation — please specify when ordering

FIRST FLOOR — 2,192 SQ. FT.
SECOND FLOOR — 248 SQ. FT.

TOTAL LIVING AREA:
2,440 SQ. FT.

REAR OF HOME AS ATTRACTIVE AS FRONT

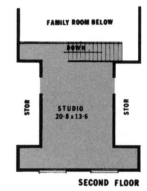

FAMILY ROOM BELOW

DOWN

STOR · STUDIO 20·8 x 13·6 · STOR

SECOND FLOOR

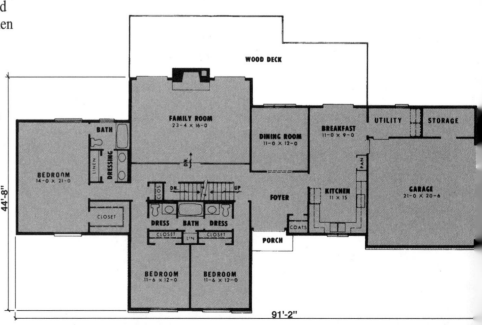

WOOD DECK

BATH

FAMILY ROOM 23-4 x 16-0

DINING ROOM 11-0 x 12-0

BREAKFAST 11-0 x 9-0

UTILITY

STORAGE

BEDROOM 14-0 x 21-0

DRESSING

LINEN

CLOSET

DN

UP

FOYER

KITCHEN 11 x 15

GARAGE 21-0 x 20-6

CLOS

DRESS BATH DRESS

COATS

CLOSET LIN CLOSET

PORCH

BEDROOM 11-6 x 12-0

BEDROOM 11-6 x 12-0

44'-8"

91'-2"

PRICE CODE C

ONE-OF-A-KIND

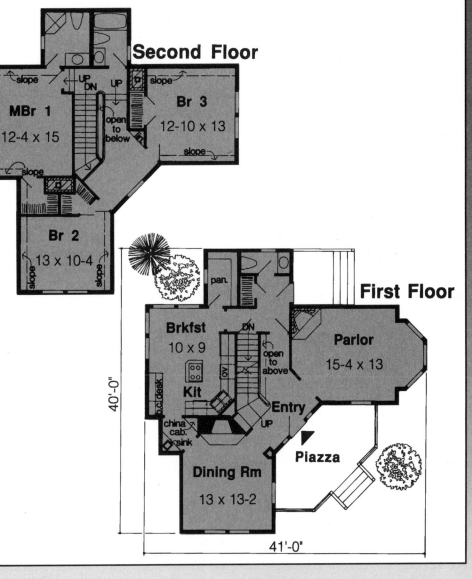

Second Floor

No. 20365

■ This plan features:

— Three bedrooms

— Two and a half baths

■ A porch sheltering the entry

■ A fireplaced Dining Room with warmth and atmosphere

■ A corner fireplace adding a focal point to the Parlor

■ An island Kitchen with a Breakfast area and walk-in pantry

FIRST FLOOR — 955 SQ. FT.
SECOND FLOOR — 864 SQ. FT.
BASEMENT — 942 SQ. FT.

TOTAL LIVING AREA:
1,819 SQ. FT.

PRICE CODE F

UPPER DECK AFFORDS ROADSIDE VIEW

No. 10768

■ This plan features:

— Five bedrooms

— Two and one half baths

■ A wetbar in the Family Room, built-in seating in the Breakfast Room, and an island Kitchen with a planning desk and room-sized pantry

■ A magnificent Master Suite including a fireplace, access to a private deck, an abundance of closet space and a tub in a bow window setting

FIRST FLOOR — 2,573 SQ. FT.
SECOND FLOOR — 2,390 SQ. FT.
BASEMENT — 1,844 SQ. FT.
CRAWL SPACE — 793 SQ. FT.
GARAGE — 1,080 SQ. FT.

TOTAL LIVING AREA:
4,963 SQ. FT.

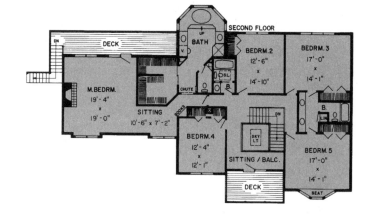

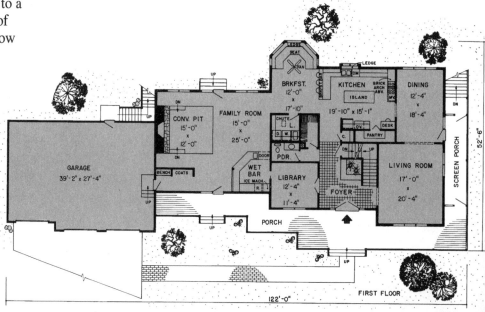

PRICE CODE D

Modern Living with a Farmhouse Feel

No. 20222

- ■ This plan features:
- — Four bedrooms
- — Two full and one half baths
- ■ A large Living Room equipped with a fireplace
- ■ A well-equipped Kitchen that serves both the informal Breakfast Area and the formal Dining Room with equal ease
- ■ A cooktop island that doubles for a snack bar and a built-in pantry in the efficient Kitchen
- ■ A large walk-in closet and private Master Bath in the Master Suite
- ■ Three additional bedrooms, one with a walk-in closet, that share use of a full hall bath

FIRST FLOOR — 1,488 SQ. FT.
SECOND FLOOR — 893 SQ. FT.
BASEMENT — 801 SQ. FT.
GARAGE — 677 SQ. FT.

TOTAL LIVING AREA:
2,381 SQ. FT.

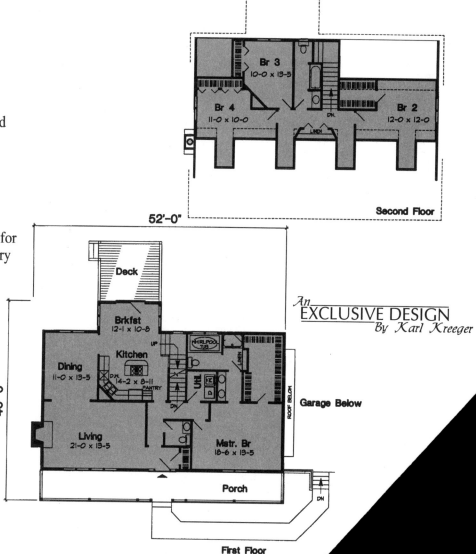

An
EXCLUSIVE DESIGN
By Karl Kreeger

PRICE CODE D

INTERESTING CONCEPTS

An
EXCLUSIVE DESIGN
By Energetic Enterprises

No. 24253

■ This plan features:

— Three Bedrooms

— Three full baths

■ A vaulted ceiling in the Living Room

■ Sunny Dining Room with bayed window

■ Modern Kitchen with cooktop island and double sinks

■ A vaulted ceiling in the spacious Family Room with fireplace

■ Master Bedroom with bayed window, vaulted ceiling and skylit Master Bath

■ Additional Bedrooms share

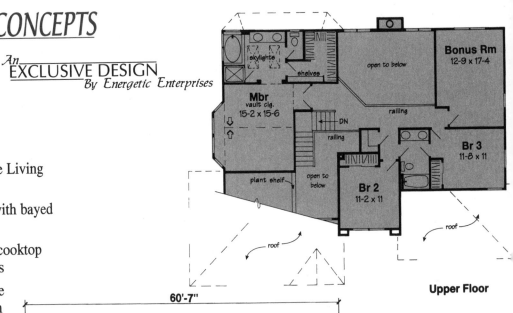

Upper Floor

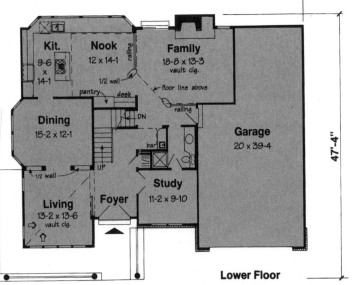

Lower Floor

PRICE CODE B

TRADITIONAL TRANSOM WINDOWS ADD APPEAL

No. 90396

 This plan features:

— Three bedrooms

— Two full and one half baths

 A vaulted ceiling in both the Living and adjoining Dining Rooms, accentuated by a fireplace

 A well-appointed, sky-lit Kitchen which easily serves the Dining Room

 A first floor Master Suite with a dramatic vaulted ceiling and private patio access

 A private Master Bath with double vanity and walk-in closet

FIRST FLOOR —
1,099 SQ. FT.
SECOND FLOOR —
452 SQ. FT.

TOTAL LIVING AREA:
1,551 SQ. FT.

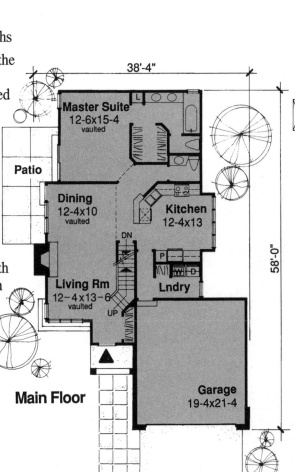

Main Floor

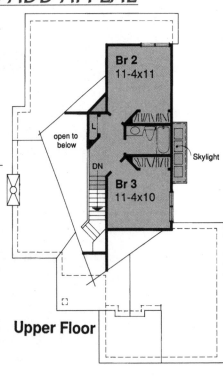

Upper Floor

PRICE CODE B

LIVING ROOM IS FOCUS OF HOME

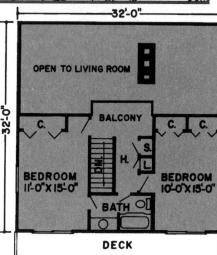

No. 10328

■ This plan features:

— Three bedrooms

— One and one half baths

■ A well planned traffic pattern connecting the Dining Area, Kitchen, laundry niche and bath

■ A balcony overlooking the open Living Room on the second floor

■ Sliding glass doors opening to the deck, a fireplace and a sizable Living Room

FIRST FLOOR — 1,024 SQ. FT.
SECOND FLOOR — 576 SQ. FT.
BASEMENT — 1,024 SQ. FT.

TOTAL LIVING AREA:
1,600 SQ. FT.

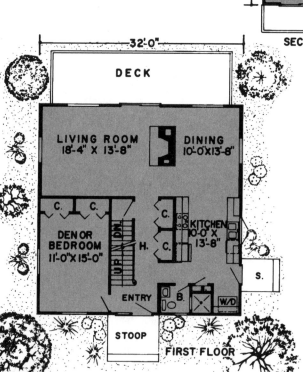

PRICE CODE D

No. 90420

■ This plan features:

— Three bedrooms

— Two full and one half baths

■ A spacious, sunken Living Room with a cathedral ceiling

■ An isolated Master Suite with a private bath and walk-in closet

■ Two additional bedrooms with a unique bath-and-a-half and ample storage space

■ An efficient U-shaped Kitchen with a double sink, ample cabinets, counter space and a Breakfast area

■ A second floor Studio overlooking the Living Room

■ An optional basement, slab or crawl space foundation — please specify when ordering

FIRST FLOOR — 2,213 SQ. FT.
SECOND FLOOR — 260 SQ. FT.
BASEMENT — 2,213 SQ. FT.
GARAGE — 422 SQ. FT.

TOTAL LIVING AREA:
2,473 SQ. FT.

1SOLATED MASTER SUITE

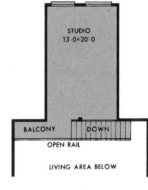

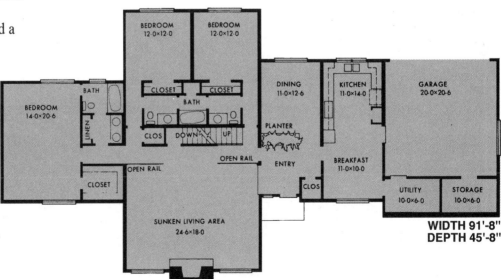

WIDTH 91'-8"
DEPTH 45'-8"

PRICE CODE C

COUNTRY KITCHEN AND GREAT ROOM

No. 90419

- This plan features:
— Three bedrooms
— Two full baths
- Front porch, dormers, shutters and multi-paned windows
- An eat-in country Kitchen with an island counter and bay window
- A large utility room which can be entered from the Kitchen or Garage
- A Great Room with an informal Dining Nook and double doors opening to the rear deck
- A Master Suite featuring a walk-in closet and a compartmentalized bath with a linen closet
- An optional basement, slab or crawl space foundation — please specify when ordering

FIRST FLOOR — 1,318 SQ. FT.
SECOND FLOOR — 718 SQ. FT.
BASEMENT — 1,221 SQ. FT.
GARAGE — 436 SQ. FT.

TOTAL LIVING AREA:
2,036 SQ. FT.

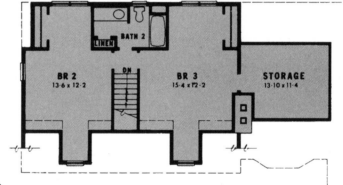

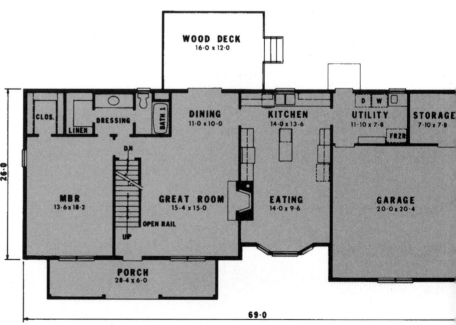

PRICE CODE C

o. 20223

This plan features:

- Three bedrooms

- Two full and one half bath

A sheltered entry leading directly into a comfortable Living Room with a boxed front window and a cozy fireplace

A octagon-shaped Dining Room with two walls of windows and easy access to the Deck, Kitchen and Living Room

A well-equipped and efficient Kitchen with a double sink, loads of counter and storage space and adjacent to a Utility Room

A convenient entry from the Garage for unloading groceries

A lovely Master Suite with a decorative ceiling, a double, walk-in closet, and private Bath with an over-sized shower and double vanity

Two additional bedrooms sharing a full, double vanity bath

FIRST FLOOR — 892 SQ. FT.
SECOND FLOOR — 960 SQ. FT.
BASEMENT — 892 SQ. FT.
GARAGE — 486 SQ. FT.

TOTAL LIVING AREA:
1,852 SQ. FT.

FAMILY PLAN HAS MANY COZY COMFORTS

An
EXCLUSIVE DESIGN
By Karl Kreeger

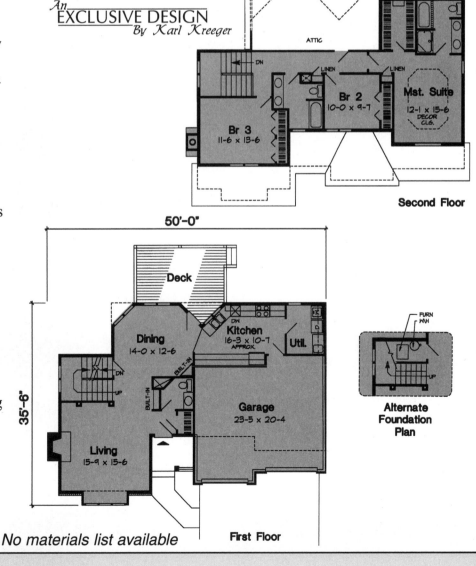

No materials list available

PRICE CODE E

No. 93333

■ This plan features:

— Four bedrooms

— Two full and one half baths

■ A formal Living Room featuring wrap-around windows and direct access to the front Porch and the cozy Den with built-in book-shelves and a window seat

■ An elegant, formal Dining Room accented by a stepped ceiling

■ An efficient Kitchen equipped with a cooktop island/eating bar, a double sink with a boxed window, a huge walk-in pantry and a Dinette with a window seat and an atrium door leading to the Deck

■ A bright, all-purpose Sun Room, with glass on four sides adjoining an expansive Deck

■ A Family Room, with a tray ceiling topping a circle head window and a massive, hearth fireplace, also accessing the Deck

■ A private Master Suite with a decorative ceiling and a luxurious Bath

WHISPERS OF VICTORIAN STYLING

No materials list available

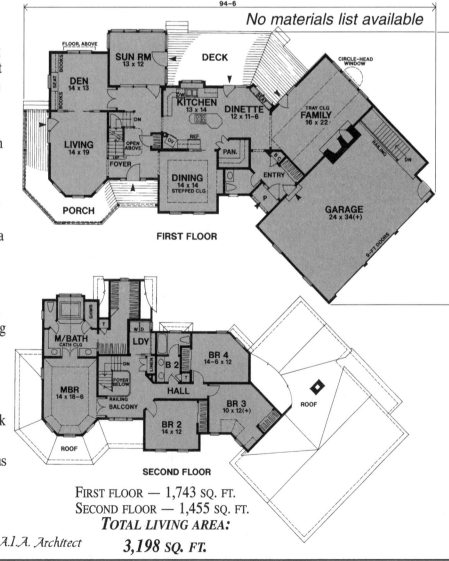

FIRST FLOOR — 1,743 SQ. FT.
SECOND FLOOR — 1,455 SQ. FT.
TOTAL LIVING AREA:
3,198 SQ. FT.

An
EXCLUSIVE DESIGN
By Patrick Morabito, A.I.A. Architect

PRICE CODE B

COMPACT VICTORIAN IDEAL FOR NARROW LOT

No. 90406

■ This plan features:

— Three bedrooms

— Two full baths

■ A large, front Parlor with a raised hearth fireplace

■ A Dining Room with a sunny bay window

■ An efficient galley Kitchen serving the formal Dining Room and informal Breakfast Room

■ A beautiful Master Suite with two closets, an oversized tub and double vanity, plus a private sitting room with a bayed window and vaulted ceiling

■ An optional basement or crawl space foundation — please specify when ordering

FIRST FLOOR — 954 SQ. FT.
SECOND FLOOR — 783 SQ. FT.

TOTAL LIVING AREA:
1,737 SQ. FT.

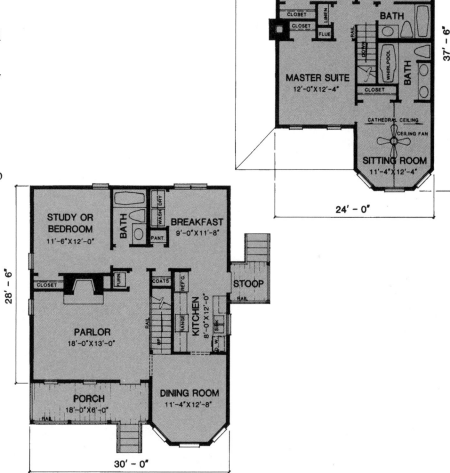

PRICE CODE C

COUNTRY LIVING

No. 90410

■ This plan features:

— Three bedrooms

— Two full and one half baths

■ An eat-in country Kitchen with an island counter and bay window

■ A spacious Great Room with a fireplace flowing easily into the Dining area

■ A first floor Master Suite including a walk-in closet and a private compartmentalized bath

■ Two additional bedrooms sharing a full bath with a double vanity

■ An optional basement or crawl space foundation — please specify when ordering

FIRST FLOOR — 1,277 SQ. FT.
SECOND FLOOR — 720 SQ. FT.

TOTAL LIVING AREA:
1,997 SQ. FT.

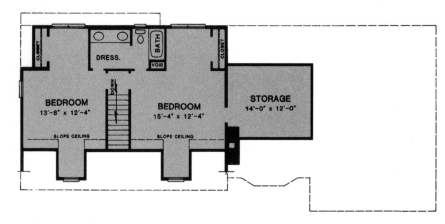

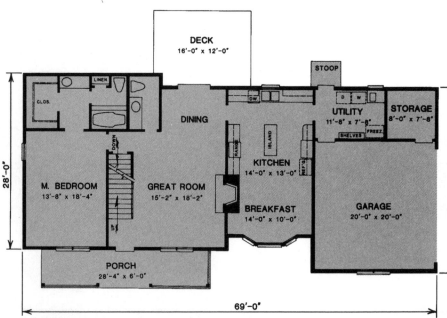

PRICE CODE D

FEELINGS OF NOSTALGIA

No. 24252

■ This plan features:

— Three bedrooms

— Two full and one half bath

■ A vaulted ceiling in the Foyer to give a first impression of spaciousness

■ A Great Room with skylights, a wetbar and a fireplace

■ A Kitchen that is equipped with an island, a built-in cooktop and a planning desk

■ A sunny, informal Eating Nook

■ A formal Dining Room convenient to the Kitchen

■ A vaulted ceiling in the Master Suite which boasts a private bath and a walk-in closet

■ Two additional bedrooms that share a full hall bath

■ An upstairs Study Room close to the bedrooms

■ A Bonus Room for future expansion

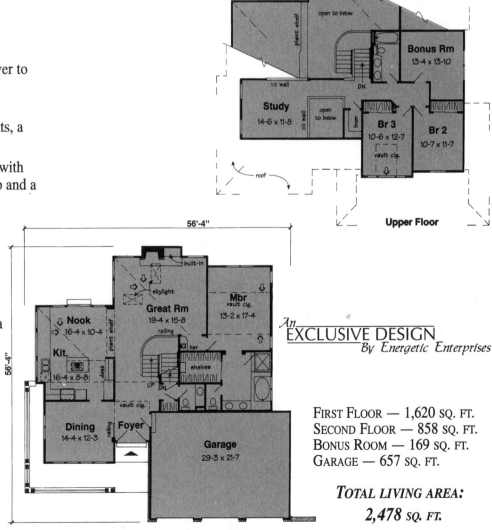

An EXCLUSIVE DESIGN
By Energetic Enterprises

FIRST FLOOR — 1,620 SQ. FT.
SECOND FLOOR — 858 SQ. FT.
BONUS ROOM — 169 SQ. FT.
GARAGE — 657 SQ. FT.

TOTAL LIVING AREA:
2,478 SQ. FT.

PRICE CODE D

ATTRACTIVE HIP AND VALLEY STYLE ROOF

No. 24262

■ This plan features:

— Four bedrooms

— Two full and one half bath

■ A see-through fireplace between the Living Room and the Family Room

■ A gourmet Kitchen with an island, built-in pantry, and double sink

■ A Master Bedroom with a vaulted ceiling

■ A Master Bath with large double vanity, linen closet, corner tub, separate shower, compartmented toilet, and huge walk-in closet

■ Three additional bedrooms, one with walk-in closet share full hall Bath

FIRST FLOOR — 1,241 SQ. FT.
SECOND FLOOR — 1,170 SQ. FT.

TOTAL LIVING AREA: 2,411 SQ. FT.

ALTERNATE KITCHEN

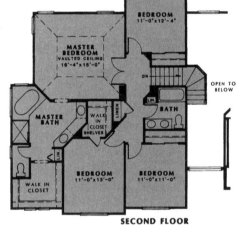

SECOND FLOOR

An EXCLUSIVE DESIGN
By Energetic Enterprises

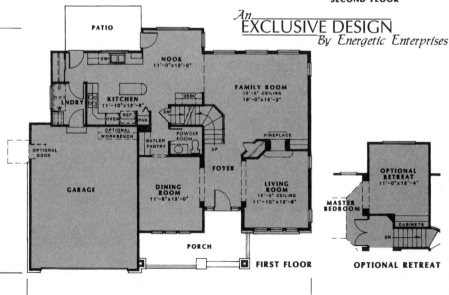

FIRST FLOOR

OPTIONAL RETREAT

PRICE CODE E

ON A GRAND SCALE

No. 93332

This plan features:

— Three bedrooms

— Two full and one half baths

■ An inviting, front Porch wrapping around the unique octagon shape of the Parlor and Master Bedroom above

■ A formal Parlor opening into the Family Room, with a hearth fireplace, for easy entertaining

■ A stepped ceiling accenting a charming bay window in the formal Dining Room

■ A large, island Kitchen with a double sink, a built-in pantry and a peninsula counter/eating bar leading to a large Entry with access to both the Garage and Laundry Room

■ Sliding glass doors in the Dinette leading to the Sun Room, with a cathedral ceiling

■ An elegant Master Suite with a tray ceiling, a room-sized, walk-in closet, and a plush Bath, featuring a raised, corner window tub and two vanities

An
EXCLUSIVE DESIGN
By Patrick Morabito, A.I.A. Architect

FIRST FLOOR — 1,484 SQ. FT.
SECOND FLOOR — 1,223 SQ. FT.

TOTAL LIVING AREA:
2,707 SQ. FT.

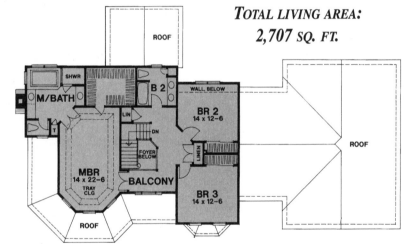

SECOND FLOOR

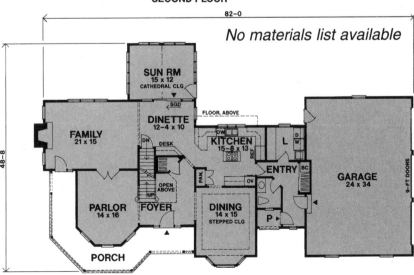

No materials list available

FIRST FLOOR

PRICE CODE B

OLD-FASHIONED COUNTRY PORCH
DESIGN NO. 93219

An EXCLUSIVE DESIGN
By Jannis Vann & Associates, Inc.

■ This plan features:
— Three bedrooms
— Two full and one half baths
■ A traditional front Porch, with matching dormers above and garage hidden below, leading into an open, contemporary layout
■ A Living Area with a cozy fireplace visible from Dining Room for warm entertaining
■ A U-shaped, efficient Kitchen featuring a corner, double sink and pass thru to Dining Room as well as a bright Breakfast area with access to the Sundeck
■ A convenient half bath with a laundry center on the first floor
■ A spacious, first floor Master Suite with a lavish Bath including a double vanity, walk-in closet and an oval, corner window tub
■ Two large bedrooms with dormer windows, on the second floor, sharing a full hall bath

FIRST FLOOR — 1,057 SQ. FT.
SECOND FLOOR — 611 SQ. FT.
BASEMENT — 511 SQ. FT.
GARAGE — 546 SQ. FT.

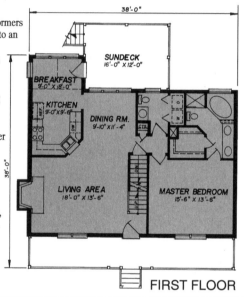

FIRST FLOOR

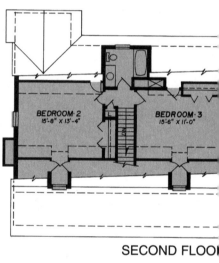

SECOND FLOOR

TOTAL LIVING AREA:
1,668 SQ. FT.

TWO STORY INTERIOR DRAMA
DESIGN NO. 92600

■ This plan features:
— Three bedrooms
— Two full and two half baths
■ Sunken Great Room with wetbar and corner fireplace, leads to an angled outdoor deck
■ Second floor Loft overlooks both Foyer and Great Room below
■ Two upstairs Bedrooms share access to a full bath with dual vanities and a dressing area
■ Luxurious main floor Master Bedroom wing features a private deck, both his-n-her walk-in closets, enormous Bath complete with tub, shower, two sinks, and private commode facilities
■ Pantried Kitchen with an angular counter flows into the multi-windowed breakfast room, which provides outdoor deck access
■ Two half-baths strategically located: one off the laundry room and the other off the foyer
■ Two-car garage has large storage area with double door access to the rear of the property

FIRST FLOOR — 2,245 SQ. FT.
SECOND FLOOR — 710 SQ. FT.

TOTAL LIVING AREA:
2,955 SQ. FT.

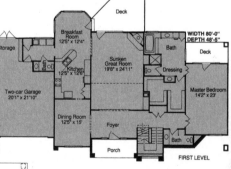

WIDTH 80'-0"
DEPTH 48'-5"

FIRST LEVEL

No materials list available

SECOND LEVEL

PRICE CODE C

DESIRABLE FAMILY PLAN
DESIGN NO. 20208

This plan features:

- Three bedrooms
- Three full baths
- A sloped ceiling in the Living Room with a fantastic fireplace
- A spacious U-shaped Kitchen and adjoining Dining Room with access to the deck
- A Master Suite with large walk-in closet and a private Master Bath with a vaulted ceiling
- Two additional bedroom sharing a full bath

FIRST FLOOR — 989 SQ. FT.
SECOND FLOOR — 932 SQ. FT.
BASEMENT — 950 SQ. FT.
GARAGE — 475 SQ. FT.

TOTAL LIVING AREA:
1,921 SQ. FT.

An
EXCLUSIVE DESIGN
By Karl Kreeger

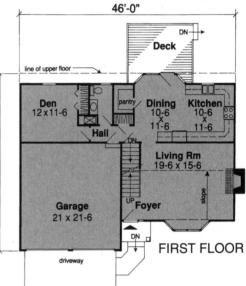

46'-0"

36'-0"

Deck

line of upper floor

Den
12 x 11-6

pantry

Dining
10-6 x 11-6

Kitchen
10-6 x 11-6

Hall

DN

UP

Living Rm
19-6 x 15-6

slope

Garage
21 x 21-6

Foyer

driveway

DN

FIRST FLOOR

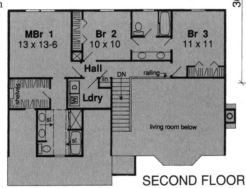

MBr 1
13 x 13-6

Br 2
10 x 10

Br 3
11 x 11

Hall

DN

railing

lin

W D

Ldry

shelves

sl.

sl.

living room below

SECOND FLOOR

PRICE CODE E

MASTER SUITE OFFERS PRIVACY

DESIGN NO. 24318

- This plan features:
— Four bedrooms
— Two full baths
- A large covered porch and dormer windows creating a friendly invitation to enter
- A Living Room with a beamed ceiling and atrium door access to the Patio
- A Dining Room adjoining the Living Room and Kitchen making entertaining easy
- An efficient, U-shaped Kitchen with a curved counter that serves as a pass-through and a snack bar
- An exclusive Master Suite on second floor offering a quiet place with a double vanity Bath
- Three bedrooms on the first floor sharing a full hall bath

FIRST FLOOR — 1,044 SQ. FT.
SECOND FLOOR — 354 SQ. FT.

TOTAL LIVING AREA:
1,398 SQ. FT

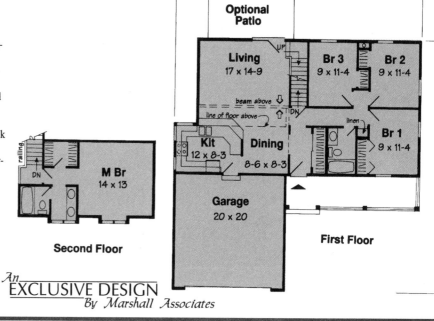

46'-0"

Optional Patio

Living
17 x 14-9

Br 3
9 x 11-4

Br 2
9 x 11-4

beam above

line of floor above

Kit
12 x 8-3

Dining
8-6 x 8-3

linen

Br 1
9 x 11-4

Garage
20 x 20

First Floor

railing

DN

M Br
14 x 13

Second Floor

An
EXCLUSIVE DESIGN
By Marshall Associates

LOVELY SECOND HOME

DESIGN NO. 91002

- This plan features:
— Three bedrooms
— One and one half baths
- Firedrum fireplace warming both entryway and Living Room
- Dining and Living Rooms opening onto deck that surrounds the house on three sides
- A crawl space foundation only

FIRST FLOOR — 744 SQ. FT.
SECOND FLOOR — 288 SQ. FT.

TOTAL LIVING AREA:
1,032 SQ. FT.

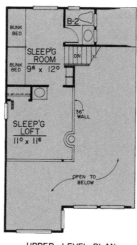

BUNK BED

B-2

SLEEP'G ROOM
9⁶ x 12⁰

DN

36" WALL

SLEEP'G LOFT
11⁰ x 11⁶

OPEN TO BELOW

UPPER LEVEL PLAN

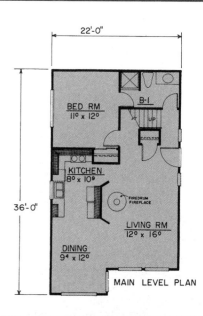

22'-0"

BED RM
11⁰ x 12⁰

B-1

UP

KITCHEN
8⁰ x 10⁹

FIREDRUM FIREPLACE

36'-0"

LIVING RM
12⁰ x 16⁰

DINING
9⁴ x 12⁰

MAIN LEVEL PLAN

ISTINCTIVE WINDOWS LIGHT UP CONTEMPORARY

DESIGN NO. 20310

This plan features:

- Three bedrooms
- Two and a half baths
- A Master Bedroom with a volume ceiling, walk-in closet and private Master Bath
- A fireplaced Great Room flowing into an elegant Dining Room with floor to ceiling windows
- An island Kitchen with an eating Nook and easy access to the Dining Room

RST FLOOR — 1,263 SQ. FT.

COND FLOOR — 483 SQ. FT.

ARAGE — 528 SQ. FT.

ASEMENT — 1,263 SQ. FT.

TOTAL LIVING AREA:
1,746 SQ. FT.

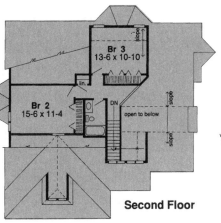

Br 3
13-6 x 10-10

Br 2
15-6 x 11-4

lin.

DN

open to below

slope

slope

Second Floor

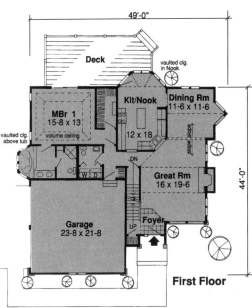

49'-0"

Deck

vaulted clg.
in Nook.

Kit/Nook

Dining Rm
11-6 x 11-6

MBr 1
15-8 x 13

vaulted clg.
above tub

volume ceiling

12 x 18

slope

slope

DN

44'-0"

Great Rm
16 x 19-6

Garage
23-8 x 21-8

UP

Foyer

First Floor

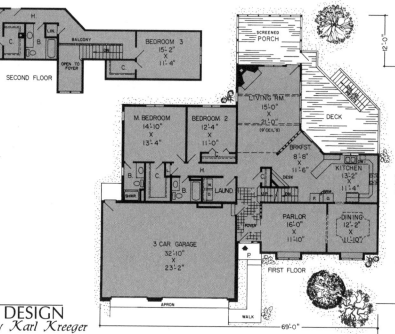

CORNER FIREPLACE WARMS LIVING ROOM

DESIGN NO. 10581

- This plan features:
— Four bedrooms
— Three baths
- A Parlor, Formal Dining Room, Kitchen, Breakfast Room and Living Room revolving around a central staircase
- A Laundry room located near two bedrooms for convenience
- A screened porch and deck which can be accessed from the large Living Room or the spacious Kitchen area

FIRST FLOOR — 1,916 SQ. FT.
SECOND FLOOR — 740 SQ. FT.
BASEMENT — 1,916 SQ. FT.
GARAGE — 814 SQ. FT.
SCREENED PORCH — 192 SQ. FT.

TOTAL LIVING AREA:
2,656 SQ. FT.

An
EXCLUSIVE DESIGN
By Karl Kreeger

LUXURY PERSONIFIED

DESIGN NO. 92623

- This plan features:
— Four bedrooms
— Three full baths
- A tray ceiling in the formal Living Room and Dining Room with corner columns pulling these two rooms into a unit, to create a large and charming area for entertaining
- An island Kitchen which includes a corner sink with windows to either side, flooding the counter with natural light
- A sunken Family Room with a cozy fireplace
- A luxurious Master Suite with double walk-in closets, a sloped ceiling and a private Master Bath
- Three additional bedrooms, sharing a skylit full bath, with laundry chute located close by
- A balcony overlooking the foyer with a plant shelf, arched window and skylight

FIRST FLOOR — 1,365 SQ. FT.
SECOND FLOOR — 1,288 SQ. FT.

TOTAL LIVING AREA:
2,653 SQ. FT.

No materials list available

PRICE CODE C

FRIENDS AND FAMILY WILL LOVE THIS PLAN

DESIGN NO. 20207

This plan features:

- Three bedrooms
- Two and a half baths
- A striking exterior featuring a variety of wood sidings, brick, curved front windows and a covered entrance way.
- A large Living Room and Dining Room flowing into each other, providing an elegant area for entertaining
- An island Kitchen with breakfast bar efficiently serving the Dining Room and the Breakfast Room
- A cozy, but open, Hearth Room offering a massive fireplace
- A spacious Master Suite with a Sitting Room, a walk-in closet and a skylit Bath with a corner tub and double vanity
- Two additional bedrooms sharing a full hall bath

FIRST FLOOR — 1,086 SQ. FT.
SECOND FLOOR — 986 SQ. FT.
BASEMENT — 1,086 SQ. FT.
GARAGE — 533 SQ. FT.

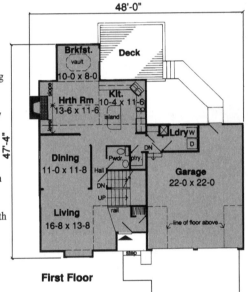

First Floor

48'-0"
47'-4"

Brkfst.
vault
10-0 x 8-0

Deck

Hrth Rm
13-6 x 11-6

Klt.
10-4 x 11-6
island

Ldry

Dining
11-0 x 11-8

Pwdr pntry
Hall
DN
UP
rail

Garage
22-0 x 22-0

Living
16-8 x 13-8

line of floor above

step

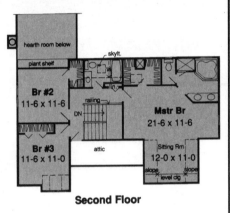

Second Floor

hearth room below
plant shelf
skylt.

Br #2
11-6 x 11-6

railing
DN

Mstr Br
21-6 x 11-6

Br #3
11-6 x 11-0

attic

Sitting Rm
12-0 x 11-0
slope   level clg   slope

TOTAL LIVING AREA: 2,072 SQ. FT.

An
EXCLUSIVE DESIGN
By Karl Kreeger

PRICE CODE E

PRICE CODE D

TRADITIONAL SUN CATCHER

No. 20096

- ■ This plan features:
- — Three bedrooms
- — Three and one half baths
- ■ Windows and skylights in all shapes and sizes, giving this home an airy feeling
- ■ A sky-lit Breakfast nook off the Kitchen
- ■ A large rear deck accessible from the Living Room and Breakfast nook
- ■ Three bedrooms opening to a balcony overlooking the floor below
- ■ A Master Suite with a walk-in closet, double vanities, and a raised sky-lit tub

FIRST FLOOR — 1,286 SQ. FT.
SECOND FLOOR — 957 SQ. FT.
BASEMENT — 1,286 SQ. FT.
GARAGE — 491 SQ. FT.

TOTAL LIVING AREA:
2,243 SQ. FT.

An
EXCLUSIVE DESIGN
By Karl Kreeger

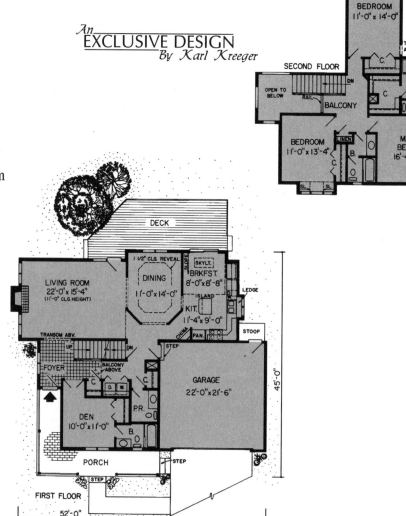

Ignoring Copyright Laws Can Be A $1,000,000 Mistake

Recent changes in the US copyright laws allow for statutory penalties of up to **$100,000** per incident for copyright infringement involving any of the copyrighted plans found in this publication. The law can be confusing. So, for your own protection, take the time to understand what you can and cannot do when it comes to home plans.

——— *What You Cannot Do* ———

You Cannot Duplicate Home Plans

Purchasing a set of blueprints and making additional sets by reproducing the original is *illegal*. If you need multiple sets of a particular home plan, then you must purchase them.

You Cannot Copy Any Part of a Home Plan to Create Another

Creating your own plan by copying even part of a home design found in this publication is called "creating a derivative work" and is *illegal* unless you have permission to do so.

You Cannot Build a Home Without a License

You must have specific permission or license to build a home from a copyrighted design, even if the finished home has been changed from the original plan. It is *illegal* to build one of the homes found in this publication without a license.

What Garlinghouse Offers

Home Plan Blueprint Package

By purchasing a single or multiple set package of blueprints from Garlinghouse, you not only receive the physical blueprint documents necessary for construction, but you are also granted a license to build one, and only one, home. You can also make any changes to our design that you wish, as long as these changes are made directly on the blueprints purchased from Garlinghouse and no additional copies are made.

Home Plan Vellums

By purchasing vellums for one of our home plans, you receive the same construction drawings found in the blueprints, but printed on vellum paper. Vellums can be erased and are perfect for making design changes. They are also semi-transparent making them easy to duplicate. But most importantly, the purchase of home plan vellums comes with a broader license that allows you to make changes to the design (ie, create a hand drawn or CAD derivative work), to make an unlimited number of copies of the plan, and to build up to three homes from the plan.

License To Build Additional Homes

With the purchase of a blueprint package or vellums you automatically receive a license to build one home or three homes, respectively. If you want to build more homes than you are licensed to build through your purchase of a plan, then additional licenses may be purchased at reasonable costs from Garlinghouse. Inquire for more information.

You've Picked Your Dream Home!

You can already see it standing on your lot... you can see yourselves in your new home... enjoying family, entertaining guests, celebrating holidays. All that remains ahead are the details. That's where we can help. Whether you plan to build-it-yourself, be your own contractor, or hand your plans over to an outside contractor, your Garlinghouse blueprints provide the perfect beginning for putting yourself in your dream home right away.

We even make it simple for you to make professional design modifications. We can also provide a materials list for greater economy.

My grandfather, L.F. Garlinghouse, started a tradition of quality when he founded this company in 1907. For over 85 years, homeowners and builders have relied on us for accurate, complete, professional blueprints. Our plans help you get results fast... and save money, too! These pages will give you all the information you need to order. So get started now... I know you'll love your new Garlinghouse home!

Sincerely,

TYPICAL WALL SECTIONS

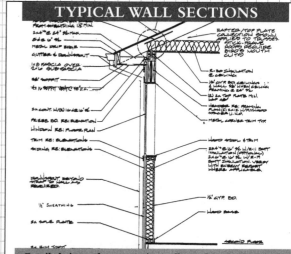

Detailed views of your exterior walls, as though sliced from top to bottom. These drawings clarify exterior wall construction insulation, flooring, and roofing details. Depending on your specific geography and climate, your home will be built with either 2x4 or 2x6 exterior walls. Most professional contractors can easily adapt plans for either requirement.

KITCHEN & BATH CABINET DETAILS

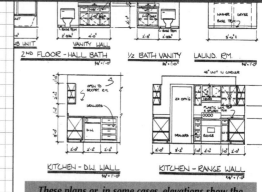

These plans or, in some cases, elevations show the specific details and placement of the cabinets in your kitchen and bathrooms as applicable. Customizing these areas is simpler beginning with these details. Kitchen and bath cabinet details are available for most plans featured in our collection.

EXTERIOR ELEVATIONS

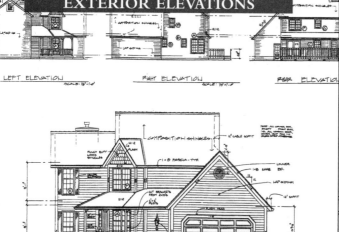

Exact scale views of the front, rear and both sides of your home, showing exterior materials, details, and all necessary measurements.

DETAILED FLOOR PLANS

Showing the placement of all interior walls, the dimensions of rooms, doors, windows, stairways, and other details.

ke Your Dream Come True!

for home designs by respected professionals.

FIREPLACE DETAILS

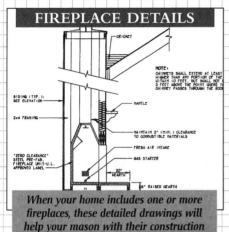

When your home includes one or more fireplaces, these detailed drawings will help your mason with their construction and appearance. It is easy to review details with professionals when you have the plans for reference.

TYPICAL CROSS SECTION

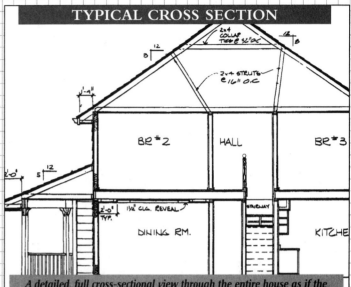

A detailed, full cross-sectional view through the entire house as if the house was cut from top to bottom. This elevation allows a contractor to better understand the interconnections of the construction components.

FOUNDATION PLAN

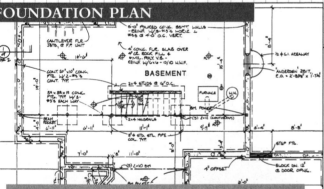

With footings and all load-bearing points applicable to your home, including all necessary notation and dimensions. The type of foundation supplied varies from home to home. Local conditions and practices will determine whether a basement, crawlspace or a slab is best for you. Your professional contractor can easily make the necessary adaption.

SCHEMATIC ELECTRICAL LAYOUTS

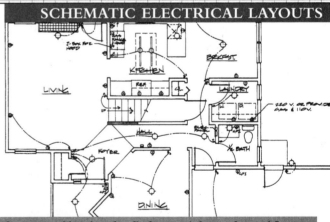

The suggested locations for all of your switches, outlets and fixtures are indicated on these drawings. They are practical as they are, but they are also a solid taking-off point for any personal adaptions.

ROOF PLAN

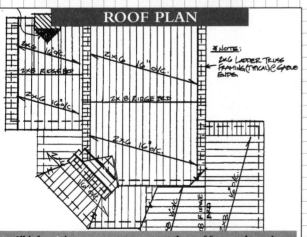

All information necessary to construct the roof for your home is included. Many blueprints contain framing plans showing all of the roof elements, so you'll know how these details look and fit together.

STAIR DETAILS

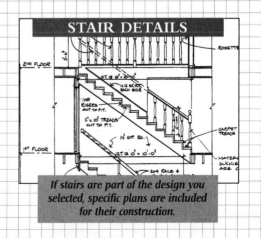

If stairs are part of the design you selected, specific plans are included for their construction.

GARLINGHOUSE OPTIONS & EXTRAS
MAKE THE DREAM TRULY YOURS.

Reversed Plans Can Make Your Dream Home Just Right!

"That's our dream home... if only the garage were on the other side!"

You could have exactly the home you want by flipping it end-for-end. Check it out by holding your dream home page of this book up to a mirror. Then simply order your plans "reversed". We'll send you one full set of mirror-image plans (with the writing backwards) as a master guide for you and your builder.

The remaining sets of your order will come as shown in this book so the dimensions and specifications are easily read on the job site... but they will be specially stamped "REVERSED" so there is no construction confusion.

We can only send reversed plans with multiple-set orders. But, there is no extra charge for this service.

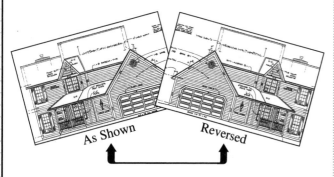

As Shown   Reversed

Modifying Your Garlinghouse Home Plan

Easy modifications to your dream home such as minor non-structural changes and simple material substitutions, can be made between you and your builder and marked directly on your blueprints. However, if you are considering making major changes to your design, we strongly recommend that you purchase our reproducible vellums and use the services of a professional designer or architect. Modifications are not available for plan numbers 90,000 and above. For additional information call us at 1-203-343-5977.

Our Reproducible Vellums Make Modifications Easier

With a vellum copy of our plans, a design professional can alter the drawings just the way you want, then you can print as many copies of the modified plans as you need. And, since you have already started with our complete detailed plans, the cost of those expensive professional services will be significantly less. Refer to the price schedule for vellum costs. Call for vellum availability for plan numbers 90,000 and above.

Reproducible vellum copies of our home plans are only sold under the terms of a license agreement that you will receive with your order. Should you not agree to the terms, then the vellums may be returned unopened for a full refund.

Yours FREE With Your Order
FREE
SPECIFICATIONS AND CONTRACT FORM

provides the perfect way for you and your builder to agree on the exact materials to use in building and finishing your home before you start construction. A must for homeowner's peace of mind.

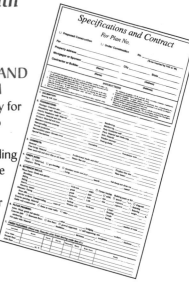

Remember To Order Your Materials List

It'll help you save money. Available at a modest additional charge, the Materials List gives the quantity, dimensions, and specifications for the major materials needed to build your home. You will get faster, more accurate bids from your contractors and building suppliers — and avoid paying for unused materials and waste. Materials Lists are available for all home plans except as otherwise indicated, but can only be ordered with a set of home plans. Due to differences in regional requirements and homeowner or builder preferences... electrical, plumbing and heating/air conditioning equipment specifications are not designed specifically for each plan. However, detailed typical prints of residential electrical, plumbing and construction guidelines can be provided. Please see next page for additional information.

Questions?

Call our customer service number at 1-203-343-5977.

How Many Sets Of Plans Will You Need?

The Standard 8-Set Construction Package

Our experience shows that you'll speed every step of construction and avoid costly building errors by ordering enough sets to go around. Each tradesperson wants a set — the general contractor and all subcontractors; foundation, electrical, plumbing, heating/air conditioning, drywall, finish carpenters, and cabinet shop. Don't forget your lending institution, building department and, of course, a set for yourself.

The Minimum 5-Set Construction Package

If you're comfortable with arduous follow-up, this package can save you a few dollars by giving you the option of passing down plan sets as work progresses. You might have enough copies to go around if work goes exactly as scheduled and no plans are lost or damaged. But for only $40 more, the 8-set package eliminates these worries.

The Single-Set Decision-Maker Package

We offer this set so you can study the blueprints to plan your dream home in detail. But remember... one set is never enough to build your home... and they're copyrighted.

New Plan Details For The Home Builder

Because local codes and requirements vary greatly, we recommend that you obtain drawings and bids from licensed contractors to do your mechanical plans. However, if you want to know more about techniques — and deal more confidently with subcontractors — we offer these remarkably useful detail sheets. Each is an excellent tool that will enhance your understanding of these technical subjects.

Residential Construction Details

Eight sheets that cover the essentials of stick-built residential home construction. Details foundation options - poured concrete basement, concrete block, or monolithic concrete slab. Shows all aspects of floor, wall, and roof framing. Provides details for roof dormers, eaves, and skylights. Conforms to requirements of Uniform Building code or BOCA code. Includes a quick index.

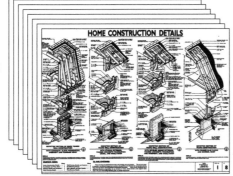

$14.95 per set

Residential Plumbing Details

Nine sheets packed with information detailing pipe connection methods, fittings, and sizes. Shows sump-pump and water softener hookups, and septic system construction. Conforms to requirements of National Plumbing Code. Color coded with a glossary of terms and quick index.

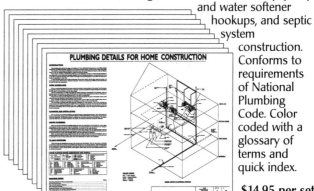

$14.95 per set

Residential Electrical Details

Nine sheets that cover all aspects of residential wiring, from simple switch wiring to the complexities of three-phase and service entrance connection. Explains service load calculations and distribution panel wiring. Shows you how to create a floor-plan wiring diagram. Conforms to requirements of National Electrical Code. Color coded with a glossary of terms and a quick index.

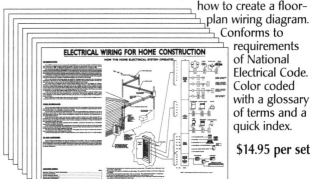

$14.95 per set

Important Shipping Information

Your order is processed immediately. Allow 10 working days from our receipt of your order for normal ground delivery. Save time with your credit card and our "800" number. Our delivery service must have a street address or Rural Route Box number — never a post office box. Use a work address if no one is home during the day.

Orders being shipped to Alaska, Hawaii, APO, FPO or Post Office Boxes must go via First Class Mail. Please include the proper postage.

Only Certified bank checks and money orders are accepted and must be payable in U.S. currency. For speed, we ship international orders Air Parcel Post. Please refer to the chart for the correct shipping cost.

An important note:

All plans are drawn to conform to one or more of the industry's major national building standards. However, due to the variety of local building regulations, your plan may need to be modified to comply with local requirements — snow loads, energy loads, seismic zones, etc. Do check them fully and consult your local building officials.

A few states require that all building plans used be drawn by an architect registered in that state. While having your plans reviewed and stamped by such an architect may be prudent, laws requiring non-conforming plans like ours to be completely redrawn forces you to unnecessarily pay very large fees. If your state has such a law, we strongly recommend you contact your state representative to protest.

VISA BEFORE ORDERING PLEASE READ ALL ORDERING INFORMATION **MasterCard**

Please submit all Canadian plan orders to:
Garlinghouse Company
20 Cedar Street North, Kitchener, Ontario N2H 2W8
Canadian Customers Only: 1-800-561-4169/Fax #: 1-519-743-1282
Customer Service #: 1-519-743-4169

ORDER TOLL FREE— 1-800-235-5700
Monday-Friday 8:00 a.m. to 5:00 p.m. Eastern Time
or FAX your Credit Card order to 1-203-343-5984
All foreign residents call 1-203-343-5977

Please have ready: 1. Your credit card number 2. The plan number 3. The order code number ⇨ H52S1

GARLINGHOUSE 1995 BLUEPRINT PRICE CODE SCHEDULE:
Additional sets with original order $20

PRICE CODE	A	B	C	D	E	F
8 SETS OF SAME PLAN	$280	$290	$300	$315	$330	$350
5 SETS OF SAME PLAN	$240	$250	$260	$275	$290	$310
1 SINGLE SET OF PLANS	$180	$190	$200	$215	$230	$250
VELLUMS	$395	$410	$425	$445	$465	$495
MATERIALS LIST	$25	$25	$25	$30	$30	$35

DOMESTIC SHIPPING*	1-2 Sets	3+ Sets
UPS/RPS Ground Service	$6.50	$8.50
First Class Mail	$8.00	$11.00
2-Day Express	$16.00	$20.00
Overnight Express	$26.00	$30.00

INTERNATIONAL SHIPPING	1-2 Sets	3+ Sets
Canada	**$11.00**	**$15.50**
All Other Nations	$40.00	$52.00

*Plan Numbers 90,000 & Above For Domestic Shipping —
Standard Express 3-5 Days -- $20.00*

Canadian Orders and Shipping: To our friends in Canada, we have a plan design affiliate in Kitchener, Ontario. This relationship will help you avoid the delays and charges associated with shipments from the United States. Moreover, our affiliate is familiar with the building requirements in your community and country. We prefer payments in U.S. Currency. If you, however, are sending Canadian funds please add 40% to the prices of the plans and shipping fees.

GARLINGHOUSE ─ Blueprint Order Form ─ Order Code No. H52S1

Plan No. _____
☐ As Shown ☐ Reversed (mult. set pkgs. only)

	Each	Amount
8 set pkg.		$
5 set pkg.		$
1 set pkg. (no reverses)		$
____ (qty.) Add'l. sets @		$
Vellums		$
Materials List		$
Residential Builder Plans		
____ set(s) Construction	@ $14.95	$
____ set(s) Plumbing	@ $14.95	$
____ set(s) Electrical	@ $14.95	$
Shipping		$
Subtotal		$
Sales Tax (CT residents add 6% sales tax, KS residents add 6.15% sales tax)		$
Total Amount Enclosed		**$**

Prices subject to change without notice
Payment must be made in U.S. funds
Foreign Mail Orders: Certified bank checks in U.S. funds only

Credit Card Information
Charge To: ☐ Visa   ☐ Mastercard

Card # | | | | | | | | | | | | | | | | |

Signature _____ Exp. ____ / ____

Send your check, money order or credit card information to:
(No C.O.D.'s Please)
Please Submit all <u>United States</u> & <u>Other Nations</u> plan orders to:
Garlinghouse Company
P.O. Box 1717
Middletown, CT 06457

Please Submit all <u>Canadian</u> plan orders to:
Garlinghouse Company
20 Cedar Street North
Kitchener, Ontario N2H 2W8

Bill To: (address must be as it appears on credit card statement)

Name_____

Address_____

City/State_____ Zip_____

Daytime Phone (   ) _____

Ship To (if different from Bill to):

Name_____

Address_____

City/State_____ Zip_____